DANGEROUS RIVER

DANGEROUS RIVER

R.M. PATTERSON

**CHELSEA GREEN
PUBLISHING COMPANY**
POST MILLS, VERMONT

Published by arrangement with
Stoddart Publishing Co. Limited,
Toronto, Ontario, Canada

CATALOGUING IN PUBLICATION DATA
Patterson, R.M. (Raymond Murray, 1898-   )
     Dangerous River

ISBN 0-930031-26-1

1. South Nahanni River Valley (N.W.T.) - Description and
travel.   2. Northwest Territories - Description and travel -
1906-1950.*   3. Patterson, R.M. (Raymond Murray), 1898-   .
Journeys - Northwest Territories - South Nahanni River Valley.
I. Title.

FC4195.S6P38   1989   917.19'3
F1100.S6P38   1989

To Gordon Matthews

Contents

Foreword

This book is the story of the Nahanni country in the Northwest Territories of Canada and of an attempt to find the lost gold of that little-known land. The attempt failed, so this must also be the story of a failure — but it was a failure that succeeded in so many other ways that, if life could be entirely filled with such defeats, I for one would never ask for any victory.

The tale departs from established tradition in two ways, beginning with the dust cover on which the reader will fail to find the customary stern, iron-featured man of the North gazing with frosted eyelashes into the steel-blue distance, his wolfish sled dogs crouching at his feet. We were never able to see ourselves in that heroic light, and, as for the North itself, we found a friendly country and a happy, well-stocked hunting ground. Secondly, I am glad to say that we added little to the world's biggest curse—its stock of scientific knowledge. I have to confess that I once fell from grace so far as to take compass bearings and estimate

distances: later on, with these data, I produced a map of the Flat
River and a small booklet entitled "The Flat River Country,"
copies of which were deposited with the Topographical Survey of
Canada and with the National Museum at Ottawa where, for a
number of years, they were the only sources of information on
that bit of the Territories. But apart from that, nothing. We
travelled because we liked the life—and, of course, hoped to find,
buried at the far end of the rainbow, the crock of gold.

Having, then, made it quite clear to the prospective reader that
his mind is in no danger of improvement at my hands, let me now
explain a couple of points that may otherwise seem obscure.

Any quotations that are without a reference are from a detailed
diary which was written up from day to day, at the time.

If certain passages seem a little vague as to topography it must
be remembered that we (Gordon Matthews and I) went into the
South Nahanni not primarily to trap but to prospect, and what we
found there, or did not find, must, for some time yet, remain our
own secret.

For the rest, we left that lovely country as we found it, by which
I mean that no forest fire resulted from any action of ours. We
killed game only when we needed food for ourselves or our dogs,
and no wounded animal was ever allowed to get away. Everything we hit we killed, and nothing was shot uselessly with the exception of one mountain sheep that was swept away down the
rapids. That, I claim, is a clean record.

Finally, I should like to thank the members of the Royal Canadian Mounted Police detachment at Fort Simpson of that time,
wherever they may be today, for their kindness and hospitality,
and similarly the Gentlemen of the Hudson's Bay Company's
establishments of Fort Nelson, Nelson Forks, and Fort Simpson.
To all others who sheltered us or helped us on our way I think I
have made it plain that we were indeed grateful.

My thanks are also due to Asst. Commissioner C. E. Rivett-
Carnac, O.C. "E" Division R.C.M.P., for his assistance in ob-
taining information regarding the early days on the Nahanni—to
Miss Conway of the files room of the *Edmonton Journal* for her help
also in this respect—to Miss Wolfenden of the Provincial Archives

Library, Victoria, B.C., whose deep knowledge of the books in her care led to the recording here of the earliest references to the South Nahanni—to Mr. Clifford P. Wilson, editor of *The Beaver*, for his permission on behalf of the Hudson's Bay Company to use again certain photographs of mine previously published in his pages—to Major C. G. Matthews for the use of the photograph of him and the dog team in Lower Canyon—and to Mr. A. J. Pickford of the British Columbia Forest Service for his rendering of the maps.

R. M. P.

Shoal Harbour,
Sidney,
British Columbia,
Oct. 6th, 1953.

1

The Legend

"To the West, low down and dimly seen, were the twin ranges of the Mimbres—those mountains of gold whose desert passes rarely echo the tread of human foot. Even the reckless trapper turns aside when he approaches that unknown land that stretches northward from the Gila; the land of the Apache and the fierce Navajo."

The Scalp Hunters, Mayne Reid

In the winter of 1926-7 I had to go home to England from Canada on some family business. To one accustomed by now to the glittering sunshine of sub-zero winters the weather in London that January was even fouler than usual, so much so that it became almost a duty to stay indoors and try to forget the fog and the soot-laden sleet and the rain. So I came back from the city on this particular afternoon by way of Harrod's and picked out a book from the library there; then I took myself home to a blazing fire and a deep armchair—and the noises of London faded, and I found myself back in the wilderness, following a strange, new trail.

The book was Michael H. Mason's *The Arctic Forests*. There were a couple of maps in the back of it—a physical map of Alaska, the Yukon Territory and the Mackenzie River valley, and a coloured ethnographical chart of the same area. The Yukon-Mackenzie divide, land of my boyhood dreams, was shown as a dotted line, named (inaccurately) "Rocky Mountains" and running vaguely between the heads of dotted rivers, themselves vague and their courses only guessed, north to the Arctic Ocean. Reaching up into the southern portion of these so-called Rockies, and rising near the heads of the Pelly, which are the furthest

3

heads of the Yukon, there was a river. It was (inaccurately) shown as a straight line and it had a couple of tributaries; it seemed to be about two hundred and fifty miles long, and it ran southeastwards into the Liard which, itself, is the West Fork of the great Mackenzie. The river led into the country that I had always wanted to see (or seemed to lead there, for how was I to know that it was only on the map at all from the reports of Indians and prospectors?), and its name was the South Nahanni.

The ethnographical chart placed the South Nahanni in a large beige-coloured area that ran all the way from the Wind River in the Yukon to the heads of the Sikanni Chief in British Columbia. The word "Nahanni" was written large over this area: a section of Mason's book was devoted to *The People of the Arctic Forests*, and I turned the pages, looking for this unfamiliar name. There it was: "Nahanni (people of the west)" it ran. ". . . They are a hardy, virile people, but have suffered much from white influence. They are hostile to strangers, and many white pioneers have been done to death by them. This tribe was for many years under the complete domination of one woman, supposed to be partly of European descent."

That was interesting: and it would be fairly easy, I could see, to reach the South Nahanni; all I would have to do would be to throw a canoe into the Peace River and follow the water down north—down the Peace and the Slave and through Great Slave Lake to the Mackenzie. Then, at Fort Simpson, one would turn up the Liard to the mouth of the South Nahanni, and from there north-west into the lonely mountain country of the Yukon divide, the land of the wild white sheep. Sometime soon I would do that, I decided—and strangely enough I never doubted that I could, though exactly what I proposed to use in place of experience has since often puzzled me. I was extremely accurate with a punt pole and could place a punt where I wanted it to an inch, but the art of handling a canoe had been acquired entirely on the Cherwell and the Isis—a very gently school of rivercraft.

I turned again to the maps: I could probably sell the canoe in the fall at one of the fur trading posts in the Sikanni Chief country and walk south, carrying a pack, the two hundred miles or so to

Fort St. John on the Peace—there must be some kind of a trail. That would be some time in October, but it would still not be too late to build a raft and float or sail down the two hundred miles of river between Fort St. John and Peace River Crossing, even if I landed in there with the river running ice. And that would close the circle and bring me back to my starting point: I could either ride north from there on the old Fort Vermilion trail to my Alberta homestead, or catch the train south to Edmonton, whichever seemed to be the thing to do.

I had had a run of luck lately, and I could afford to make this journey this very summer if I wished. The homestead would be safe; my nearest neighbour would keep an eye on it for me, and the horses could run out on the range. I began to measure distances on the map: tomorrow I would go to Canada House and see what, if anything, they could tell me about the Nahanni.

Late July found me poling a sixteen-foot canoe up a mile-wide river. The sun blazed down out of a cloudless sky, and it was hot and still—a hundred in the shade at the very least. The brown, swirling flood glittered and flashed in the bright light of the noonday sun: it seemed to come from a bell-shaped mountain that rose in the west out of the flatlands of the forest country. From this mountain a steep, scarped range stretched away to the north and faded from view: to the south of it there was nothing, and no foothills could be seen to east or west of it. The range had been coming closer for several days now: it seemed to quiver in the heat of that blazing noonday, and deep blue shadows were already lengthening on its eastern face: it gave promise of clear springs and icy streamlets full of trout, clean gravel beaches and cool nights, and I urged the canoe towards it, longing to be clear of this mosquito-ridden plain.

The big, brown, swift-flowing river was the Liard—the Rivière aux Liards or the Courant Fort of the old voyageurs, the West Branch of the Mackenzie. The mountain was Nahanni Butte, and northward from it ran the Nahanni Range. But I did not know those names then and there was no map to show them to me: all I knew was that the mouth of the South Nahanni, where it met the

Liard, lay just beyond the bell-shaped mountain: there was a trading post there, I had been told in Fort Simpson, but it would not be occupied. There was an Indian village, too, they had said, but it would be deserted also; all the Indians would be away up to Fort Liard for treaty money and supplies. And that, I thought, bearing in mind the description of these Indians in Mason's book, was all to the good.

I had heard a thing or two by now about this strange river with the beautiful name. Hundreds of miles away, at Fort Smith on the Slave River, someone had heard that I was headed for the South Nahanni.

"So you're going up the Big Nahanni? Boy, you've bitten off something this time! They say there's canyons in there thousands of feet deep, and the water coming through faster'n hell."

"But people have got through, haven't they?"

"Oh, I guess they have just got through—years ago. But canyons—and sheer! Thousands of feet!"

"If people have got through, there must surely be some ledges or something where a man can tie a canoe and camp and sleep?"

"I don't know. There ain't many that have come back to tell about it. Men vanish in that country. There was some prospectors murdered in there not so long ago, and down the river they say it's a damned good country to keep clear of. . . ."

And then there had been that man in the Hudson's Bay store at Fort Resolution, and de Meldt at Hay River on the Great Slave. They had said it all over again but with more detail. The Nahanni? There was gold in there somewhere—coarse gold and lots of it away up beyond those deep canyons. Deadmen Valley was tucked away in there some place—hadn't I heard of it? A valley between two canyons where the McLeods were murdered for their gold in 1906. No man ever knew what happened to them, but they were found—at least their skeletons were—tied to trees, with the heads missing. Laugh that one off! And enough men had disappeared in there since then that it was considered best by men of sense to leave the Nahanni country alone. But there was another lunatic who meant to try his luck in there—I would most likely run into

him on the way down the Mackenzie. Albert Faille,[1] his name was; he'd been trapping on Beaver River near the outlet of the Great Slave, and now he'd got the Nahanni bug into his head. Red Pant, the Indians called him because he always wore great, heavy work pants of scarlet stroud. He'd pulled out with his canoe just a couple of days ago, and with them red pants on him a blind man couldn't miss him. . . .

I had seen Faille, a day or two later, at Wrigley Harbour, a little bay on an island where the Mackenzie spills out of the Great Slave Lake. There he was, a small, red-trousered figure on the distant shore: I had got my canoe and camp stuff loaded up on the scows of a mining outfit that was going downriver, and we had waved to Faille and passed by without stopping.

But there had been no nonsense or beating about the bush, with regard to the Nahanni, at Fort Simpson. There had been a succession of drinks in the upstairs of the old Hudson's Bay house, with the sun pouring in through the low windows, lighting up odd piles and bales of fur and all the queer implements and contrivances that a hundred years of the fur trade had drifted up into this old attic. Spilled over the floor lay the mail and an opened case of Scotch, for the first boat of the year had just gone by to the Arctic. As we kicked the mail about and extracted our own I listened to them: they were saying good-bye to me for ever, and they became more eloquent with each successive drink. The Nahanni, they said, was straight suicide. The river was fast and bad, and if a man ever did get through those canyons what would he find in that little-known country of the Yukon divide? Gold— gold without end, guarded quite likely by horned devils for all anybody knew to the contrary, but certainly by the wild Mountain Men—Indians who never came in to any trading post either in the Yukon or in the Northwest Territories. They lorded it over the wild uplands of the Yukon-Mackenzie divide and made short work of any man, white or Indian, who ventured into their country. Just ask the Indians here or, better still, the Indians at Fort

[1]Pronounced Faley.

Wrigley. Why, you couldn't bribe them with all the marten in the North to go back west more than thirty miles from the Mackenzie! No—we'd better all have another drink and be sensible and forget about the South Nahanni. . . .

One way and another I had plenty to think about as I brought the canoe upstream on that hot July afternoon.

It was the McLeod saga, more than anything else, that spread the Nahanni legend—even to the extent of earning for it, at the hands of one enthusiastic press writer, the title "Dark River of Fear."

There were three McLeod brothers involved in the finding of the Nahanni gold—Willie, Frank and Charlie. They were, according to Jack Stanier, a veteran prospector of Fort Liard, the sons of Murdoch McLeod, the Hudson's Bay factor at that post, and they were "raised as Indians."

An Indian of the Nahanni country had been helped and befriended by old Murdoch, and in return he had told the McLeods of an Indian working of gold somewhere away up the Flat River, the Nahanni's biggest tributary, and close to the boundary of the Yukon Territory. The young McLeods were fascinated by this tale of treasure hidden behind the mountain ranges which rose from the plain, ridge piled upon ridge, across the Liard from their home. They mulled it over from every angle and planned some day to go and see for themselves; it was not far away, perhaps a hundred and fifty miles as the crow flies—though vastly further as he walks, and with an untold amount of grief on the trail between.

Their chance came, oddly enough, not at Fort Liard but when they were "outside," in Edmonton of all places, six hundred miles (again by flight of crow) to the south and east. Why they started from Edmonton we are not told: perhaps they had sold some fur there to advantage, or they may have been outside, working for good wages in order to finance the trip. Possibly somebody grub-staked them in return for a share in the venture—but anyway, according to Charlie McLeod, there now began an Odyssey of the North that rivals anything that even Jack

London's fertile imagination could bring forth.

The brothers hit the trail in January, 1904. They took the train to Vancouver, and from there they took the boat up the foggy inland passage to Wrangell in the panhandle strip of Alaska. The salt water of Wrangell Sound is cut by the fresh water of the Stikine River, but it is never completely frozen. However, the McLeods bought dogs and an outfit at the settlement and somehow got themselves freighted off Wrangell Island and dumped on the solid ice of the Stikine. They went north up the Stikine against the bitter winter wind that blows there without ceasing from the plateau to the sea, through the gorges and the sombre forests of the Coast Range, past great glaciers that crawl down right to the river bank in this land of heavy snow, and they came after a hundred and fifty miles of trail to a drier, colder country and to the little post of Telegraph Creek. They went on from there, north by east, and in time they crossed a modest little gravelly ridge, not too far from Tanzilla Butte, and the ice of a long, narrow lake met their eyes: the lake ran straight into the north for some thirty odd miles; its southern end was no more than half a mile away, at the foot of a little hill down which the trail wound through the trees to the shore. The gravel ridge was the divide between the Pacific and the Arctic Oceans, and the lake was Dease Lake; they were once more on water that flowed to the Liard.

Down the windswept surface of the lake went the little party, two men breaking trail, pounding down the snow with their snowshoes so that the dogs could travel, and one man handling the dogs and the load. The brothers passed by old gold mining camps, long since deserted; then they came to the north end of the lake where the mountains begin to close in. They followed the ice of the winding Dease River for a hundred miles down into the Cassiar Mountains and through them into the rolling country of the Liard Plain. They came to the Liard, but their trail led north, and they took to some smaller river—it may have been the Hyland—and they followed it for a hundred and fifty miles or more; and the days came and went, and still the trail led on, and they had long since lost all track of time. They were in the mountains of the south-eastern Yukon now; and that country can warm up in the wintertime under the southwest wind, or it can drop down with the north wind to sixty and seventy below zero till the aurora crackles in the black night sky, and by day a sun that is without heat peers through a drifting veil of glittering frost particles. And it can do either one or the other at any time, just as easy as kiss your hand.

Sometimes the sun shone out of a deep blue sky, warm and life-giving, for spring was on its way to the Northland, and the days were growing longer. And sometimes it hung in the sky, rayless like a ball of copper in a sky of brass: a circle of light would be round it, with blazing sundogs to right and left of it, and horns of light growing out of the circle—and it would be colder than hell. Sometimes the spring blizzards would take a parting kick at the McLeods, and sometimes they travelled under a sea of heavy, driving cloud, with warm, wet snowstorms clogging and soaking into their snowshoes. And when men and dogs were full of moose meat all was well, but when they were empty the cold could reach them through their mitts and furs and parkas, and things were not so good. And then they made camp and hunted. . . .

"We came to the MacMillan Range," Charlie McLeod says, but God knows where or what that was, for the only MacMillan Range on the map today is away west towards the Yukon River, three hundred miles from the Nahanni country. And in the end they came to the upper Flat River, and there they found Cassiar Indians with coarse gold—"some big stuff," Charlie says, "up to $2 and $3 a nugget." Spring was at hand now, so they made camp beside the creek from which the gold had come and looked the country over. Charlie doesn't say what became of the Cassiar Indians, whether they stayed or went away. From what took place afterwards one imagines that they must have gone: they cannot have been overjoyed at the arrival of the McLeods. The brothers called the creek Gold Creek. The prospect, apparently, was a small one—and quite likely the Indians had taken the cream off it. They panned for a while, and also used Indian-made sluice boxes which they found there, but the largest bit of gold they got was worth no more than fifty cents, and they didn't get much; they filled a toothache-remedy bottle with gold.

Then they took two of the Indian sluice boxes (which would be made of planks hand-hewed or whipsawed from local timber) and made a sort of a box of a boat for the run downstream to the Nahanni and home. They were about twenty miles, Charlie says, above what they called The Cascades of the Thirteen Drops, which is what we later came to know as the Flat River Canyon; so, in order to reach their home, they had to travel about a hundred and ten miles down the Flat River in their box-like contraption, roughly the same distance down the Nahanni, and finally eighty miles up the Liard.

They started off light-heartedly enough and tried to run the Canyon, as dirty a piece of water as you could wish to see, but at the first of the thirteen drops they swamped and lost everything, including the bottle of gold—salvaging only a rifle and thirty shells.

They went back to Gold Creek and got themselves a moose. Then they went to work, shifted some more boulders and panned out some more gold. Finally they made a boat out of two more of the Indians' precious sluice boxes, and made a trackline out of thin strips of moosehide so that they could lower their outfit down the worst places in the river. And somehow they got their crazy bateau safely down through the canyons to Nahanni Butte and home to Fort Liard.

Glad, possibly, to settle down for a while after this long trip, Willie McLeod went to work for the Hudson's Bay Company. But no prospector can ever permanently settle down: as he works at some humdrum job he keeps running over his last trip in his mind and building up new theories; he can soon see what mistakes he made, just where he took the wrong line and exactly what he ought to have done. . . .

Willie soon had it all figured out to his own satisfaction, and in 1905 he set off again for the Nahanni, taking with him Frank and an unnamed Scottish engineer. There was a vague story that Willie had lost a large amount of gold "when his canoe upset," but that he still retained a small bottle, containing about five ounces, which had been held in a sash wrapped round his waist;

with this, it was said, he drew the Scotsman into it. The little party disappeared up the Nahanni, and a year went by and there was no sign of them.

Charlie McLeod started a search for his brothers which ended in 1908 with the finding of the bones of Willie and Frank in their camp by the Nahanni. They were found in the mountain-ringed valley that lies between the Lower and Second Canyons of the Nahanni: the valley was named that day by Charlie McLeod's party—they called it Deadmen Valley, and to this day it bears that name.

The McLeods' camp in Deadmen Valley was in the spruce on the left bank of the Nahanni, not far below Second Canyon Mountain. The dead men had been supposedly on their way out: one of them had always had a habit of leaving messages on bits of wood, blazed trees and so forth, and here, true to form, he had written one—on a split sled runner, this time: "We have found a fine prospect," it ran.

There was no trace of the white man: he is either unnamed, or referred to as Weir or Wilkinson. Nobody seems to know much about him: one version of the story traces him to Telegraph Creek with $8,000 in dust and nuggets, and another claims that the Mounted Police traced him as far as Vancouver, where he apparently had with him $5,000 in gold: from there the trail was lost. If this white man killed the McLeods and went out by way of the upper Liard and the Dease to Telegraph Creek and Vancouver, one is tempted to ask why the deed was not done up the Flat River near the Yukon border, instead of down in Deadmen Valley with all those weary miles to retrace upstream alone.

The murdered men were apparently shot while in their sleeping bags, one report says. And then G. M. McLeod, Charlie's son, steps in with an interview to the *Calgary Albertan* for February 19th, 1947—a time when the press had seized on this old tale and had created a furore about the Nahanni and its tally of dead men. "River of Mystery" they called it, and by many another wild title, including that of "Headless Valley," for they had fastened onto that feature of the story in particular. The Alaska Highway Handbook went one better. "The jumping off point," it said of

Fort Nelson, "for The Valley of Vanishing Men."

G. M. McLeod added some further detail: his two uncles were found and buried by Charlie McLeod. Their heads were gone and could not be found so "Charlie buried them without their heads." There were seven witnesses present, and a cross was set up. "One brother was found lying in their night-bed face up, and the other one was lying face down, three steps away, with his arm outstretched in a vain attempt to reach his gun which was at the foot of a tree, only another step from where he fell. The blankets were thrown half across his brother as if he'd left the bed with a leap." The murderer took no valuables, nothing but the gold.

G. M. McLeod should have known what he was talking about since the murdered (?) men were his uncles. The story is quite different from the one that I had heard at Fort Simpson, which was that the skeletons of the McLeods were found tied to trees and minus their heads. But there is something queer about both these accounts to anyone with experience of the North: the story of one of the most recent tragedies of the Nahanni country will show why.

In the spring of 1949 a man called Shebbach died of starvation at the mouth of Caribou Creek on the Flat River. He had threaded his way through the mountains on foot, in the fall of 1948, from the nearest point on the Alaska Highway, some two hundred miles by trail south by west from Caribou Creek. His partner was to have gone by river, taking in supplies, but when Shebbach got to the mouth of Caribou Creek, mapping out in his head, no doubt, the wonderful feed he was going to have, he found nobody there and no grub in the cache. And nobody came, and winter shut down on the land.

He had come in carrying a .22 rifle and living off the country. Eventually his supply of .22 cartridges gave out, and his diary became a record of forty-two days of starvation. Then he died. I had the story from Kraus, a prospector-trapper, who lives down by Nahanni Butte, the only white man—except Faille who is a nomad and whom no man can pin down to any one spot—to make his home on the Nahanni. Kraus questioned the forty-two days' starvation period, but that is quite possible. When Jack Hornby with Adlard and Christian died on the Thelon River they lived on scraps, whiskey jacks, odds and ends and bits of wolverine hide until Christian, who kept a diary[1] and who was the last to die, had starved for over sixty days. Kraus, who is game warden for the Nahanni area, was sent up in the summer of 1949 to see where Shebbach was. He found him at Caribou Creek, but not all in one place—the bears had broken into the cabin and what had been Shebbach was scattered all over the flat—just a mess, Kraus said, scraps of clothing here and there and bits of bone that had been gnawed and dragged about by "bears, wolves and every other damned thing that could chew."

Deadmen Valley is just as full of bears and wolves as the Caribou Creek country: how was it, then, that the McLeods were found so neatly tied to trees, or lying just as they had been killed and with camp so little disturbed, even to the hastily thrown back blanket, that those who found them could say exactly what had happened? For everything to have been in such good order the murder would have to have been committed only a few days, at the most, before the search party arrived, and that in itself would have been a strange coincidence, for it was three full years from the time that Willie and Frank and the Scotsman had started up the Nahanni. Not only that, but there would still have been a chance of catching the murderer, for he would not have had time to get out of the country.

To balance all this we have a statement by Flynn Harris made at Fort Simpson to a correspondent of the *Edmonton Journal* and published in that paper on December 23rd, 1929. Flynn had had a wide and varied experience of the North and, in 1929, he had been Indian Agent at Fort Simpson for seventeen years. He was very jealous of the good name of his Indians, even to the point of asking me, when I was going out in 1929, to go to the *Edmonton Journal* office and try to put an end to "all these damn fool stories about the head-hunting Nahany Indians." Here follow Flynn's comfortable words:

"There's no denying there have been some sudden deaths on

---

[1]"Unflinching" by E. Christian (John Murray, 1937).

the Nahanni, but no Indians were responsible for them. The most romantic incident on the Nahanni—the death of the McLeod boys many years ago, after they were supposed to have located a fabulously rich gold mine—has never been accepted as a case of murder by men familiar with the river, though it has always been broadcast as such.

"I personally am convinced that they starved to death and that the clues held up as proofs of crime were the work of wolves or other animals that discovered the bodies. As far as the gold is concerned there has been a good deal of talk about it—mostly by natives who are prone to exaggerate, or by gullible visitors. . . . In itself the Nahanni lives up to its reputation, however. It is a nasty piece of water, and an arduous and dangerous waterway for the best of navigators."

The Mounted Police are even more definite. In a letter to me, dated from Ottawa, October 27th, 1952, the Departmental Secretary writes:

"The McLeod case was investigated by the Force in 1909 and the conclusion reached was that they died from starvation and exposure. It was proved that they started on the trip ill-equipped and short of supplies, having only 50 pounds of flour and 5 pounds of tea when they left Fort Liard, N.W.T. The case was reopened in July, 1921, and further investigation substantiated the initial conclusion."

And in the same letter, in answer to a second question of mine, the D.S. went on to say:

"As to Jorgenson, we have no file or record of such a person being reported missing in the South Nahanni Country. In all probability a man by that name could have made a trip into that country and, like many other prospectors and trappers, returned to the outside safe and sound."

There you are, and you can take your pick. But there must be *something* hidden away at the bottom of this well-muddied pool—and this something, whatever it is, must rest at least half way between the calm official denials, and the gorgeous inventions of the out-going prospector or trapper, inspired by Bacchus to a bewildering flood of traveller's tales. For my part I cannot see that a really effective investigation can be made of events for which there can be no witnesses—bygone events, the very signs and traces of which must have been blurred or wiped out, even for Charlie McLeod's party, by time, animals and weather. As to the five pounds of tea and the fifty pounds of flour, I question whether that means very much. It obviously would not last three men for very long, but they may have meant to travel light and live off the country and, if they had plenty of salt, matches and rifle cartridges, it would be easy enough to do so in that paradise of wild game. Scurvy can be avoided by means of fresh, wild fruit and by eating freshly killed meat only partially cooked: even salt can be dispensed with, for a time at least, by eating raw or very lightly cooked fresh meat. But if one knew what the McLeods' original plan was, that would help in reaching a decision: whether they planned to come out in the late fall of 1905 or whether they intended to winter up on the Flat River—in other words to what extent they were *overdue* when their brother and his party found them. But the case was officially closed, and that was that.

That brings us to Jorgenson, the man without a record. Jorgenson was Poole Field's partner, and in the early nineteen hundreds the two of them had a trading post over in the Yukon Territory on the Ross River, one of the heads of the Pelly. The Ross and the South Nahanni head close together: both partners had heard of the lost McLeod mine and wondered what lay on the Nahanni side of the divide, and around 1910 Jorgenson went over to see. Two years later an Indian came in to the Hudson's Bay post at Pelly Lake where Poole Field happened to be. The Indian brought word from Jorgenson who had built himself a cabin some two hundred miles away, near the mouth of the Flat River and on ground that has since been washed away by the Nahanni. There was a map and a message for Field to come quickly—Jorgenson had struck it rich.

Field went, as soon as he could get away, by the same route that Jorgenson had taken—over the Yukon-N.W.T. divide and down the Nahanni. He found the cabin burned to the ground and Jorgenson's skeleton lying between the cabin and the river:

Jorgenson's bones were bleached, Field said, "so he must have been dead nearly two years." A new Savage rifle that he had taken with him from Ross River was gone. And the map had directed Field only to Jorgenson's cabin site and not to his prospect.

Poole Field—who later married one of Flynn Harris' half-breed daughters and became a well-known character on the Liard and the Nahanni—is dead now, and the above account is taken from an old interview in which he may well have been wrongly reported. Other stories were that Jorgenson had evidently been walking from the cabin to the river for a bucket of water when he must have seen something that scared him, dropped the bucket, run towards the cabin to get his rifle and been shot in the back: that a rifle lying by his side with two empty cartridges showed that he had made a fight for his life: that he was found without his head but with his rifle and, conversely, with his head and without his rifle. Try and get at the truth of anything connected with the Nahanni in the old days—even the headless motif is dragged into it! To round off the Jorgenson story there is a report that Field found the Savage rifle in a store at Fort Simpson but could not trace the man who had traded it there—an unlikely yarn, since good rifles were not so common in trade nor the population so numerous in those days that a trader would not be able to remember and identify the man.

Other men vanished, quite probably through perfectly natural accidents such as the breaking of a trackline or the upsetting of a canoe, a broken leg, a rockfall, a disagreement with a grizzly. . . . One mistake is quite sufficient when a man is travelling alone. And the Nahanni became a river that men avoided, except for the odd summer prospecting party—and the Indians and Poole Field.

Faille and I broke the spell in 1927. They said good-bye to us in Fort Simpson, but we turned up again, and Faille has gone on turning up again ever since. He disappears into the wilderness of the upper Nahanni, and no man, white or Indian, sees him; and always they say of him, "This time he's done it once too often." But he appears again, perhaps after two years have gone by, a little more bent but cheery as ever, and indestructible as bronze.

Then Charlie McLeod went back in to the upper Flat River,[1] after an absence of thirty years, guiding three prospectors, and I went back with Gordon Matthews, and the news got around, and men became certain that we "had something back in there." A minor stampede to the Flat River was touched off in 1929: Gilroy's party was typical of this particular excitement; they went in travelling light, they had no intention of wintering in there and all they wanted to do was to find the lost McLeod "mine," pick up a quick fortune and get out. Gilroy told me a thing or two about the trip that may be of interest here. Gilroy, incidentally, was strong as a bull, square-built with tremendous shoulders on him and designed by Nature for carrying a pack; he and his two companions, Hay and Hall, tackled the approach to the Flat River from a new and daring angle.

They went in by way of the Long Portage and Fort Nelson in 1929, and they were on the Nahanni by May. There their troubles began: late May and most of June is flood time on the Nahanni, and Gilroy and his partners ran into all the grief in the world. The brown, tearing flood was high, and it stayed high, and if ever it relented and dropped a little then, sure as fate, up it came again. On June 1st, Gilroy says, the Nahanni rose ten feet in four hours. The partners got through the Lower Canyon and Deadmen Valley, and through the short Second Canyon into the Little Valley, and there they made camp on June 9th at Scow Creek, a small creek that comes in from the south-west. They had had enough rivering to do them for quite a while.

They decided, round the fire that night, to hit out next day up this creek that came roaring down past their camp, and to follow it until they got to the height of land between the N.W.T. and the Yukon. Then they would travel northwestwards along the divide, shooting their meat as they went, until they found some stream that would lead them down to the Flat River near Gold Creek. And so they set out next morning, Gilroy and Hay carrying heavier loads than Hall, who believed in travelling light and had packed himself accordingly. The going was difficult in the steep,

[1]See Chapter 4, "Fall of the Leaf."

narrow valley, but evening found them camped in a little clump of firs well up into the timberline country, tired, tempers short and Hall grumbling about the slowness of the other two and the pile of junk they insisted on carrying.

The next morning Hall let fly, at breakfast time, with a few well-chosen words: if Gilroy and Hay wanted to make packhorses out of themselves, let them. As far as he was concerned, to hell with it! A rifle and a mosquito net would do for him and he would wait for them on Gold Creek, or wherever the stuff was, with his claims staked; and they could stake alongside him when they got there—if they ever did. And, with that, he slung his little pack over his shoulders, picked up his rifle and hit the trail. Some time later they caught a glimpse of him climbing, away up a long valley against a background of grey boulders, green grass and alpine flowers. And then they saw him again, once, silhouetted for a moment against the blue, summer sky—and that was the last time that any man ever set eyes on Angus Hall.

Gilroy and Hay travelled on across the alpine country, keeping above timberline by day and dropping down at nights to camp by some small patch of balsam fir. They ate enormously of meat and, since there was a limit to what they could carry and still make time, they shot an animal almost every day—mostly bears, Gilroy said. They travelled northwest, and eventually they dropped down to what they thought was the Flat River; but it was Caribou Creek, and they had to climb up again and cross another divide to reach the upper Flat River. Their arrival on the Flat was a memorable occasion. They were dog-tired, and they trudged slowly across a big river flat, thinking of all the nice kinds of grub that they hadn't got with them, wondering if there would be fish that they could catch for supper, and swatting at the mosquitoes. Then they smelt wood smoke: a party of four prospectors had gone in by river, and they were just finishing supper when Gilroy and Hay staggered in. So supper was made ready all over again, and Gilroy and Hay blew themselves out, "till we pretty nearly burst," on all the things they'd been dreaming about. A wonderful bit of timing, that meeting was—a man wouldn't pull that off so sweetly and neatly twice in a lifetime.

The two parties joined forces and went on up the river. Somewhere, in a patch of hardpan, they found the track of a hob-nailed boot—a right foot with nine nails in it; Gilroy took particular note of it. Hall had been wearing nailed boots, and they thought now that he must be somewhere ahead of them, but they could never find him although they did their best, making big smokes and firing rifles from time to time. It was not until a year later that Gilroy told me of this, and I explained to him that it must have been an old track of mine[1] from the preceding September that had stayed fresh under the snow and had not been appreciably dimmed by the rain.

In the end they came to Gold Creek—a tough-looking spot; boulders, boulders and boulders, little gravel and no gold. Floods and spring run-offs had swept down the creek since the Indians and the McLeods had taken the pay out of it years before, and nothing more could be got at without immense labour and a tremendous rooting about in the overburden—if there was anything there at all. The odd thing about this venture was that all the upper Flat River country lay around these diggings, crying out to be prospected, and yet to Gilroy's party, and again and again to others, this creek seems to have acted as a fatal magnet.

Two of the river boat party, Hill and Cochrane, hit the creek about three miles upstream from the others and found the remains of a small shaft and a broken down dam, old cartridges and a whipsaw. They also found messages on a blazed tree left by four men who had come there from the Yukon in April, 1921. These men had left a cache with some dog harness in it: under their names—Langdon, Rae, Brown and Smith—on the old blaze was a pencilled message which read, "Liard Smith and Indian arrived on June 15th, 1921," and then further writings stating that the four Yukon men had left Gold Creek on June 25th and June 27th, 1921, in two parties. Brown and Rae went on down the Flat River, blazing a tree at Irvine Creek and leaving a record on it which I found in 1928. Liard Smith was probably the Smith who lived and trapped in the lonely country on the Liard near Smith

[1]See Chapter 4, "Fall of the Leaf," Page 146.

River, beside the great hot springs where the Alaska Military
Highway runs today. Pencilled writing on an old blaze like this
will remain fresh and legible for many years, preserved from the
weather by the overhanging spruce branches and by a thin film of
gum that runs over it as the tree seeks to heal the wound.

While Hill and Cochrane were poking around in the debris up
the creek, Gilroy and the rest were further downstream examin-
ing old, grey, bleached sluice boxes of whipsawed lumber and a
tremendous upheaval of boulders: this may have been the spot
where the McLeods got their gold and built their box-like boats in
1905. But Gilroy and his party found nothing else in the country
to keep them there: a few colours of gold here and there, but that
was all. Summer merged into fall, and they dropped downriver
and picked up the other boat at Scow Creek and went out—six
now, out of the seven who had started, for the Nahanni had ex-
acted a toll of one.

Then, in 1931, Phil Powers went in to trap on the Flat River
and failed to appear when the ice went out in the spring. Constable Martin, Special Constable Edwards, Poole Field and Faille
were sent in to look for him, for it was no longer 1905: the
R.C.M.P. were in charge of the country now, and they like to
keep a tidy record of the missing. In the fall of 1932 the search
party found Powers' burned cabin up the Flat, about thirty miles
from Gold Creek, and his charred skeleton. There was only one
odd thing about the find, but it was decidedly odd: the signs
showed that the fire occurred at the beginning of the winter of
1931, but, nailed to one of the uprights of the cache, was a piece of
paper with the words: "Phil Powers finished Aug, 1932."

By 1933 Canada was in the depths of the depression of the thirties: nobody had any money, and men and airlines (which were
then starting up and having a very tough time making ends meet)
were desperate for work and freight. Gold was high, it was the one
stable thing in a collapsing world, and the magic word could be
relied upon to start a bunch of optimists stampeding in any direction. Conditions were ideal for trotting out the McLeod story
once again. We were about to hear more of the same old creek up
the Flat River.

This time the yarn was complete, even down to the inevitable map and a dream. The map was produced by Father Turcotte of the Oblate Fathers at Fort Liard. It had been given to him, many years previously, by Father Gouet who was as much of a trader and prospector as he was a priest, and by Willie McLeod. The map had lain forgotten among Father Turcotte's papers: the word "gold" was on it in two places, and the Father gave it to Jack Stanier, the old prospector of Fort Liard.

Stanier roped D——(wrong initial), an employee or ex-employee of the Hudson's Bay Company, into it, and the pair of them got themselves flown in to a lake on the Flat River. They came out with some placer gold in their possession: and here, according to the published story,[1] Stanier was indeed fortunate to have chosen D—— as his companion. D——, it would seem, could see further through a stone wall than most, as the old saying went; and one night, when things were not looking too bright for our prospectors, he dreamed a dream. The next morning they went up the creek: round a bend they came to a barren-looking spot: from the wall of the gulch on one side a slide of rock and gravel had come down, and out of the slide stuck some unnatural-looking pieces of wood. D—— rushed forward: "That's the place," he cried—and, by God's truth, it *was* the place, and those were the pick and shovel handles of the long-dead McLeods! Most remarkable!

"You can kick the gravel heaps," one newspaper said, "and see the gold gleaming like butter." Nobody, of course, wanted to stop and consider why all this wealth had remained unnoticed by previous parties: off went the usual collection of hopefuls headed by the dog-musher, Harry McGurran, who had hauled the winter mail on the Mackenzie for many years—and river freighters and a certain air line had work for a while. The excitement was maintained for a little time by odd paragraphs in the Edmonton papers to the effect that "the Nahanni gold fields are yielding good pay," but inevitably it fizzled out, and peace came again to the Flat River, and the moose and the caribou were once more free to

---

[1] See the files of the *Edmonton Journal*.

breed and restock the country, unmolested by men.

After this brief interval of romantic buffoonery things got back to normal. Faille came and went and sometimes others would come, too: and sometimes the Nahanni, the green, shadowy, driving river, would stir a little in its dreams and reach out and take its toll: in 1936 Eppler and Mulholland disappeared and, in 1940, Holmberg—and Shebbach starved to death in 1949, at Caribou Creek. And there were others, too. As Flynn Harris truly said, "The Nahanni is a nasty piece of water, and an arduous and dangerous waterway for the best of navigators."

2

South Nahanni River

"It is one of the four rivers that flow out of Paradise.
And the country is very bright, gay and beautiful."

Clavijo, Ambassador to the Court of Tamerlane

T he afternoon was blistering hot. The bell-shaped
mountain had become a blue silhouette against the bluest of summer skies, for its eastern face was now deep in the shadow. Behind
the mountain lay the dangerous river, and sweating up the Liard
towards it came one who was far from being the best of
navigators. Behind, however, though still out of sight and earshot, came the man whose name, above all others, was to be
associated with the Nahanni for the next quarter of a century—Albert Faille. The Nahanni has probably never seen a finer
canoeman, and to watch Faille search out the weak spot in a riffle
and plant his canoe's nose exactly there, and neither to the right
nor to the left by even a hand's breadth, is like watching a fine
swordsman seeking for an opening, feeling out his adversary. He
was of Swiss descent, born in Minnesota, that land of lakes and
clear streams: mountains were in his blood as well as rivers and
he, too, was heading for Nahanni Butte on that July afternoon,
sitting in the tail end of his canoe and listening to the song of his
little outboard as it churned up the Liard.

It had been a devil of a day. The night before had been hot, for
there was hardly any darkness and no time for the earth to cool.
The early morning was dead still and hot: it was the worst morn-

27

ing for mosquitoes that I ever saw. As the sun rose, the hum outside my net rose to a savage thrumming note: I counted the brutes
on a certain area of the net, and then I multiplied that out and
made a very conservative estimate of the number in the air. Why,
dammit, there were two thousand of the maddening insects waiting out there, shouting for my blood! It wasn't even worth fighting with them over breakfast; I would go straight on and stop and
breakfast when the breeze got up. So I reached out from under the
net, grabbed a pot of cold rice and raisins and got it inside with me
and had some of that. Then I dressed myself and oiled my face and
hands with citronella and put on my bit of head protection—a
square yard of mosquito netting, folded cornerways into a triangle
of double thickness. I put this over my head like a shawl, crossed
the ends under my chin, put them round the back of my neck and
fetched them to the front again and tied them there, tucking them
down into my shirt which I buttoned up tightly. Then I crammed
a hat on to my head over the netting, crawled out, tore camp to
pieces, threw it into the canoe and grabbed the pole and went on.

I came at last, between three and four in the afternoon, to a
sandbar in the middle of the Liard. There was lots of driftwood
there and no green vegetation to harbour mosquitoes: the sand
threw back the heat of the sun in such a fierce blast that no mosquito could have lived there anyway, for they like greenery and
dampness and part shade. Soon the fire smoke was going up and a
little breeze came down from the mountains: I bathed and shaved,
and cooked and ate a meal that was long overdue and felt a new
man. I had rounded Swan Point, and Nahanni Butte lay due west
against the sun with mountainous white thunderheads climbing
into the sky behind it. That explained the frantic behaviour of the
mosquitoes—a storm was on its way. South Nahanni was about
five miles from my sandbar; I could make it that same evening if I
got at it right away: and so I packed the lunch outfit back into the
grub box, loaded the canoe and hit the river.

Very soon the distant whine of a kicker broke the evening
stillness: in half an hour or so it was close behind. I turned and
looked to see who it might be: but there could be no doubt about
it, there was only one pair of those red pants in the country! It was

Faille, and he was standing up in his canoe and beckoning to me to swing out into the stream. As I came near he set the steering of the kicker and ran forward over his load.

"Throw me a line," he shouted, "and I'll give you a tow."

I threw him the trackline, which was fast to the ring in the nose of my canoe, and climbed on board the freight canoe. Faille passed my trackline round a forward thwart of this canoe while I made fast a canoe pole with a couple of half hitches in the trackline up against the ring. Quickly we shoved the two canoes apart till there was space between for the Liard current to slip freely past without boiling up and over the gunwales. Then the pole was made fast to Faille's canoe and the line adjusted and tied at the forward thwart: the two canoes then rode parallel at the distance set by the fixed pole. All this time we had been travelling slowly upstream. Faille next went back and turned the handle over to full speed and then, bawling at each other above the full-throated howl of the kicker, we got down to the serious business of introducing ourselves.

The sun had gone down behind the thunderclouds which were crawling up into the blue behind the Butte, golden rimmed and throwing dark shadows into the eastern sky. The current had slackened as we crept forward into the wide sweep of water where the two big rivers meet: the Butte and the fiery sunset and the dark green forest were reflected in the calm water, and the water itself was no longer brown; it ran a silty green for we were in the current of the Nahanni. There were cabins ahead of us and caches, and we made straight for them and tied up and carried our bedding and grub boxes up the bank. Faille produced a key from some hiding place in a log wall, and before very long we were sitting down, in Poole Field's cabin, to our first meal on the South Nahanni. It was Sunday, July 24th, 1927.

The cabin was piled full of boxes, sacks and kegs except for a little clear space round the stove and table. It was Hudson's Bay Company freight, dropped off there by the company's gas boat, *Liard River*, a few days before on her way up to Fort Liard and Fort Nelson. There was no Bay post here; there was only the little trading post run by Jack LaFlair, the independent trader. In fact there was not trade enough on the Nahanni for two establishments to exist profitably side by side. The Bay knew that quite well, but to it the Northwest Territories were still Rupert's Land, and an independent trader was an eyesore, an untidyness to be cleaned up as soon as possible. Hence this outfit, and there was a rumour that the Bay was going to establish a new post at the Hot Springs, forty miles up the Nahanni at the mouth of the Lower Canyon, with a view to drawing Jack's Indians up there and killing his trade. But nobody could be found to tackle the job of dragging this trade outfit up the river through the fast channels of The Splits, so it stayed where it was and Poole Field ran a post down there by the Butte for a time, and then others—but in the end Jack LaFlair outstayed them all. It was more than just a trading outpost to him—it was home.

By the time Faille and I had finished supper the lightning was already playing along the mountains to the west and the mosquitoes, knowing that it was now or never, swarmed into the cabin with redoubled fury. Every action became subservient to "the importunate Bizz of the Moskettoe": we put a bucket in the doorway with some embers in it, and green grass and fireweed on the embers. That fixed the mosquitoes, and it fixed me, too: I retreated outside and set up my tarpaulin lean-to between two trees and made my bed and set up my net beneath it. Faille was made of sterner stuff: he groped around in the choking fog in the cabin, heaving bales and boxes right and left until he had cleared himself a bedground on the floor, on the Jorrocksian principle of "where I dines I sleeps." Being an optimist he hoped he could shut the door and keep the mosquitoes out without bothering with a net—an error in judgement, he admitted next morning at breakfast.

The storm broke with a blaze of lightning on the summit of the Butte. Down came the rain, whole water, and by morning it had set in for a day's downpour. The mosquitoes were drowned, most of them, or frozen by the torrents of icy rain and we were never again seriously bothered with them. All day it poured and we stayed in the little cabin, cleaning up, cooking, reading and swapping the various yarns we had heard about the Nahanni. We put markers in the sand at the edge of the river to gauge its rise after this heavy rain: by evening the Nahanni was on the climb, and we eyed it sourly; every fresh inch of height meant so much more weight of water against us. We talked as we watched the rising flood: he was headed for the Flat River, Faille told me. He would be the first white man to winter up the Nahanni for seven years, he said, and we were the first ones to tackle the river alone in that time.

Next morning it was cold and misty, and we loaded up and waited for it to clear. I drew my canoe tarp over the load and tucked it in and adjusted the trackline in an insane kind of fixed "bridle" that somebody had shown me down by the lower rapids of the Liard. Fortunately Faille saw it.

"What's that rigging you've got on your canoe?" he asked.

"The way the line's fixed? That's the bridle for tracking."

"Well, whoever showed you that must be crazy. Keep that rigging the way it is and in two day's time you'll be walking out of here without your canoe, talking to yourself. How much line have you got?"

"A bit over eighty feet."

"That'll do. Let me have it, and I'll show you——"

He undid the bridle, took off some kind of a jockey stick that was lashed across the forward thwart and chucked it into the river. Then he tied one end of the eighty-foot line to the ring in the nose of the canoe and the other end to the rear seat.

"That's all you need," he said. "Now watch me."

He pushed the canoe into the river and started to walk up the shore with the bight of the line in his left hand. The canoe wasn't far enough out, it was heading for a rock, so Faille passed the line through his hand in a forward direction: this let the nose of the canoe fall away from shore and drew the tail in: the current did the rest and the canoe swung outside the rock, avoiding it, and was straightened again by a pull on the forward end of the line: it was brought in close to shore, as Faille walked, by a jerk on the canoe's nose and then sent flying out into the stream again by a pull on the rear end. It was one of those beautifully simple things

that any fool can understand—and it was flexible and perfect.
With that and a strong hand on the paddle and the ability to use a
pole a man can go anywhere.

Faille was letting the canoe drop downstream again.

"You can line down with that rigging, too," he said, "but it's
not so easy as going up. You can make time upriver that way,
with a light load, just as fast as you can walk, as long as you've got
a good tracking beach. But don't be afraid to let the canoe right
out into the current, outside the shore eddies and into deep water
whenever you can. Try to track her in shallow water and she'll
suck down to the bottom and pull like a lump of lead."

Patches of blue sky were appearing. Then the sun broke
through, the mist rolled away from the river and at noon we
started. The canoes were hitched together as before, since the first
eight miles of the Nahanni, where it winds like a serpent in two
tremendous oxbows at the foot of the Butte, is all quiet water. A
couple of hours later the first swirl of fast water hit us and Faille
pulled in to a shelving bank of gravel. As we unhitched we looked

at the prospect ahead: the wooded banks and quiet, sheltered water had given place to a wide-open flood plain strewn with sand-bars, shingle islands, wooded islands, huge driftpiles, and queer, dead-looking forests of snags where uprooted trees had lodged and settled on the river bottom and now, swept clean by ice and floods of all their branches, projected bleakly from the water, their broken tops pointing down river. Through this desolation rushed the Nahanni in, perhaps, two main channels and a maze of smaller ones. From a wooded bank nearby came the thudding lash of "sweepers"—trees that have been undercut by the floods into the river, but which still cling with their roots to the bank, lashing and beating at the water which drives through their branches. From all sides in this wasteland of the river came the noise of rushing water—it was the foot of The Splits.

Faille held out his hand. "Well, friend," he said, "here's where we part. Good luck to you." We shook hands and he shoved out into the current, pulling on the kicker's starting cord.

I arranged the pole and paddle so that they were handy for

TRACKING WITH SINGLE LINE

quick action. The spare paddle was lightly tied to a thwart in a position where it could be quickly freed and grabbed in the event of the other one being broken or lost: there was a split second once, in the Lower Canyon when I almost lost a paddle—fending the canoe off the canyon wall I thrust hard at the rock, and the blade of the paddle slipped neatly into a crevice and jammed there. The instinctive wrench brought it straight out again: had it stuck it would have been a case of hold on and be pulled out of the canoe, or let go and be whirled down the river plucking hurriedly at the ties that held the spare paddle. So it had to be handy. The sling straps of the rifle, a .303 Lee-Enfield sporting model, were fastened round the rear thwart, and the rifle itself was tucked in under the big canoe tarp, easy to get at quickly. A +8 Zeiss monocular in its leather case was strapped to the rear seat of the canoe. All seemed to be in order, so I flicked the canoe out into the current on the trackline and started upstream, wading in the shallows. I travelled for two or three miles and then made camp on a wooded island: the canoe was a bit too much down in the nose for this swift water and tended to sheer more than need be when coming out of an eddy—I could easily fix that by re-packing and shifting the weight further back. Later on I found that, on a long stretch of tracking, it paid to put a sizable rock in the canoe just forward of the rear seat to replace some of my own weight, and so to hold the nose well up and out of the grip of the eddies.

It was cold and clear that evening, and there were no mosquitoes: the cold rain had done them in, at least for the time being. So there was peace, and after supper I walked up to the head of the island: the usual driftpile was there, a huge affair of logs and dead trees, hopelessly entangled, piled and jammed there by many a June flood. It had been there a long time for big, old logs on the downstream end of it were rotten now; poplar and willow seedlings were sprouting out of them. In fact the driftpile had probably started the island in the first place, causing it to form in the eddy which it had created so many years ago. I climbed to the top of it and looked around. The sun was setting in the northwest, and the low, evening light threw into relief every boil and whirlpool on the surface of the racing river: other channels could be seen, gleaming here and there beyond other bars and islands in the cold, yellow light of the low sun. The water level was dropping now, but a little drift was still coming down the river after the thunderstorm and the rain. Round the bend above came a dead, drifting tree, its old broken roots black and queerly swaying against the golden, dark furrowed river. It seemed to be going very oddly, something was drawing it into the far bank—and then one saw the reason why, for a great bull moose emerged with deceptive slowness from the water, shook himself in a shower of diamonds and clattered away over the stones to plunge into the next channel—a prehistoric-looking beast, silhouetted against the evening sun.

From all around came the rush and swirl of the river and once, from half a mile upstream, an awe-inspiring roar as fifty yards of bank and a dozen tall trees crashed into the water. The Nahanni was at its old game again, undermining and cutting into the river the islands it had built up and the trees that had grown on them. The trees might hang on there as sweepers for a time; then they would be swept away by the floods or the running ice, to fetch up in some monstrous driftpile behind which the silt would gather again to build the island to grow the trees for the river to knock down once more in the fullness of time—world without end. I climbed forward to the end of the driftpile: one could feel it vibrating as the river drove into it, through it and underneath it, splitting on it into two channels. Let yourself get swept backwards in a canoe into one of these things and it would be the end of you: and the same applied to those lashing sweepers under the cut-banks—trapped, smashed and thrust under.

The next morning I was up at four and so were the sun and a small breeze. It was cloudless and perfect and never a mosquito from dawn to dusk. That was just as well, for The Splits presented other problems besides driftpiles and sweepers and the steady drive of fast water. As with most flood plains and deltas the main channel was high, and in this case pretty well in the centre, mid-way between the Twisted Mountain and Jackfish Mountain.[1]

[1]1927—it has shifted since then.

From this main channel there branched off, at acute angles, side chutes and channels, sometimes with a swift drop of three or four feet, leading off water from the main stream into lower channels, from which the process would be repeated into winding outer channels that were lower still. In a number of places the "shorn and parcelled" Nahanni is, by this means, as much as two miles across from outer channel to outer channel—it is easy to imagine the maze of islands in between.

Through this network of waterways I worked the canoe all that day, backing down out of impracticable channels to seek for some way around, sometimes crossing the heads of the side chutes and sometimes swept down them, but only to wade up once more on the upstream side, waist deep in water perhaps, hauling the canoe. That night my camp faced the Twisted Mountain, and from somewhere below it I could see a blue drift of wood smoke hanging in the evening air—it was from Faille's campfire.

Just to make tracking difficult, there was a north-west wind the following morning, and a little smoke haze drifted into the Nahanni country. I passed Faille's empty canoes turned upside down on the sand of a little bay where the shoulder of the Twisted Mountain shelves off into the river. The outfit was spread around on the rocks, drying and airing in the wind. Faille and his dogs were away somewhere—after a moose I supposed, but he told me afterwards that he had been looking for convenient trees where he could build a cache—the Nahanni was too strong for his small kicker and a full load; he had cached half the outfit there, and he would come down again and pick this stuff up in the fall.

A howling gale was blowing at midday, so I stopped and made a fire in the shelter of some trees. The trees came to an end a little way upstream: beyond them was a sunlit waste of grey stones, gay with the purple flowers of the willow herb that were dancing there in the wind. Something moving caught my eye from that direction as I knelt by the fire, frying bacon with one hand and doing things to the tea pail with the other. I looked up and saw a medium-sized black bear going as if the devil were at his heels. He was tearing across the stony flat towards the channel in which my canoe was tied, the bank of which, in front of him, was undercut and about four feet above the water. That didn't bother him one bit: he never checked his speed for even a fraction of a second; he leapt into the air, sailed out from the bank and hit the Nahanni with a shattering bellyflopper, sending a minor tidal wave downriver. It didn't take him long to swim the channel: out he came on the far side, pausing a moment to shake himself like a dog while a perfect fountain of spray flew from his long fur. Then away again at a lope to repeat the performance at the next channel: the shingle bars here were bare of trees, and I could see the spray fountain growing smaller every time till the bear vanished into the bush towards Jackfish River. He had evidently made up his mind to leave the country in a hurry: pottering about in his inquisitive, black-bearish way, he had probably run smack into Faille and his

dogs and given himself a thoroughly bad scare.

But lunch was ready, and I was ready for it. I had just seated myself with a mug of tea handy and the frying pan beside me on the ground when a shadow swept across camp and there was an appalling sound, as of tearing silk, right over my head. I jumped up and turned just in time to see a great, bald-headed eagle banking away from the trees—and at that moment the splitting sound was repeated as a second eagle braked and banked a few feet from my head. This was getting to be too much of a good thing, and I grabbed a towel and the rifle and waved one and brandished the other. The eagles came again, but not a third time: what they wanted, or whether the red scarf around my neck attracted them, I never knew, but there are few things more startling than that sound coming suddenly out of the blue.

I slept for a couple of hours under the trees until the wind dropped and then I went on. The Twisted Mountain fell behind and I passed the North Elbow and turned west into the sun. Camp that night was close to a sharp, foothill ridge, cut through by the river, that we later came to know as the Outpost Hills. Supper was late, and wolves were howling somewhere back on the ridges. Up a nearby snye beaver were playing about; one could hear them splashing and hear, every now and then, the resounding slap of a flat tail brought down square on to the surface of the water. The Splits lay behind, and far ahead was a range of square-looking, block-faulted mountains;[1] but where or what it was, or whether the Nahanni would take me to the foot of it, I had no means of knowing. In the dusk, as I took a last look up and down the river, a cow moose and calf walked sedately down the opposite shore.

The noonday sun blazed down into the little bay, and the rocks were hot to the touch. The wet sand by the water's edge was hidden under a carpet of shimmering blue, a host of small blue butterflies delighting in the heat: gaudy black and yellow swallowtails flickered past, gay jockeys of the sunshine in their racing jackets. Across the river the leaves of the cottonwoods glittered in the

---

[1]The Tlogotsho Range of later years.

hard, clear light, turning their grey undersides to the sun as the little breeze from the canyon stirred them. The midday fire was on the sand at the foot of the Painted Cliffs, and these, with their harsh, flaring reds and yellows, banded with ochre and blotched with dead-looking lichens, added no coolness to the scene. The sun flashed up from the eddy in which the canoe lay, and its heat was thrown back by the sand and the tall, brightly coloured cliffs: there was a faintly putrid smell about the place, for out of these cliffs, so gaily encrusted with their vivid mineral deposits, bubbled small springs, some of them warm and all tasting vilely of sulphur. There were no more islands here and, only a mile or two ahead, the river issued from a great cleft in the mountain wall—the mouth of the Lower Canyon of the Nahanni.

A short stretch of tracking after lunch brought me up into fast water, and I crossed the river to get the easier going on the right bank. The water seemed to be warmer there, and I splashed along very contentedly in the shallows, with the canoe out in deep water on the trackline and my eyes on the canyon mouth ahead.

But the water was getting warmer fast, and there was a blue tinge to it and a clearness that looked wrong, somehow, against the silty green of the Nahanni. The delicate stink of rotten eggs drifted downriver on the canyon breeze, and ahead one could see the riffle where the warm stream came into the river: this was the first landmark on the trail, the Hot Springs of the Nahanni.

I beached the canoe above the warm creek and climbed the bank. There was a good camping place there, and I marked it down for future reference. From it a trail wound off into the bush: I followed it and came in a few hundred yards to a little meadow. There was grass there, and grass is a rarity on the South Nahanni below timberline: the clearing must have been started, in the dim past, by the wild game and then gradually enlarged by man with the help, no doubt, of the animals who came to this place and killed the surrounding trees by scratching and rubbing on them and so destroying the bark. There were cleared spaces of old Indian camps, more used in an earlier day than now when treaty money and the dole of government supplies keep the Nahanies hanging around down in the Liard country through the summer months, instead of roaming freely through the mountains like their nomad ancestors. Many of the old campsites had become overgrown with an exuberance of wild roses and wild fruits—gooseberries, raspberries and red and black currants. The springs themselves were of a clear, blue water; hot, but not too hot to lie in if you picked your spring, for the temperatures varied: they welled up close to the foot of the cliff, and the cliff was the end of the western precipice of the Lower Canyon as it swept away from the river. The meadow and the alleyways through the bush had been trampled by moose and bears, but everywhere one could see evidences of a riotous, almost tropical growth of grass, flowers and bushes. There were gorgeous butterflies there, pale orange and blue, and, in the red and yellow columbines that grew in the rocks at the foot of the cliff, humming-birds were busy—tiny, flashing, bright red jewels with their wives in bronze and iridescent green. One could well understand how the story of the Tropical Valley got around: the eager young reporter, a type ever prominent on the sucker list, and the old trapper, reminiscent in some tavern, and with the memory of all this beauty to spur his tongue. . . .

Hidden away in the mountains of the North-West, and preferably somewhere in the canyons of the Upper Liard, there was a valley like the pleasant vale of Avalon from which the storms and the cold winds turned aside, where the snow never lay and winter never came. The valley was a sun trap and a Chinook trap—the only wind that blew was the warm south-west Chinook, and it blew all the time, softly through the mountain passes, bringing nothing but the gentle rain. And, better even than this, the grinding glaciers of the ice ages had passed this valley by, and there were relics there of a pre-glacial flora:[1] palm trees, even, could be relied upon to appear as the old trapper warmed to his story.

A pleasant tale, though difficult to swallow, and we all liked to think that somewhere there might be an eternal garden cached

---

[1]Not impossible, at least in a gentler climate: survivals of a pre-glacial flora are to be found alongside certain fumaroles on the Mediterranean island of Ischia.

away amongst these hills. These hot springs of the Nahanni added to the legend, and some writers made use of them in fanciful stories of the North. But the main source of inspiration was the big hot springs on the Liard, a few miles from the bridge by which the Alaska Road crosses that river today.

Near those springs a trapper named Tom Smith once had his camp, and from there, with his half-breed daughter, he ran his trapline. He was probably the "Liard Smith" mentioned as coming to Gold Creek on the Flat River in Part I. When he came in to trade his furs at the Lower Post, Fort Liard or Fort Simpson he brought with him tales of these great springs and the luxuriant growth around them—and the legend grew, not without the assistance of many willing collaborators. It was the dying kick, in Canada, of the Age of Marvels, in which, if a cartographer found himself with an embarrassingly blank space on the map, he felt free to write there whatever had pleased him most out of a tangle of travellers' tales. "Basiliskes," perhaps, or "Prester John." The Mackenzie Mountains in 1927 offered similar opportunities to the bold, inventive spirit.

Finally the Tropical Valley legend gained such force that, in 1935, Dr. Charles Camsell, the Deputy Minister of Mines, flew over the area, landing at the various supposed locations of the valley, on some lake or river as close as possible. That settled it as far as he was concerned, and the myth was officially exploded: the rampant growth in these places was properly set down to sub-irrigation by warm water and a consequent early start in the spring and, though no palm trees were seen, the official party had to ram its way through strands of wild timothy growing seven feet high. And quite likely, from the sound of it, through swarms of giant-size mosquitoes as well. A gallant effort and a vain one, for the story still persists.

There seemed to be a few mosquitoes here, too: they were gathering like vultures to the feast, and it was high time to go. As I walked back to the canoe it struck me that the fallen trees lying across the trail were unusually rotten—there was no sound wood anywhere lying on the ground. Kraus told me why in 1951: he had built a trapping cabin close to the springs some years previously, but had found it impossible to maintain—there was so much sulphur in the ground that the sill logs rotted away in two years.

I crossed the Nahanni to catch the tracking beach on the left bank. There were some old cabins there on the little flat, and a cleared space around them that had gone back completely to wild fruit. There were the best wild raspberries there that I have ever tasted, masses of them and just as good and just as large as any garden varieties. And there were black currants and red currants, and any open patch of stony ground was covered with fat, ripe, wild strawberries. I ate till I could eat no more, and then I filled the tea pail with raspberries and put it away in the shade, in the nose of the canoe.

The Nahanni was quiet here: no sound came from it except sometimes a gentle lapping of the water on the stones. As one looked upstream, north-west into the canyon, the river swung to the right and disappeared between the towering walls. Two big cottonwoods close by the cabins had just been felled by the beavers; the chips could not be more than a day old; some of the tender shoots had been eaten and some of the bark gnawed off the branches. It was late in the afternoon now, and the shadow of the great cliff above the Hot Springs was creeping across the river towards the old cabins: there was a faint blue haze, perhaps of smoke, in the air, and the edge of the shadow was visible in the haze. Thousands of wildly gyrating bugs danced in the warm, still air. They danced most thickly, or so it seemed, along the shadow-line—whirling pinpoints of silver light in the sunshine, vanishing utterly as they passed into the shadow of the canyon wall.

The beach down by the canoe was tramped and churned as if all the moose on the Nahanni had yarded there. As I shoved the canoe out into the current a stone rolled with a clatter on the far shore: I looked up and saw a bull moose walk down to the river to drink, just above the sulphur stream. I have passed the Hot Springs eleven times since then and camped there for several days, but always, when I think of the place, I see the picture of that first afternoon with its humming-birds and columbines, the bugs, the bull moose and the beaver cuttings.

I poled the canoe on into the shadows, and it was not long before I was in the water up to my waist hauling the canoe "by the snoot," as Faille called it, up Lafferty's Riffle. This riffle—the second strongest in the Lower Canyon—had, in those days, built up for itself a great, crescent-shaped bar of shingle reaching halfway across the river. The main stream flowed round the end of the bar and roared down the steep drop, foaming and bellowing under the cliffs. The rest of the river had cut channels for itself through the bar and the water raced down these in swift, brawling chutes, each one strong enough to sweep a man off his legs and most of them too deep to wade. I had not met anything like this before, and I had not yet developed the "bar technique" that I built up later from experience. The affair at Lafferty's Riffle that last evening of July was simply a brute, head-on collision between me and the Nahanni. All I brought to the contest was a certain in-born river sense and an ability to see what water was going to do with a canoe before it had done it. Using this and the experience gained in The Splits, I reached the head of the riffle after a hard struggle—soaked but victorious. The riffle had changed greatly when I saw it twenty-four years later, in 1951: it had become a much simpler affair, a straight hill of water.

The river made a sharp turn to the left (as one faced upstream) and in the middle of the next reach was a bar of sand and shingle with plenty of driftwood lying about on it. There I made camp, and very soon a fire was blazing on the sand, a few wet rags of clothing dangled from the roots of stranded trees, and I was warm and comfortable in old cord riding trousers, heavy shirt and sweater. The last rays of the sun went off this east-west reach as I was having supper, and I soon found myself reaching for a mackinaw jacket. The contrast, in one week's travel, between this canyon world of cool breezes and cold, rushing waters and the sweaty, mosquito-infested plain of the Liard was almost unbelievable.

After supper I walked up to the head of this shingle island. At the upper end of the reach the river swung sharply to the right, or north, so that in every direction—upstream, downstream and on either shore—one was faced with the tremendous canyon walls.

They rose sheer from the talus slopes at their feet, with mosses and dwarf firs growing on the ledges: limestone and sandstone they were, in level strata, but the colours of the rocks were fading now and the cliffs were turning blue in the twilight. From all sides came the noises of swift, clashing water.

Never in my wildest dreams had I hoped to see anything like this. Away in the distance, at the foot of the island, the tiny flame of the campfire could be seen, flickering and winking: wreaths of blue wood smoke from it were drifting away down the canyon. Somewhere I had seen something for which this wild scene might have been the prototype: it was a fantastic engraving of the last survivor of the human race cowering in the dusk beside his puny fire at the bottom of some vast, shadowy canyon—a monstrous gash into the heart of a dead world. This place was it, as near as any man would ever see it. Gordon Matthews and I camped several times on this bar in the following year, and we came to know it as the Last Man Camp.

The Lower Canyon must be about fourteen miles long, and it took me two days to get through it. The place that nearly stuck me was not far above that first camp: there is an island in the river there, and an island well out into the stream usually means trouble since the current, splitting on the point of it, is thrown hard against the cliffs on either shore. The result is that each side is sheer and deep, affording no tracking beach and no poling bottom. This island was no exception to the rule; in fact, it was worse than most of these obstructions: the river raced past it in a fast riffle, and each bank was a sheer rock wall. There was only one thing to do—wade the canoe upstream from the upper point of the island until the last possible inch had been gained and the canoe floated level with the breast pockets of one's shirt. Then spring in off the river bottom, grab the paddle and let drive with it, all out, and try to catch the tail end of a sandy beach on the right shore before being swept backwards down the riffle.

Twice I was whirled down close under the canyon wall, and the third time I made it—just. The hardest thing in making one of these crossings off an island is to balance the canoe at exactly the right angle before jumping in. An inch or two off centre and the canoe will sheer as you jump—and you might as well make a fresh start. The nose of the canoe must split the current exactly, with the very slightest bias towards the shore you are making for. When you have it that way, jump and put all you know into it!

And why doesn't the canoe upset when you jump in? And what about the load? You must fetch in two or three quarts of water every time you try this stunt—surely the whole outfit must get completely soaked by the end of the day?

Well, for one thing you're not using a round-bottomed, tipply pleasure canoe: you're using a work canoe. I had a sixteen-foot Chestnut, Prospector Model, thirty-six inches wide and fourteen inches deep—a canoe with beautiful lines but fairly flat-bottomed: load three or four hundred pounds of outfit into that and you've got a pretty stable canoe—something you won't upset at all easily. You can stand up and pole in it, you can crawl about over the load in it and pull yourself upstream by handholds in the canyon wall, and you can put all your weight onto the gunwale on one side of it and still it won't upset from that cause alone.

Faille had an eighteen-foot freight canoe—also a Chestnut. His canoe was forty-six inches wide and eighteen inches deep, and when that was loaded down solid you could go for a stroll over the load and it would barely alter the trim. Faille was using a 3 1/2 h.p. outboard, and he had it out on a home-made bracket, not off to one side as one sometimes sees them, but where it should be—directly behind the stern of the canoe. He had no use for a square-ended canoe, specially shaped to take an outboard, and, after running one down the Cache Rapid two years ago, neither have I.

As to water in the canoe, that was easily dealt with. I always laid, lengthways on the bottom, three light, dry spruce poles: over them was spread a large double-proofed tarpaulin, the "canoe tarp." One edge of this was pulled up level with the gunwale of the canoe, and the perishable part of the load—flour, sugar, ammunition, clothes, films, etc.—was then laid in the bight of this big tarp and packed solid. When this was done the ends of the tarp could be folded up, and the loose bunch of tarpaulin on the far side of the canoe could be pulled across under the thwarts and

tucked in *outside* the section that was level with the gunwale, between it and the side of the canoe. If that was carefully done the
canoe could dive through a wave in a riffle, or have six inches of
rain water slopping about in it from an over-night thunderstorm,
and still the load would be perfectly dry. The three spruce poles
on the floor of the canoe would allow this water to drain back into
the tail whence it could be bailed. Anything like a waterproofed
tent, a sleeping bag in its proofed cover, axes, cooking pots and so
forth would be packed where they were most handy, outside the
tarp. A sharp, light axe always lay ready for action, under the
rear seat of the canoe. The trackline of heavy sash cord lay on top
of the canoe tarp, coiled in such a way that it would pay out swiftly
and easily, without getting snarled up, as one jumped for shore
holding the line in either hand. On top of all this lay the pole,
shod end to the rear, point tucked into the canoe's nose, where
also was to be found a roll of birch bark for the lighting of a fire.

That passage through the Lower Canyon was the sort of thing
that comes to a man perhaps once in a lifetime—if he's lucky. The
scenery is the finest on the Nahanni, and the weather was
perfect—clear, with cold nights and blazing hot days. And it was
all strange and new: rounding a bend was like turning a page in a
book of pictures; what would one see, this time, and would this
next reach hold, perhaps, some insuperable obstacle? But it never
did, and always one found some way around by means of some
new trick with the line or the pole.

The battered old diary is a bit faded now but still legible: "At
4.30 I came to a point of rocks where there was the worst chute of
all, so I tied the canoe and climbed on over the rocks to see what I
could do to pass through it, but I could see nothing for one man
alone except to go up as far as possible in the eddy and then
unload and portage—over big, tumbled rocks. So I went back and
camped and beached the canoe to dry out the load. Think this
must be the end of the canyon as I could see a wider country
ahead and blue ranges of mountains in the distance, standing out
sharp against the sun. Walls of the canyon here must be 800-foot
precipices—almost sheer."

It *was* the end of the canyon, and the big riffle was the Cache

Rapid: there was an old cache back in the bush behind the little bay of black sand where the canoe was beached, and it got its name from that. And the wide open country ahead was Deadmen Valley, though I was not to know that until I reached Fort Liard in September. After supper that evening I went up on to the point of rocks: the low evening light coming through the gap from Deadmen Valley struck across the riffle and threw the big waves into full relief: it was a wild-looking piece of water. . . .

Next morning I cached some heavy stuff back in the bush near the old cache: then I loaded up and was just going to start up the eddy when I heard the noise of Faille's kicker. One could just see a speck of movement far down the reach, a mile or more away. Up he came, slowly: he had his light canoe with him, towing alongside his eighteen-footer. I waved him into the little bay, pointing out some sunken rocks that lay just off shore: we arranged our mouths in grins of greeting; it was no use trying to say anything with that kicker running. Right at the psychological moment, when he was swinging in but was still well out in the current, the outboard conked, the grins were wiped from our faces, and Faille grabbed a paddle and faded backwards down the Nahanni trying to drive his unwieldy outfit in to shore: in the sudden silence, and before he got out of earshot, I heard from across the water the spirited prelude to a discourse on outboard motors that he was evidently composing. . . .

Quite a while later he reappeared, and this time the programme went off without a hitch; soon his canoes were nosed into the sandy shore and we were shaking hands.

"My God," Faille said, "who'd have thought it would be like this? This is *some* canyon: a thousand feet, I'd call it—"

"I figured about eight hundred," I broke in.

"No! A thousand anyway—maybe more."

We were both a little out in our reckoning, and the charitable will remember that, from the fish's eye viewpoint, which was what we had been getting, the great walls are very much foreshortened. The following year I twice carried an aneroid barometer from the river level to the plateau, and I found that the main walls in the lower part of the Canyon rose a good 1,500 feet practically sheer: then, set back by one or two talus slopes, the topmost cliffs stood a clear 3,000 feet above the Nahanni, while the plateau through which the canyon was cut sloped up another 1,500 feet to its highest point.

We christened this chute the Cache Rapid and then proceeded together to line first one and then the other of the small canoes up the rocky shore to an eddy at the head of the drop—one of us on the line and the other fending the canoes off the rocks with a pole. Then Faille went back and brought up his freight canoe by means of the little outboard; and the way he did it with that low horsepower kicker and through those big waves, so sweetly and easily, was a fine thing to see.

By the time he got up to the eddy I had a fire going and the tea water boiling. We ate our lunch there and then tackled the two strong riffles that lie above the Cache Rapid. We went up side by side, and all was going well when Faille's kicker, with that flair for timing that these accursed tea-kettles seem to possess, conked in a bad spot. As luck would have it he was swept in toward shore, and as soon as he was in shallow enough water he jumped overboard and grabbed his big canoe. He couldn't advance a step in that racing water with that heavy load; all he could do was to stand there, in up to his waist, and hang on till I had beached my canoe and waded out to him. Then, step by step, Faille on the "snoot," snout or nose, and myself on the tail, we waded his outfit up to the head of the riffle and to a safe landing. There I left him tinkering and went back and brought up my canoe and went on, past the Little Butte, a five-hundred-foot, tree-clad rock that overhangs the river, and into Deadmen Valley.

The bit of water we had just come up is the strongest on the Nahanni below the mouth of Flat River. I had had enough canyon for a while and was glad to see something new—and some quiet water. I found "a lovely reach of calm water,[1] glittering in the burning sunlight. The walls fell back and gave place to a wide valley surrounded by forested mountains. Streams of water clear as glass came pouring down from clefts in the rock. . . ." It was

[1]Christened by Starke, in 1928, "Patterson's Lake."

my first introduction to the mysterious valley where the McLeods had been killed twenty years before.

But today it was just another valley in the mountains, and I poled and tracked the canoe on westwards—past Ram Creek, past the mouths of Prairie Creek, past Wheatsheaf Creek, one eye on the glittering river and the other on the towering masses of boiling, white cumulus clouds, anvil-headed, that were climbing over the western range. Thunder was rumbling somewhere back in those mountains: then the sun went in behind the cloud masses, lightning flashed, and a drifting skirt of rain trailed down the valley of the Meilleur River. I had left it almost too late: "I made a rush for a spot sheltered by trees and just managed to get a big fire lit, my tarp up, and myself and things flung under it and the stuff in the canoe covered, when down she came—came with a flash and a bang—whole water! Sand blew off the bars, spray blew off the river, smoke blew in from some fire in the Yukon: lightning, thunder, rain, a whole gale—and all the time the sun shone, pale yellow through the rain, over a mountain and under a cloud—it looked just like hell."

Typical Deadmen Valley stuff, that: throw everything at you at once, all in ten minutes, and then turn out all sweet and smiling five minutes later. Mosquitoes suddenly appeared at suppertime so I set up my net under the tarpaulin and went to bed at ten.

I woke at four to a lovely morning. The rim of the sun was just climbing over the mountains above the Dry Canyon, and I lay there, in bed in great comfort, lazily watching the river and the rising sun and dreaming about getting up. Something was swimming the river up there: it was a bull moose, and he was going to climb out on to that shingle island; and Faille needed meat for himself and his dogs, and I could find a home for a few steaks. I rolled over in bed and reached for the rifle; then I pushed up one side of the mosquito net and arranged my mackinaw jacket, which was serving as a pillow, so that it would make a good rest. Then I waited. It was five hundred yards to that moose—he was probably pretty safe from me.

His great bulk emerged from the water, shining in the low morning sun. He walked slowly across the island, and I fired as he reached the centre of it: he stopped dead, and there was a second's pause: I was just going to shoot again when his knees crumpled under him and he pitched forward and on one side. He gave a couple of kicks, and I wondered for a moment if he was going to start to kick himself into the river. But no, that was all: one could get up and dress now and light the fire and have breakfast with the day well begun; Faille would probably be along soon, and there would be moose for everybody—moose galore.

I had my canoe unloaded and ready when Faille came up: we got into it and reached the island after some hard paddling. There we dealt with the moose, returning soon afterwards to camp and to a capering, excited trio of dogs, with a heavy canoe load of moose meat. By this time the wind had got up: it blew harder and harder, bending the tree tops and drifting the sand off the big bar into the bush towards Prairie Creek. Neither of us could travel: a canoe in a high wind is about as manageable as a cork bobbing about on top of the water. And neither of us cared very much—a day on dry land, after The Splits and the canyon and the Cache Rapid, was very welcome: "So we bathed and cooked, and washed and mended our clothes, and lunched off moose liver and bacon and still it blows." Faille wandered off into the bush, and I swilled out my canoe and then turned it bottom up, patched one or two places and put on a coat of grey canoe paint. It needed it: The Splits and the sharp rocks of the canyon had left their marks on it. While I did this I kept an eye on two appetising-looking mulligans that were simmering gently over the fire: they had everything in them from sage and red pepper to wild onions, dried potatoes, rice and the leaves of Labrador tea, all on top of a rich foundation of the tenderest of the meat. Later on I fished and then baked bannock for our supper.

Faille and the dogs reappeared towards evening, and we cut a few steaks off the tenderloin and set about getting supper.

"I like this valley," he said. "It's a good country, and if I wasn't headed for Flat River I'd stay here and put in the winter. A man could make a good catch of fur here."

"Why don't you stay, then, if you like it so much?"

"No! Flat River, that's my destiny!"

From that camp we pushed on upriver, through the maze of bars and channels that we called The Second Splits. Faille faded from view; in a place like this he could make better time than I could: I travelled nine or ten miles and camped halfway through the Second Canyon: ragwort was growing there and big, purple wild asters, and the place was alive with the humming of wild bees.

I went on and into the Little Valley, past Scow Creek where an old scow, battered and useless, lay drawn up into the bush. I entered the Third Canyon, a mountainous country where the canyon walls are less well defined but often more spectacular than they are anywhere in the lower canyons. And I passed through the Gate of the Nahanni where the walls close in, and the quiet, green river glides silently between tawny precipices that climb a thousand feet sheer into the sky. And at the head of the Gate the canoe's nose swung to the left, northwestwards into the long reach of the Red Screes. At the top of that reach I saw Faille's tracks on a sand-bar, and shortly after that I made camp on the right bank.

Round the next bend I found Faille. His canoes were drawn up on the beach on the left bank, and his mosquito net was set up a few yards away, by a little creek. Smoke was curling up from his breakfast fire, but there was no other sign of life about the camp. The Nahanni ahead looked tough—sheer cliffs on either side, a rock in the middle, a strong riffle and no poling bottom. One would have to portage.

I crossed over and beached my canoe beside Faille's. I found him stretched out on his eiderdown under his net reading a life of Father Lacombe: he was fed up with life and for the moment, discouraged.

"This Nahanni," he said, "she's a tough river. Never lets up: just a steady drive all the time. And the way that kicker eats gas, bucking this current, Flat River had better show up soon!"

He rolled out, and we had some coffee and made our plan of action: we would portage all our stuff about a quarter of a mile along the top of the cliff on this left bank, and down to a little bay at the head of the riffle. Then we would paddle the canoes across the river and try to get on to a ledge in the canyon wall that Faille had spotted, from which, if the ledge didn't peter out, we could track the canoes upstream till we were above the riffle and above the head of the portage. Then into the canoes again, if we could climb down to them, and back across the river to the portage bay where all the outfit would be waiting for us. Simple. There was only one other "if" in the performance—if we didn't make a straight crossing of the Nahanni to the ledge without losing any ground, we would miss the ledge and be swept backwards over a three-foot drop caused by a projecting reef of the canyon wall. And the only chance of making a straight crossing was to tackle it with empty canoes.

Faille by now was completely cheered up by the prospect of action and the chance of outwitting the river, and we went straight at it. He cut out an old trail from camp over the first half of the portage: I cut out the second half and made a good trail down into the little bay. Then we portaged everything except the canoes, poles and paddles; and when that was done we sat down in the bay where our stuff was and cooked and ate a tremendous meal, "because if we make a mess of that crossing it'll be a long, cold day before we see grub again—if we ever do." And then we walked back to the canoes—which, incidentally, we could have portaged too, like the rest of the stuff, but what fun was there in that?

Faille tackled it first: he bounced away over the waves and, after a struggle, made it and waved to me to come: landing on that ledge seemed to be easier than it looked from where I was standing. Then I took my paddle and shoved out from shore. I gained ground at first until I hit the riffle, and then, for about ninety seconds there seemed to be water racing past me in all directions as the canoe skimmed across towards Faille. The roar of the river over the reef was getting closer—and then the current slackened, the canoe gained a foot or two, and I caught the tail end of the ledge where it shelved off into the water.

"That beats portaging!" Faille was saying, delightedly. "We fooled the Nahanni that time! Now, if this ledge only holds. . . ."

It held. It did better than that—it widened into a magnificent paved boulevard, big enough to take a farm wagon and team. As it widened it sloped upwards till it was twelve or fourteen feet above the water, and then it levelled off. As we walked along this paved highway with the empty canoes skimming along below us on the tracklines we wondered how we were going to get down, for the cliff was sheer or overhanging; but the obliging ledge carried on just as far as we needed it and no more; then it sloped gently off into the river in a natural ramp, and we got into the canoes again and whirled across the river to the portage bay.

Faille went back for his second canoe while I made camp and got some water boiling. Then we bathed, re-loaded the canoes and made our sleeping places under the trees. The day ended with a terrific supper, at which a delicacy of Faille's construction, Norwegian Logging Cake, held the place of honour, preceded by enormous moose steaks; and then, when all was done, we sat for an hour or so smoking and talking on a drift log by the fire, close to the water's edge.

The river ran due south here, and the gorge lay in the evening shadow. The last light of the sun struck full on the mountain at the foot of this long reach: one looked down a hill of tossing, boiling water towards it, with every wave and every whirlpool in strong relief, cold and blue: the river fetched up against the base of the mountain and then swung to the left and disappeared. The grey limestone mountain was turning to a soft rose colour in the sunset light. . . .

"I'll bet we're the first men to use that ledge," Faille was saying. "You can't see it at all from here, and you can only just see it in certain lights from where I was camped last night. And what a river! A lifetime wouldn't be enough for a man to see all this. . . . The first men! Well, we'd better go and get some sleep."

After a breakfast that ended with wild raspberries and my last can of cream, we went on our way, and Faille's kicker soon took him out of sight. The weather was perfect, and the memory of those days of canyon travel is of colour—colour everywhere, lit by the blazing August sun. There were drifts of tall blue delphiniums and yellow arnica daisies, and there were acres of purple fireweed, almost over now and the leaves turning to their autumn red. Everywhere amongst the flowers fluttered the black and yellow swallowtails, and everywhere there was the heavy scent of spruce and fir on the warm summer air and the hum of countless wild bees. There was colour in the patches of wild fruits where the great, fat raspberries grew, and there was colour in the green river and in all the varied greens of the northern forest that clung to the canyon walls. But the canyon came to an end half a day's travel from the portage camp, and the mountains fell back a little from the river which ran here between rocky, wooded foothills. This was woodland caribou country now, and twice I saw them swimming the Nahanni—the first game I had seen since leaving Deadmen Valley, excepting for two or three black bears ambling along the banks, stopping to turn over a rock or bash a rotten log to pieces in search of grubs, dawdling and then breaking into short scampering runs as if to make up for lost time.

In camp that night just below the Flat River I noticed a faint muttering in the ground when I lay down to sleep. It came up through the mackinaw jacket which was my pillow, steadily and persistently, and I wondered what it could be. A rapid somewhere near, I thought; but in the morning there was no rapid to be seen, and I knew then that the vibration in the ground must have come from the great Falls of the Nahanni. So I was near the mouth of Flat River; that was something to know. If the map was even vaguely right those falls had to be at least twenty miles away, perhaps more, and a pretty notable affair they must be, to make themselves felt at that distance.

I passed Faille's light canoe drawn up on a sand-bar: that meant he was running out of gas and was now down to tracking and poling like myself. Then the valley opened out and divided into two, separated by a great block of a hill. The smaller valley seemed to head west while the main Nahanni went on north-westerly. I climbed on top of a driftpile and looked across the water with the glass: from the westerly valley seemed to come water of a deeper, clearer green, no doubt that of the Flat River. It came slowly, almost dead water, and was sheared off, as with a knife, by the silty, glacial green of the Nahanni as it swept round the outside of a bend. One would have to be careful there on the way down, passing from such fast water into water with no current at all. Shove the canoe's nose head-on into that slack water while its tail was still in the Nahanni current and the results would be quite spectacular—rather like shoving a fishing rod through the front wheel of a bicycle while racing downhill. I had done that once, in my early days, and I was not at all keen on trying a watery version of it.

I tracked on upriver. By the way Faille's footprints were dug into the gravel he must have been tracking here, too. Then, after a quarter of a mile or so, one could see where he had coiled his trackline and stepped into his canoe to make the jump across and into the mouth of the Flat. I pulled out my rifle and fired a shot into the air to let him know that I had gone by: without gas and with the other half of his gas and load still cached down at the Twisted Mountain, I knew that he would go no further than the first good building site. All he would be looking for now would be the nearest good bunch of building spruce with a reasonably good landing close by.

The Falls are nearly twenty miles upstream from the mouth of the Flat River, and those twenty miles, as I was soon to find out, are the worst on all the lower river. Short canyons of red and yellow rock through which the river boils and races, rock strewn in dry summers of low water and with five- and six-foot waves in the riffles: powerful eddies that drive a loaded canoe upstream on a slack trackline too fast for a man on the shore, clambering frantically over the tumbled rocks, to keep pace with it: sharp rocks onto which the eddies or the waves from the big riffles drive the canoe, slicing its canvas: whirlpools, driftpiles, sheer cliffs with deep, racing water at their feet—all these are crowded close in those twenty miles as if to test the spirit of the voyageur to the breaking point. I travelled late that day; I passed the Flat River and camped late. There was no time to lose: autumn was on its way, the first reds and browns were appearing in the undergrowth, scarlet of wild rose, deep crimson of choke-cherry and blueberry, and that night I saw the aurora streaming out of the north-east in rainbow-coloured fire.

The next day at noon I came to an old camping place facing

west, and I landed there and made my midday fire. The axe cuts were all old: if Faille was right and we were the first white men up here in seven years, then nobody had come this way at all in that time, for the Indians made no use of canoes for upstream travel; they reached their hunting grounds in wintertime, using dog teams and travelling over the river ice or the level alpine tundra country, coming down the Nahanni or the Beaver River in springtime in skin boats of moosehide with their families, dogs and catch of fur.

So there was nobody in all the Nahanni country except Faille and myself, unless there was any one in somewhere on the head-waters from the Yukon side or from the North Nahanni. That gave us about six thousand square miles apiece, if not more—elbow room enough, anyway, even for a couple of solitary eccentrics of the lone-wolf variety. I liked that camp, I decided, as I sat there on the grub-box, munching away at bacon and bannock and drinking tea: I had travelled steadily for a week, and now I would take a half day on shore and refit. It was necessary, for the river had taken its toll.

First of all I unloaded the canoe, dried it out and did some patching on it with heavy canvas, tacks, glue and shellac. Then I came a step nearer home and did some much needed patching on myself: I had been wearing crepe rubber-soled running shoes, mostly without socks, and light drill trousers; the shoes were sliced and torn from wading the canoe over reefs of sharp slate and shale, and my feet and legs were in the same condition as the shoes. The cold water driving at them all day long with its tiny particles of glacial silt had prevented these gashes from healing thoroughly, and the result now was a network of blue tattoo marks that would have done credit to a freak in a circus. I did what I could with them and exchanged the battered old shoes for the soft comfort of moccasins. Then I baked a couple of bannocks, upending the caky mixture in a frying pan before a glowing mass of charcoal and turning and browning it till it was done and ready to cool. Meanwhile rice and raisins were cooking in a small pot and a mixture of dried fruit in another—there was a lot to be said for this river travel where one could carry cooked food in the canoe in its native pot: that was something you couldn't do with pack-horses. And the long fire on the river sand—no other form of travel gave one that so easily and safely. Two long, dry drift logs are laid parallel, about six inches apart, and a fire is lit between them. As this fire grows, it can be spread lengthways between the logs, and then, when cooking operations start, the pots and frying pans are stood each one on a couple of green poplar or willow sticks laid in Vs across the two large logs. Laid so, in Vs, the green sticks cannot roll, and the array of pots and pans sits in safety over the fire as well as if on a stove, thus cutting down the amount of swearing necessary to the getting of supper by about seventy per cent. But that evening no pot dared to upset: supper cooked itself while I bathed and shaved, and I sat down to it feeling clean and slack and easy: this was the way to enjoy this golden summer—and I ate tremendously and watched the shift and play of light and colour on the river and the wild chaos of the folded hills. This camp, I thought, must be about seventeen hundred feet above sea level, judging from the barometer readings—a nice, comfortable altitude, though nothing that one could saddle with the blame for this appalling appetite.

I looked around for the rifle: the last of the moose was in the pot, and the camp needed meat; and I always went out in the evening anyway, when there was time after supper—along the river beaches or to the top of some nearby hill. I went straight back into the woods and then up a tangled slope of alder thickets and small firs onto the bald summit of a hill that I had seen as I came up the river. Soon I was comfortably settled in a little hollow in the turf with my back to a warm rock, and I pulled my field glass out of its case to see what I could see. A small breeze was blowing from the west, warm and dry, but the heat of the day was over and, if there was any game in the country, it should be on the move now. First of all I looked west, up the glittering river, planning my trip for the morrow as far as I could see up the Nahanni before it lost itself in a jumble of hills: I had it all sorted out and fixed in my head and was just going to turn away when a caribou stepped daintily out of the bush and walked down to drink at the river's edge: he looked upstream and then down, and then, suddenly as if something had alarmed him, dashed into the water, swam the river and disappeared into the bush on the far bank. I looked down towards camp and saw a blue wisp of smoke rise above the trees and drift upstream: there must have been some eddy in the wind down there, six hundred feet below, or else the ground breeze had switched—something had certainly scared that caribou.

I hitched myself around to the right and took a look at a big, stony mountain that lay to the north; there was a green patch on it, and white specks were moving across the green—a dozen or fifteen head, whatever they were; it was too far to see. It didn't look like a goat mountain—it looked like a sandstone mountain, and it was rounded and nowhere precipitous: and suddenly it dawned on me that I was looking at my first *Ovis dalli*, the white sheep of the North. I stared and stared: the white animals stood out sharply against the green grass in the intense light of the setting sun, but even with the powerful glass one could only just see that these were not the massive outlines of goat but sheep with their graceful legs and lighter movements. Well—ten to one, since they were in the country, I would be seeing more of them—and I swung the glass over the bush below. There was a little lake there that I had noticed before, ringed round with tall spruce: the western side of it was deep in the evening shadow, but the sun still touched the eastern shore. Something was flashing there; it was an old bull moose, and he was feeding on some kind of water weed as he stood in the shallows; the great head would disappear beneath the water and then raise out of it again festooned with weed and shedding a glittering cascade of drops that sparkled in the sun. The fantastic, heraldic-looking beast was in his proper setting there, against that background of dark forest and dark brown water— and he would stay there unmolested as far as I was concerned; what I wanted was meat on the river and not back in the bush, and preferably a sheep or a caribou; now that I had no chance of meeting Faille a moose was too much meat to kill.

A cow moose and calf came out of the bush about a mile away, crossed a stony wash and disappeared again amongst the trees: truly this country was full of game; every sand-bar on the river was a maze of tracks that told the story plainly enough for all to read. Meanwhile the shadow was creeping over the valley, eating up the little hills. All that could be seen now of the moose in the pool was an occasional gleam of water as that monstrous head broke the surface in pursuit of the delectable weed. The sun slid down behind the mountains in the north-west, the breeze dropped, and all the faint rustlings of the grass and flowers were stilled, leaving only the quiet murmur of the river down below.

I overslept and was roused at six by the sun which was blazing down, as usual, out of a cloudless sky. A little after seven I hit the river and poled on up the reach that I had seen the night before from the hill. Where the caribou had swum the river there was a tangle of tracks, some moose but mostly caribou: it was evidently a regular crossing place—there was probably a lick, not too far away, that attracted all the game. Shortly after that the walls of a low canyon closed in and I became busy, dealing with the hazards of the river.

About ten I came to a little bay, beyond which the canyon walls went on again, thirty to forty foot sheer on either side, with no beach and with a swift current between them. At the far end of this canyon reach I could hear the roar and see the boiling white water of a bad rapid.

The only thing to do was to beach the canoe and walk ahead some five or six hundred yards along the cliff to a rock point from which it looked as if one could see down onto the rapid. There were faint signs of an old trail: it took the easiest way through the bush, back from the cliff edge, and then dipped down to a great, sandy bay above the rapid; no doubt it was the old portage trail. I turned aside from it and pushed through the screen of trees onto the point. I stood still there for quite a time, just looking—and then I sat down and looked some more. It was an amazing sight, though by no means designed to make the voyageur burst into any hymn of thanksgiving: it was the Figure-of-Eight Rapid, the most dangerous bit of water on the lower river—now known as Hell's Gate.

The Nahanni swept downhill here, at great speed, round a right-hand bend: suddenly, at the foot of the bend, the river made a right-angle turn to the left, entering the low-walled canyon. But the current and the whole volume of the Nahanni could not make that sharp turn: the mass of water was hurled clean across the river in a ridge of foaming six-foot waves, to split on this point of rock on the right bank, thus forming two whirlpools, the upper and the lower. It would be almost equally difficult, one could see, to run this rapid either upstream or downstream: the only way would be to climb on to this surging hill of water at a fine angle and to drop off it on the far side in the same way and as soon as possible. The trouble was that if the canoe was driven up too soon on to this "ridge of the white waters" it would be swamped by the big waves—and if it climbed on to it too late or stayed on it too long it would be hurled across the river and smashed, with its occupant, on to this rock point on which I was sitting. I looked down at the boiling water beneath: if one looked long enough, straight down, it seemed that the water stood still and that it was the point itself that was moving, surging upstream like the bow of a destroyer.

I walked back to the canoe and took out my axe and rifle, my packsack and some food and clothes, and laid them on the beach in case I lost the whole outfit but managed to get to shore myself: then I started up into the canyon.

I tried that rapid three times, but the current in the canyon was stronger than I had thought, and I was not able to get speed enough on the canoe to drive it up onto the crest of the riffle that barred the way. Twice the canoe climbed the ridge, close under the big waves, only to be flung across the river and driven down the canyon, almost touching the cliff on the portage side. At the third and last attempt the eddies worked in my favour: the canoe was climbing the hill of racing water with speed enough (I thought) to take it on and over, when suddenly a gust of wind blew down the river, the nose swung off course, and the canoe slid down into the lower whirlpool. It started to spin—and then was lifted on the upsurge of a huge boil from below. It was like the heave of one's cabin bunk at night in some great Atlantic storm. Then the water fell away from beneath the canoe, and I caught a glimpse of the white waves of the rapid, a long way above, it seemed. The canoe rose once more and spun again, and then at last the paddle bit into solid water and drove the outfit out of the whirlpool and down the canyon for the last time, taking a sideways slap, in passing, from a stray eddy and shipping it green as a parting souvenir of a memorable visit.

Persistence is one thing and plain obstinacy is another. That last frolic with the rapid had set my mind at rest: some other fool could try his luck at running the thing in a light canoe—I would portage. And I put into the bay, beached the canoe, took the axe and started to cut out the portage trail.

By suppertime the whole outfit, including the canoe, was lying on the sand in the big bay at the head of the portage. Supper was in the nature of a celebration and included two fool hens split in half and fried: these courageous birds had been eating blueberries

along the trail and had obligingly stuck their heads in the way of
bullets from the Luger instead of seeking safety in flight—hence
the name.

After supper I strolled back along the trail and cut into the sides
of a couple of the old blazes that marked the path. I counted the
rings: thirty years, as near as dammit, since they were made; that
looked as if some, at least, of the Klondikers had got this far, and I
wondered whether they had won through in the end to their El
Dorado on the Yukon River, or whether the Nahanni or the Indians could best tell what became of them.

From the rock point I watched the river for a while: then I went
back to camp and studied the rapid from river level. Evening is
the time to see fast water; the midday sun seems to flatten out the
waves and smooth down the smaller boils and eddies, but the low
evening light throws every movement of a river into sharp relief,
just as the cool evening air seems to release and intensify all the
varied sounds of moving water. So it was on this evening. The
angry voices of the rapid would drop for a moment to a troubled
muttering, and then rise again as suddenly to a wild clamour as a
fresh crest of waves reared up and hurtled across the river to split
on the rock point. It was plain from here that the little canoe could
never have made it in time through the gap between the big,
unclimbable waves and the rock—and I went a few steps further
down the firm sand of the shore to get a better view of the turmoil
at the foot of the point. Suddenly there was a rush and a surge,
the whole surface of the upper whirlpool heaved up, and I found
myself standing knee deep in the water: that was evidently the
nature of the thing—it filled and emptied according as the waves
divided on the rock point. Fortified with this valuable piece
of knowledge I hung my dripping moccasins in a tree and went
to bed.

The next day was one of blazing sunshine and joyous venture
on the river, winding up with an unseemly fracas in camp at suppertime. Camp, that evening, was under the cottonwoods on a
sandy beach in an eddy at the foot of some fairly strong water. Immediately behind was a low cliff, the continuation of a canyon
wall, and the beach came to an end a few yards below camp,

against the cliff and at the head of a riffle. I made a long, double-log fire halfway between the water and the cliff, and on it I sat several pots—tea water, washing water, prunes and rice, and the mulligan pot with the last of the moose soup in it and a couple of partridges in the soup. Then I threw my bedroll down by a big spruce at the foot of the cliff, took off a soaking wet shirt and hung it on a tree to dry and went to bail the canoe which had shipped water on the last crossing of the river.

As I bailed I heard a grunting noise from upstream: a cow moose and her calf were swimming the river; the calf was having a tough time of it in the fast water, and the cow was talking to it and encouraging it. She probably intended to land where I had beach-ed the canoe, but she saw me and headed straight for the bank, landing about a hundred yards upstream. The calf, however, had been doing its utmost and had nothing in reserve: it was swept downriver and into the eddy, from which it splashed ashore about fifteen yards below camp.

I was in the classic situation—in between mother and child; and mother weighed about eight hundred pounds, and a decided-ly querulous note was creeping into her grunts. The calf let out a feeble bleat, and the cow came a little closer, grunting angrily: I waded ashore and gently took down the rifle from a tree close to the canoe where it was hanging. Then I waded into the river to see if I could get around the calf and chase it back upstream to its mother: out of the corner of one eye I could see that the soup was boiling over; the tea pail also had a fine head of steam up, and no doubt the rice was burning—and I silently cursed the whole tribe of moose right back to its remote beginnings. Anything but a prehistoric-looking beast like that would have had sense enough to stay out of camp!

I was in the water now, as deep as I could get, the rifle held high in one hand and the other busily engaged in unknotting the red silk scarf that was round my neck. The calf was watching me: heaven send the little fool wouldn't lose his head and take off down the canyon and get himself drowned; if he did the cow would blame it all on me and come charging through camp and wreck everything—and stop a bullet, when all I wanted was peace. But the calf never moved, and I came dripping out of the river below him and walked up the bank. He seemed to be petrified: not so the cow, however. She was working herself into a fine frenzy and pawing at the sand—a bad sign, that. It was high time to get that calf on the move.

I came right up behind him, flapped the red scarf suddenly and let out one devil of a yell. I had intended to fire a shot over him as well, just to speed him on his way, but there was no need for that—he was already going faster than mortal moose calf had ever gone before. And how perfectly it was all working out! He would pass between my bedroll and the fire; no damage would be done, and there would still be time for me to salvage something of my supper from the ruins of what might have been. . . .

But how completely the picture changed, all in a fraction of a second! Just as the calf drew level with it a little breeze from the west flapped the shirt that was drying on the tree: he gave a blat of terror and shied sideways, stumbling over the long logs of the fire. Over went everything, but particularly the mulligan pot which he sent flying ahead with his front feet. He then bucked over the fire and landed with one hind foot through the stout bail handle of the mulligan pot, which somehow stayed with him for about three jumps and then, as he freed himself from it with a vicious kick, sailed into the river, from which I rescued it. That was the end of the party, and, judging by the row that came from up the beach, the guests were leaving in a hurry. Supper was a wreck, the partridge mulligan had gone down the river, and the calf had pretty nearly squared the pot for me; I spent half the night hammering it round again with the back of an axe.

From that camp I could hear the muffled thunder of the Falls, but just how near they were it was impossible to tell. That night was cold and clear, and the next day was cloudless and blazing hot, which was just as well as I was in the water more often than on it. It was the toughest stretch of river that I had struck: the water was very fast and it was rock strewn, and there were no good tracking beaches, only piled up talus slopes and great, misshapen blocks of stone, tumbled from the canyon walls and wet from the waves. Over these one clambered, trackline in hand, tearing trousers, bashing shins, while the canoe, riding upstream on the borderline between the eddies and the stream, did its best to throw one off balance, or to whirl end for end as it raced up in an eddy on a slack line and then sheered out into the current.

Another endearing feature of these rock-strewn canyons by the Falls is that there is practically no good poling bottom: either the iron-shod pole hits a rock just below the surface, usually on the slant and so giving no purchase, or else it drops down into a chasm between two huge rocks and does its best to jam there: and on that heaving, racing water one cannot afford to lose time between strokes.

"I tracked on round the point, only to find yet another canyon with its red and yellow walls and curious battlements and pinnacles, and the water wilder than ever. I pushed on up to the head of the reach, and there at last I was stuck at a point where two fast riffles sprang out, one from each side of the canyon, and met in a boiling chaudière of wild white water. . . ."

So that was that: I had come about a hundred and thirty miles from Nahanni Butte in a couple of weeks' travelling time, with two portages, and here was the "insuperable obstacle": I couldn't tackle this with a loaded canoe, and it looked like a poor risk even with an empty one. And there was no portaging this time—the far side of the canyon was sheer wall with no beach, while just above this point of rocks where I was standing there was a tremendous cape of sandstone, sheer and forbidding. Just below the cape a powerful eddy raced upstream, and past the foot of it surged the big waves of the nearside riffle. Beyond the cape the canyon swung to the right and disappeared from view. The vibration of the Falls could be felt in the rock, but all sound of them was deadened and lost in the uproar of the clashing riffles and the rough water of this reach.

A worse place to camp it would have been difficult to find. The point caught the full blaze of the sun all day long: it consisted simply of a tumbled slope of jagged rock, and there was no landing beach and no shade; the few miserable spruce that poked up out of the stones were thin, stunted and curiously grey-looking. However, I had no intention of going back without seeing the

Falls, so this wretched spot was going to be home for a day or two; and the first thing to do was to get the canoe out of the water before the canvas was worn through, fretting against the rocks. I unloaded and piled the outfit back from the water and then lifted the canoe out, turning it upside down to drain and dry.

It was four o'clock by Nahanni (estimated) time; the day was still young enough for a little climbing, and supper could wait till the cool shadow of the sandstone point fell on this blistering rock pile of mine. I took a good swig of water and a bite of chocolate, gathered up the field glass and the aneroid and started towards the foot of the cliff. On an afterthought I came back and added the Luger to the load, running my belt through the holster strap: there might be partridges in the bush.

I went up a rockslide in a coulee between the pinnacles of the canyon wall, raising the warm dust and eating raspberries and the ripe fruit of the wild roses. The coulee was like an oven with the afternoon sun blazing into it: there were sheep tracks and sheep droppings in it and the tracks of a grizzly bear: here and there one could see a very faint game trail, but mostly it was rock slide, and one had to tread delicately and surely to avoid starting an avalanche of loose stones. The coulee led out on to a great hill, covered with birch, jackpine and silver spruce and floored with low-bush cranberries. I went up that till the forest gave place to grass and kini-kinik, and I saw in front of me a round, bare hill. And on the top of the hill, just showing, was a bronze-coloured thing—it looked like the end of a large log that had been squared off with a saw, but it couldn't be that up here where, more than likely, no man had ever been. Yet there seemed to be rings and a grain in it. . . .

By God's truth it was no log! It was a most noble set of horns, and presumably the horns were attached to a ram of the Dall sheep—for of the animal nothing was visible except a very little of the head. I drew the pistol from its holster and snapped the safety catch forward. . . . But it was too far, so I swung round the hill a little and went up silently, like a cat, the moccasins making no sound on the gravelly slope. I came on him suddenly at about fifty yards range, and he sprang up and faced me, white and magnificent against the deep blue sky. There was no time to waste, so I aimed between his eyes and fired. The ram stood still for at least a second: I was afraid I had missed him, and I fired twice, quickly, at his body this time, and saw each bullet strike. He gave a plunge and disappeared over the far side of the hill, leaving a light puff of yellow dust floating against the blue. I sobbed and sweated up and over the top after him, praying to all the gods to keep him out of canyons and let me get in a finishing shot. But there was no need: he was lying dead in a grassy hollow, against the trunk of a little birch tree.

He was a beautiful ram. Later on, when Faille and I put a steel tape on the head, we found that one horn measured forty inches on the outside curve and the other one thirty-nine: they were both thirteen inches in circumference at the base. The first bullet was probably the one that killed him: it had struck close to the right eye, about an inch from where I had aimed, and must have gone on into the brain.

I let the blood out of the ram and then walked back up to the top of the hill and sat down to cool off and consider the next move. I took a look around; and the first thing that caught my eye was the sight of three magnificent rams standing downstream from me, each one on a bare, green knoll similar to the one that I was on. They were not looking at me: each one was standing motionless, as if carved out of pure white marble, gazing across the canyon towards some distant mountains. The nearest ram was about four hundred yards away, and the glass showed me that each one had a head as good or better than the one I had shot. Across the river there were two more splendid rams standing like statues, snow white in the dazzling glare of the westering sun.

The knoll was seven hundred feet above camp, according to the aneroid. Down below there I could see most of that last rough reach of the Nahanni, olive green and flecked with white. It looked almost peaceful from this height, and the sound of it was only a faint murmur that came up through the hot scent of the pines. From behind the mountains in the west there came a faint drift of smoke from some far-off forest fire, perhaps in the Yukon Territory. To the south-east were the mountains through which I had come from the Liard: to the north-east, and close by, were great stone-capped mountains, pearl grey in the smoke haze: and over all this, constant so that one hardly noticed it, was the deep booming note of the Falls.

Upriver and right into the eye of the sun a cloud seemed to be hanging over the bush. Smoke, I thought, and then—my God, not a bush fire in this lovely place! But it was not acting like smoke, there was no blue in it and it stayed in one place, there was only one thing it could be—the spray from a great waterfall.

Now, even if I got benighted up here with the ram, I had to go and make sure. I started right away and cut across the hollow where the ram was and then through the bush, keeping about the same level and crossing a number of small coulees, sweating through the trees in the hot stillness of the August evening and hoping that some hill or the canyon rim would not get in the way of a speedy view. The booming was becoming louder, and I could see occasionally, through the trees, more and more of the cloud of spray. I turned towards the river after half a mile or so of this up and down travel and came out onto an open spur that stood out from the bush. And there all doubts and questionings were ended: a quarter of a mile to the west and perhaps three hundred feet below me a wild cataract flashed against the sun, and the cataract ended in a sudden drop where the Nahanni plunged over the rim of the Falls: I could see a curtain of falling water, split into two by a great tower of rock, but the bottom was hidden from me by the edge of the canyon—only a thunderous din and clouds of golden spray glittering in the yellow light of the evening sun told me that I was seeing the upper half of the Falls of the Nahanni.

Well, the other half would have to wait till tomorrow: there was still the ram to deal with, and I made my way back to him, turning over in my head various plans for getting to the foot of the Falls. Soon the meat was cut up and laid on a little platform of dry poles set across two fallen trees. I spread it out so that the air would pass through it easily, and then I covered it with green boughs: it was the best I could do for it. The head I slung on to my shoulders with a long leather latigo lace: the thing weighed like a load of lead at this end of the day, and the forward curl of the

great horns seemed bent on knocking a hole in the base of my
skull. Down through the woods I went with it, and then down the
stony chute of the coulee—sliding and cascading downhill in the
gravel and the sharp rocks and the dust. At the end of about forty
minutes or so a filthy looking object, grimy and blood-stained,
staggered out on to the rockpile which was camp, dumped the
sheep head with a groan of relief and lay down and stuck its own
head in the river.

It was twilight now and the air was chill. Luckily I had tarped
up the outfit before leaving camp, for everything seemed to be
most unusually damp—a remarkably heavy dew, I thought. But
it was not dew: a fine mist was drifting down the canyon, and it
was the spray from the Falls, which were round the point of sandstone and perhaps three quarters of a mile away: in the heat of the
day these particles of spray evaporated, but by night they drifted
down the canyon in a gentle rain.

All too soon the sun poked its nose over the canyon rim: now
was the time to get that sheep meat down the mountain before the
sun got to work on it and the flies got busy; and so I set out once
more up the game trail and into the bush—with a sack or two and
a packsack and the tea pail. All was in order at the sheep cache,
and an hour later I cascaded for the last time down the stony
coulee with a heavy load of meat and a pail full of beautiful, fat
raspberries.

I defy anybody to better that breakfast menu, or to bring to it a
better appetite: porridge, sheep liver and bacon, bannock, butter,
marmalade and tea, topped off with a bowl of raspberries and
cream. And the porridge, let me explain was no invalid dish, nor
would it ever figure on the diet sheet of a slimming movie star:
porridge as developed by me on the Nahanni consisted of a mixture of rolled oats and whole wheat, and into this was thrown a
little salt, a large pat of butter and a handful of seedless raisins.
The finished product was served in a large bowl: on top of the
porridge a thin slice of cheese was spread, and the dish was topped
with a pouring of dried milk to the consistency of cream and a lib-
eral sprinkling of brown sugar. It will be easily understood that this
porridge lays a good foundation for a good breakfast to follow.

It was a busy morning. I built a little stone wall beneath two spindly spruce to make a shadow and a cool place behind it for the sheep meat. Into the top of the wall I built an overhang of spruce branches and then, around the meat, I lit two or three smudges of rotten wood to keep the flies away—and that took care of the sheep. Then I carefully skinned the head and stretched the cape inside out on a spare paddle, with salt rubbed into it and a stick through the ears—and a weird-looking sight it was at the end of the job, but safe. Next I trimmed the meat off the skull and hung the skull in a sack in the smoke: that would do for it till I could get it down to Faille's camp and finish it in a more convenient place than this sun-blasted rockpile. I did various other odd jobs, all the time in a state of hopeless indecision. Would I try that crossing of the river or wouldn't I? The Nahanni had dropped an inch overnight: with an empty canoe one might just make it. . . .

There is such a thing as making jobs to avoid making an unpleasant decision, and that can be prolonged indefinitely until one loses heart. But suddenly, after lunch (and it may have been the good sheep meat that turned the scale), I knew that it was now or never. I turned the canoe over, strapped my field glass to the seat, laid the pole along the thwarts and put a spare paddle on the floor. Then I lifted the canoe and set it gently in the river, holding it while I laid a big rock in the nose to partly balance my weight in the tail. All was ready, and I coiled the trackline, stepped in and shoved off. There is something beautifully final in certain phases of river travel: you make your decision and pick your course, and after that the rest is all action. You are committed, and there is no turning back—you must make it or swamp. The result is a supreme peak of physical effort and a split-second awareness of changing water: and mentally a sort of cold excitement and exhilaration—a high point of living. . . .

I drove up in the eddy and hit the riffle at a fine angle and as hard and as close to the sandstone point as I dared. The canoe did its best for a second to stand on its tail—it was like riding a horse that is going to throw itself back over on to you. But the rock in the nose saved the day, and I found myself out on the smooth green water, down on my knees and digging into it like mad with the paddle. Something huge and white flashed into view as I cleared the sandstone point—it was the Falls! Well, to hell with the Falls! They could wait: this racing water was what mattered now. It was hard to get a hold of it with the paddle: it flew past so fast that it was hard to drive the paddle faster. But there was no wind, and the river could get a little grip on the empty canoe which skimmed over its surface: I was losing very little ground. But I couldn't afford to lose any at all if I wanted to catch the tail end of the beach on the right shore, and if I didn't catch it that would be that; there would be no time to swing and dodge the frothing cauldron down below. Dig, R.M.P., dig for God's sake! I was gaining a little and the beach was close. But I was missing it! Ram her in, then, and jump and pray for a bottom! I floundered into the water, trackline in hand, falling and struggling for a foothold. The canoe fetched up on the end of the line with a jerk that almost pulled me back over into deep water, but I held it and crawled ashore, sodden but triumphant. I pulled off my shirt, wrung it out and threw it into the canoe and then sat down on a rock in the sun to get my breath: that dim, archaic, reptilian ancestor who first crawled out of the waste of the waters on to some prehistoric shore must have felt pretty cocky and pleased with himself: so did I—until I realized that, in my haste, I had forgotten to bring the camera. Saddened by this discovery, I tracked on up the river.

I spent that afternoon passing from side to side over the great pool at the foot of the Falls. The sun slid down the sky and the shadows swung and deepened, but time, for me, had lost its meaning, for I myself was lost in the fascination of this place of wild, chaotic beauty. I climbed up over the rocks on either side into shadowy, dripping clefts where the ferns and mosses glistened in the never-ending rain: I came out again into the hot sunshine and hunted on the beaches for fossils of strange, queer water beasts, and then crossed over to lie on the sun-warmed rocks of the north shore. The best view was from there, where the shining rim of the Falls cut across the cloudless blue: the drop to the pool was broken by a step springing out from the southern precipice and widening to the north like the step of a turret stair: from this step sprang a glistening tower of rock that reached far above the upper step or rim and cut the Falls in two. A cloud of spray, glittering against the afternoon sun, wreathed and twisted around the sharp peak of this limestone pillar: that would be where the cataract hurled itself against the rock before taking the final plunge. A fine picture it made and a most tumultuous din, for the Nahanni here was at least as big, I thought, as the Rhône at Lyon.

The pool must be tremendously deep, and from its depths there is an upsurge of water, a sort of vertical eddy, which creates a hump of boiling water without any definite current, on which a canoe spins and twists, but goes neither up nor downstream. On the upstream edge of the hump the current sucks back into the Falls, and on its downstream side the water spills out and down the Nahanni. This simple hydrographic law I discovered for myself on my last passage across the river to the south shore. I lingered too long among the boils and eddies of the hump, spinning this way and that and enjoying from far too close the splendid sight of this tumbling curtain of the falling river.

I woke up just in time and realised that I was in the backlash current and heading for the Falls. Now, by the holy mackinaw, was the time to lay on that paddle as never before! Slowly, very slowly, and with the black fear of the river driving me on, I drew ahead across the hump and to safety in the eddy at the foot of the portage trail. I should have kept my eyes open instead of drifting, half asleep, in the canoe—but the Turks have a word for it: "God," they say, "builds the nest for the blind bird."

The portage trail ran up a precipitous coulee: there were logs set across it then for the skidding of a boat or a canoe—set there, perhaps, by the Klondikers—but those steps have vanished with the years and with the melting of twenty snows, for only Faille goes that way today. But the portage could wait for another time—I had seen all I wished, and I was anxious about that sheep head down at camp with the bear tracks all around. I took a last look at the Falls: two hundred feet, I thought, but I was wrong; Fenley Hunter came later and measured them, and the drop was three hundred and sixteen—the biggest waterfall in the Northwest Territories.

Loading up next morning, with the canoe rocking and slapping about in the waves, was not easy in spite of a log skidway that I had made. The sheep head and meat I laid in the canoe, well forward, but the cape was left on its paddle and the paddle was lashed, upended like a mast, in the nose: that, I hoped, would keep the cape above the waves and dry. It was not early: I had let the sun climb high and swing out of the east before loading so as to avoid the blinding glare on the water as I ran south-east and downriver. Then I shoved the canoe out from the rocks, jumped in and let drive with the paddle—and in a two-hour's furious run downstream I undid the work of two toiling days.

It was all new to me, this downstream work on a fast river. One thing I noticed in particular was that all movement was relative—patches of white water foamed upstream towards one like the moving waves of the sea instead of the stationary waves of a river, while the scattered rocks in midstream drove towards the canoe with a foaming wake behind them like that of a speedboat. However, the little canoe rode down safely, swaying and pitching through this mad world of racing water, with every movement exaggerated by the insane-looking figurehead in the nose. I had tried to memorize each reach as I came up, but that soon faded out in the excitement of running downstream, and the best thing seemed to be to stand up in the canoe and size up each riffle as it came along; then, with the course picked out and the decision made, sit down and paddle like fury; get the canoe travelling faster than the river and go flat out on the course planned, avoiding the big waves in the lashing tail of every riffle, dodging the eddies and following the leaping sheep-cape banner through into the quiet water.

Lunch was eaten at the head of the Hell's Gate portage, and by late afternoon the canoe, sheep and outfit had been carried through the woods and laid on the sands of the bay below the rapid. It was a lovely spot, especially after the jagged rockpile by the Falls, so I camped there overnight for the sheer joy of walking like a man again instead of hobbling over the pointed rocks like a wounded beast, and ran on down to the Flat River in the morning.

I avoided the difficult mouth of the river by making use of an offshoot of the Nahanni that cut through the point between the two rivers: it wound through thickets of willow and poplar and trickled over gravelly shallows, but in the end it ran out into the Flat River about half a mile above its mouth. There were no tracks to be seen but, a little way downstream, there were two poplars with long, white, fresh blazes on them. I walked down to see if there was a message there for me, but there was nothing but some fairly recent chips on the ground below the blazes, so I tracked on upstream and came, in about a mile, to Faille's landing.

Faille was away with his canoe. A few things were lying about at the landing, and the rest of his outfit was stacked in a tent back in the bush. Near by was a little cabin, almost finished: Faille's bed was under a big spruce, and the dogs, who seemed pleased to see me, were tied to trees by the tent.

I unloaded and beached the canoe, lit a fire by the river and had lunch. I had just finished when Faille appeared, walking along the shore with his rifle.

"So we meet again," he said. "I'm sure glad to see you."

"I saw your two blazes down at the mouth," I told him. "I figured, anyway, that you wouldn't go beyond the first bunch of good spruce."

"Blazes? I never made any blazes: where are they?"

And to this day we have never found any explanation for them, for apart from the two of us the country was supposed to be empty of men.

Faille was hungry, so I made another brew of tea, and he cleaned up the sheep mulligan and anything else that was lying around loose. He had shot a caribou a mile upstream and had come back for the dogs, leaving his big canoe by the dead animal. He went off again, and I packed my outfit up to his camp and sorted out some supplies for the trip up the Flat River: the heavy stuff I would leave here. Faille came back at dusk with a canoe load of meat and three absolutely bulging dogs: the camp chores were all done, and supper was waiting for him, with collops of sheep meat all ready floured and in the pan. We fell to and talked and ate and drank coffee till nearly midnight, and I had to give a detailed account of the river and the game between the mouth of Flat River and the Falls. We also discussed the two strange blazes a mile downstream, and I told Faille what I knew of the story of the Mountain Men and how the Mackenzie River Indians would not come up into this western country for fear of the fierce, nomad Indians of the Yukon divide; but neither of us had seen any strange track or campfire or any sign of man, and we finally arrived at the usual northern conclusion, "To hell with it, whatever it is—we can deal with it," and went to bed.

The next day broke grey and threatening and continued grey all day. After breakfast we got at it. Faille disappeared into the cabin and sang out for help whenever he needed it. I stripped and sterilized the ram's skull, mended two split paddles with snare wire, cleaned and greased our joint arsenal and generally refitted. Faille emerged from his den after we had decided that it probably wasn't going to rain, and we cut up the caribou meat and built a rack and smoked it. Faille dived inside again, and I looked after the smoke fires and baked and cooked for the two of us. At intervals we ate. Talking late over the fire that night we arranged that, unless I stumbled on to some new Klondike up the Flat River, I would return in four days time, and we would go together in Faille's big canoe to the Falls, travelling light and leaving our outfits behind in the cabin, which would be finished by then. And after that we would run down the Nahanni together to the Twisted Mountain.

Lunchtime next day found me on a spruce point facing a curiously contorted cliff. Below me was a quiet eddy and a beach of black sand, and over the sand, flipping backwards and forwards with every ripple, lay flat, shining particles of mica. The whole surface of the bay was covered with it, and it gleamed, as it flipped to and fro in the sunlight, like rich farm butter. Fool's gold, they call it, and with the black sand it was a sign of mineralization. The poplars were turning gold, too, and their gay splashes of colour stood out vividly from the black green of the spruce on the mountainside across the Flat River. It would soon be time to point the canoe's nose south and run for it.

I put out my fire and put the grub box back in the canoe. I had come to a decision on that point of spruce: I would go out and find Gordon Matthews and tell him what I had seen. He and I would come back in together, prepared to winter up here and trap, and we would try our luck at finding the lost gold of the Nahanni: this country was too good to miss; it was practically our duty to ourselves to see it while it was still young and before civilization could get its dirty paws on it. Faille wanted me to throw in my grub with his and stay—we could shoot meat enough to see us through, he said. And so I would have done, outfitting at South Nahanni, but we could get no word to the outside, and it would be thought that I had disappeared. No—better the other way: and I started to pole upstream.

Four days and three nights were spent up the Flat River. I went up some twenty odd miles, to the mouth of Caribou Creek, and then up Caribou Creek "till the riffles became too numerous and too close to make further advance by canoe worthwhile." And then I took a night camp on my back and went up into the bald mountains to the south-east.

"And a river went out of Eden:" it was the Flat River, and Eden lay here in these green, tumbled hills and stony mountains. The animals were tame and unafraid: "As I was finishing supper I heard a branch snap on the far bank, and there was a big black bear walking along . . . it was too dark to take his picture. He saw my camp at last and scampered away up the hill, pausing now and then for breath and wheezing noisily like an aged gentleman." And, "I saw a cow moose just before lunch. It never saw me but walked out of the bush about three hundred yards ahead of me on to a shingle bar—drank, splashed a little, walked by the river for a while and turned again into the woods." "At 4.30 a.m. a squirrel ran clean over my face and roused me to start the day with a burst of bad language." And it was at that same camp, before breakfast that morning, that "a caribou came out of the woods about five hundred yards away, drank and walked back—what graceful animals they are!"

The evening I saw the bear across the river there was the most

beautiful aurora borealis that I have ever seen. First it stretched
up to the zenith in long, quivering shafts of light. Then it broke
up and formed into a giant question mark and lay motionless
across the sky: that slowly faded, and it rose again waving from
north-east to north-west in long streamers of fire, and when I fell
asleep it was all over the sky in weird blobs and patches, putting
out the stars with its pale green light. I was aroused, a few
minutes later, by a heavy plunge in the water near the canoe,
which was only a few feet away, tied and riding in a gentle current. I rolled over in bed and looked over the bank: two beavers
were playing round the canoe, attracted perhaps by the glow of
the dying fire.

And now it was time to go. The four days were up, and Faille
would be expecting me. I loaded up and let the canoe slip away
down Caribou Creek: there was something unusually pleasant
about this small river on such a perfect afternoon; through the
glassy water I could see the stones fly past beneath me in the riffles
and, in the pools, the shadow of the canoe gliding over gravel
twenty feet down in the cool, clear depths. Here and there the
trees leaned out towards the centre of the stream, and the canoe
slid beneath them in the dappled shadows, green and gold. . . .
I came to Faille's camp in the dusk. A little way above his landing a reef runs across the river with one small gap in it. At high
water the whole reef is buried deep, but in the low water of a dry
summer it makes a small waterfall with this one passage in it. I
could hear the noise of the reef but, in the twilight, it was hard to
see. I stood up as the canoe slid down towards the rock outcrop;
there was a line of white across the river with the suspicion of a
black gap on the right. "I sat down and put the canoe at it, hard:
we seemed to hang in the air for a moment—then came a streak of
spray and foam, and we were in the eddy below. Faille made supper for me while I unloaded. I was very hungry."

There was one more day's work to be done on the cabin so
while Faille slammed and hammered away, I laid up and repaired
and shellacked my canoe. I baked and cooked for both of us, and

nobody complained about the food, nor was anybody poisoned by it. Then, in the intervals of shack finishing and stacking the outfit under cover, I held a laundry day (two of everything and all by now in tatters), and finally, in the last light, we cleaned up, solemnly lit the candles in the new cabin and "ate rather a marvellous supper." It was the official house-warming, and no expense had been spared. It was a roaring success, and the date was inscribed on the door—Aug. 24th, 1927. In the night we were wakened, around 3.00 a.m., by the howling of wolves.

The next night we were camped at the mouth of what Faille said was Murder Creek—the second big creek coming into the Nahanni from the north, above the Flat River. Faille had got hold of some story of violence and sudden death in connection with this stream of clear blue water when he was in Fort Simpson: the creek cut away back into richly forested mountains, and somewhere up there, Faille said, was coarse gold. He was scratting away at this very moment in the creek gravel with a shovel and a gold pan, talking hard all the time, "as a man talks who won't have much more chance of talking, except to himself, for another seven months."

The day had not been without its victory: we had come through the queer rapid without portaging. The Figure-of-Eight Rapid, Faille had called it as he stood on the rock point and looked down on the ridge of water that rushed across the river. He studied it for a long time. "Queerest piece of water on a big river that I ever saw," was his verdict as we walked back to the canoe.

Then we tried it. The first time, something seemed to explode under the canoe, and we were thrown off the ridge of water and down into the lower whirlpool. On the second attempt we came up the river, close under the cliff, with a rush and succeeded in climbing on to the racing crest of the ridge. Getting off it, however, was another matter. In a bewildering tumult of waves we hurtled across the river at an incredible speed, swinging the canoe so as to slide over into the upper whirlpool. But the river held us on the crest; we smashed with a crunch, broadside on, on to the rock point and were held there by the force of the water which started to boil into the canoe. Faille was in the stern.

"Grab the point and pull her over," he shouted.

I dropped my paddle and hauled on the rock; Faille dug into the water with his paddle, and very slowly the canoe ground across the face of the point. And then the pressure eased, and we slid gently down into the bay at the head of the portage.

Congratulations flew like rain—and when, at lunchtime, Faille found fresh tracks of lynx, fisher, wolf and marten all on the sand of one small bay, we felt right on top of the world: it looked like a good winter's hunt.

The following afternoon we came to the foot of the Falls and prospected around for a good place to take a photograph. We found it on the north shore, and there I let fly with two of our precious films—one with Faille in it and one without. Faille thought he had heard of a photograph being taken once before, but it was never developed, the camera and film being lost when a canoe upset in a rapid; so these two pictures were probably the first ones of the Falls of the Nahanni ever to reach the outside.

Then we climbed up the steep portage trail, up the stony coulee and then over a great wide avenue that had been cut through the bush, God knows when or why, as if an army was to pass that way: when I last saw it, in 1951, the bush had taken back its own again. The trail climbed high and then dropped gently towards the river, and from a little bare hill we got our first sight of the upper Nahanni, stretching on into the evening between low, forested banks, calm and beautiful like a great lake. We looked around for a good landing place, found one and blazed it for future reference; then we fell to on blueberries, cranberries and raspberries till we were stuffed and lay contentedly on the little knoll, watching the sun set behind low mountains and the shift and play of its light over the calm water. There were tamaracks growing near by: Faille got up and walked over to the nearest one.

"Come here and I'll show you something," he said.

I joined him. He was poking his finger in behind the curly flakes of the rough bark: tucked in behind each flake was a blueberry; it was the winter storehouse, the cache, of the whiskey jacks.

We slept on the rocks within sight of the Falls and woke up with

the usual puddles of spray lying on the tarpaulins we had thrown
over ourselves. I was up first and cooked breakfast before calling
Faille: he had gone to ground completely, tortoise like, beneath
his tarp. Very considerately I brought him a mug of coffee as an
eye-opener and said a few kind words in his ear, about the sun being up and things: but answer came there none, so I lifted the tarp
to see what ailed the man. It was the wrong end. I had been talking to his feet. . . .

We drove the big canoe downriver at top speed, shot through
the Figure-of-Eight Rapid in one mighty surge and lunched at
Faille's cabin. And there we were busy until darkness fell, when
we lit the candles and downed what my diary calls "a tremendous
supper."

Mist hid the Flat River that last morning at Faille's cabin,
clearing later to a perfect day. Our noonday fire was made at the
Gate of the Nahanni, by the quiet water under the Pulpit Rock;
and the spell of that tremendous place must have fallen on us
then, for we lazed too long there in the sun: the Second Canyon
lay already in the shadow when we came to it, and dusk found us
sliding down the swift channels of Deadmen Valley, straining our
eyes for our old camping place of early August. We had come
about fifty-five miles.

We hit the river from that camp as soon as the mists cleared
away and ran down out of Deadmen Valley and down the Cache
Riffles. We took the Cache Rapid close to the right shore: twice I
felt my canoe graze rocks, and then, at the last fall, it leapt over
the drop, buried its nose in foam, shipped half a bucketful and
dropped its tail end on a pointed rock. Faille touched nothing,
riding high and light in his big, empty canoe. No serious damage
was done, and we picked up my cache of grub and ran on, into the
Lower Canyon: by midday we were building our fire at the mouth
of the Hot Springs Creek. As lunch cooked we hunted out soap
and towels, and when the clamourings of the inner men had been
stilled we hit the trail for the springs. Faille made a dam and sat in
his spring: I went up to where a hot creek ran over stones in a
shallow stream, and there I lay in the sun with the warm water

flowing over me. I noticed a humming-bird busy nearby amongst the wild asters. It seemed late for that small bird to be there: the leaves were turning gold, and it was high time for him, too, to be heading south.

In the evening we came, almost in the dark and with a cold wind blowing, to Faille's cache at the Twisted Mountain: we had supper by the firelight—and for a long time afterwards we sat there, talking. Mist lay low on the river in the morning, so we worked away shifting Faille's outfit from the cache to his canoe, and I repaired the hole that the Cache Rapid had punched in mine. Then, as we ate lunch, the miracle happened again—the rolling back of the mists and the flashing into life of all the gay, autumn-coloured world. Everything was ready to go; we shook hands and said good-bye—and the canoe slipped away down the river. And for a long time, whenever I looked back, I could see Faille and the three dogs standing on the point of rock by the Twisted Mountain, looking after me. . . .

3

Deadmen Valley

"In a thousand ages of the Gods I could not tell thee of the glories of Himachal. . . ."

Traditional Hindu Text

The following May saw us—Gordon Matthews and myself—thrumming down the Liard towards the Nahanni. Gordon had been restless in Edmonton even before I came to trouble him with tales of the strange river, and it had not been difficult to get him on the move. He had listened for a while and then—"Any country," he had said, "where the Indians are still hostile and you can shoot moose from your bed and mountain sheep with a pistol is well worth seeing before the rats get at it. To say nothing of finding the McLeods' gold and making our fortunes. . . ." Promptly, and not without pleasure, he had dropped his job, and we had set to work to list and collect the things we needed for the new outfit. Now all those chores lay behind us, and we were on our way. Gordon was steering the canoes, and I lay sprawled out on the load, asleep in the sun with the dogs curled up around me. . . .

A sudden choke and a splutter broke in on the even whine of the 4 h.p. Johnson outboard: I rolled over and sat up, instantly awake, blinking at Gordon who only smiled and shook his head—evidently it was just a temporary indisposition for the thing seemed to be running happily enough again. I flattened out once more to let Gordon see ahead and twisted round so that I could get a view downstream.

I must have been asleep for quite a while for Nahanni Butte
was much closer. We were coming round the wide bend of the
Liard just above the Netla River, and the Butte lay dead ahead
and only about twelve miles away: barring accidents we would
make it in to Jack LaFlair's trading post by suppertime. The
Liard was almost a mile wide here, and it was very different from
the clear, green river that I had last seen in September. It swept
round the bend a brown, heaving mass of destruction let loose
upon the land, rising with the hot weather to an early flood, rolling a little with its own strength and speed, tearing down its banks
and carrying with it great uprooted trees and all the debris of the
mountains.

And the wind was rising from the north, whipping the surface
into waves that rolled upstream: Gordon was cutting the speed,
for the three canoes were lashed abreast and the waves were
already splashing in, waking the four dogs who raised their heads
and looked around uneasily. This afternoon wind was nothing
new: it was a daily occurrence, and we had been hitting the river
around 3.30 a.m. these last mornings in order to avoid it. But today the wind was worse than usual, and we arrived at the trading
post bailing hard and thanking our stars that the long trail in to
the South Nahanni lay behind us.

It was May 24th. We had left Edmonton by train on March
8th, and about a thousand miles of camps, dog fights and raft
trouble, ice, rapids and shallow rivers was already history.[1] And
now there was this new worry—the rivers were rising. Since the
last snowstorms in April not a drop of rain had fallen, and the
weather had been perfect—warm and sunny. A lot of mountain
snow had melted earlier than usual, and it only needed a few
heavy rains now to fetch a lot more out with a rush and turn the
Nahanni into a raging flood. There was going to be trouble; one
didn't need to be a prophet to see that, but fortunately the full extent of the trouble was still hidden from us.

We had supper with Jack up in his cabin. The Liard, he told

[1]See *Blackwoods Magazine*, July 1952, ''Interlude on the Sikanni Chief.''

us, had gone out[1] on the sixth of May and the Nahanni a few days later. The fur catch had not been good, and there was no news or sign of Faille. Two men had come down from the upper Liard, from the Devil's Portage, above Ile de Gravois and the Rapid of the Drowned. Starke and Stevens their names were, and they had run on down to Fort Simpson to get some stuff they were short of: then they were coming back and heading for the upper Flat River; the west country, they had told Jack, was getting too crowded. We had a good start of them anyway, and we had canoes: Starke and Stevens had a power scow, and Jack didn't think it could get up the Nahanni. He also told us that the general impression on the Liard was that I was a geologist and that I had run on to something somewhere up the Nahanni last summer. Otherwise why would I be coming back? Well—that would just have to work itself out; the plain truth would be altogether too fantastic a story to try to put over—nobody would be fool enough to listen to anything as simple as that.

The famous mosquitoes of South Nahanni were starting to get on the warpath so I went out to fix up my bed and stake out my mosquito net. There was no darkness now, and the Butte, with a fresh capping of snow on it, was silhouetted against the northern sunset. Down below lay the Nahanni, calm as glass and with the little, isolated butte that we called the Sphinx Rock reflected in it: from the islands and the flat lands where the two rivers met there rose the exuberant song of countless frogs—for it was May, "alliggi peesim," the "frog moon" of the Crees, and they were letting the world know it in no uncertain terms. Lulled by their joyful serenade I fell asleep.

We left LaFlair's post next morning at 5.30 and thrummed up the quiet reaches of the river, almost to the foot of The Splits, without incident. There, however, disaster struck: running along in quiet water under a high cutbank we ran the projecting boss of the gear case of the kicker into the V of a forked and sunken snag. There was a tremendous wrench as the whole weight of the three loaded canoes came, with its momentum, on to the drive shaft

---

[1]"gone out"—i.e., the ice had broken and started to run.

and housing; several things snapped, and the whole course of the summer was changed. And in an hour or two we were back at Jack LaFlair's.

There we worked for a day and managed to effect some sort of a haywire repair by means of a brace and steel bits, stove bolts, and a strip or two of metal at various strategic points to bolster up the general ruin; and with this we set out again after supper on the 26th to try our luck a second time. The kicker had a wild sort of rattle to it, but it worked unexpectedly well, and we ran up a little way and camped at Bluefish River.

Next morning we ran on into The Splits, and when we hit the fast water it soon became clear that the haywire repair job on the kicker was not going to stand up to this sort of thing. The outfit consisted of three Chestnut canoes: a sixteen-foot Prospector, which was the same size and model that I had used the summer before; a nineteen-foot Freight, a thing about the size of a fishing boat with a depth of nineteen inches and a fifty-one inch beam; and an eighteen-foot Freight that we had bought from the Bay at Fort Nelson—a shockingly battered antique with its canvas hide flapping loosely over its cedar frame, the sort of thing that a sane man would hesitate to use on a quiet lake, let alone on the Nahanni. Shoving all this against the spring flood was more than the decrepit kicker could stand: we got somehow through the Big Hole, the great U-shaped bend full of snags and hidden bars which had defeated Father Gouet, the priest-prospector of Fort Liard, and we made a little distance up into The Splits, keeping mainly to the snyes of the left bank: and then, suddenly, near the head of a fast snye that wound like a small river through the forest, a hellish din broke loose from the innards of the Johnson—the noise of devils fighting in a blacksmith's shop. The tune changed to a series of metallic hiccups without any sort of rhythm: then, thank God, the drive shaft broke with a rending crash whatever it was trying to break, the liberated engine gave a thin, whining scream of triumph—and in the blasphemous silence that followed we swept the outfit into the bank and hitched on to a tree. The mechanical period was at an end.

The sun had gone behind the clouds, and the wind was rising to a gale. By suppertime it was lashing with rain, and all night the rain came down in torrents: in the morning we bailed six inches of water out of the canoes, and the Nahanni was in full flood—an awe-inspiring spectacle from the point of the island on which we were camped.

The rain stopped in the evening, and I set to work to build a cache. The plan now was to abandon the big canoe and to relay the outfit up the river: Gordon would stay here with the dogs and hunt until the peak of the flood was passed while I would take the sixteen-footer with all it could carry and make my way up the river as far as possible—to the Hot Springs or into the Lower Canyon. There I would cache my load and return for Gordon and the dogs, returning a second time, when they were installed at the new camp, for the last load. Working on this plan we probably wouldn't get the whole outfit to the Flat River as originally intended, but we would get it to Deadmen Valley and so be assured of a good winter's trapping, and I could go on alone to the Flat. It was the best we could do.

So we hauled the big canoe up the bank and turned it upside down on a rack in the shade of the trees. Gordon greased the Johnson and stacked it away with the gas and oil beneath the canoe: then, while I built a strong, high cache—a platform set on four trees which I cut off about thirteen feet from the ground—Gordon sorted and dried the outfit, put aside the stuff for me to take, peeled the uprights of the cache to make it squirrel-proof and cut the floor poles. Between us the work was soon done, and on the first of June I hit the river.

Three days later I sat by the noonday fire looking across the main channel of The Splits to the Twisted Mountain. I was about nine miles from Gordon by flight of crow, but about three times as far if that crow had to swim behind my canoe. What with crossing channels and being swept downstream, and having to back down on one side of an island and come up again on the other, and doing all this over and over again, I had done a lot of travelling— and had had some narrow shaves in the course of it. The Splits country in flood time was a sea of racing, twisting waters, strewn with shoals and eddies and lonely driftpiles: it was just too big, too fast and too risky for a small, heavily loaded canoe without power.

And now this. Somewhere out in the middle of the half-mile stretch of water that separated me from the Twisted Mountain great trees and drift logs kept disappearing and reappearing in a very odd way—and from my fire on the low shore I couldn't see why. I pulled out the field glass and watched a big spruce go down and out of sight: there were waves out there, big waves that were invisible in this clear, blue, shimmering light—and I had to pass above them and then make land above a long line of driftpiles on the further shore. If I did it, if I made this last crossing and reached the mainland safely, I'd camp, so help me, on the Twisted Mountain till the blasted river dropped a foot—or even two. I could travel three of these dangerous days in one then, and in comparative safety: enough was enough of this sort of foolery. And I kicked out from shore and raced up in the eddy before hitting the flying current.

I must have crossed about fifteen feet above the big waves for I heard the wash of one just behind me. But there was no time to look: the loaded canoe was handling like a lump of lead, and I had to reach land somewhere above the three-hundred-yard-long driftpile under which part of the river seemed to draw into some hidden channel behind. The canoe hit the steep shingle bank with a crash and started to slide downstream: the driftpile was only about twenty yards away. I swung the canoe's nose tight in to shore and then rose up and jumped with the trackline in my left hand, throwing away the paddle which fell with a clatter on the stones. The force of my jump shot the canoe out into the current, and the jerk came on the line as I rolled over on the shingle, trying for a foothold. The heavy canoe caught the full sweep of the Nahanni and skidded me on my tail end over the stones towards the river, too frightened even to swear. But some bygone flood had half buried an old spruce root deep in the tightly cemented shingle and, struggling and fighting, I fetched up against that with both feet—and the trackline held, and I drew the canoe into shore, five yards and no more above the hungry, sucking driftpile. I made the canoe fast to the root while I went to get the paddle: then I tracked on upstream towards the camp where I had said

good-bye to Faille nine months ago. The period of flood navigation was (I thought) at an end, and nobody was sorry.

Nothing had been disturbed at Faille's cache since he and I had
left there in the fall, and I soon had my load up on the platform
and tarped over and the lean-to set up in the shade of the trees.
Camp was gay and sweet-scented with all the blossom of the wild
fruit, for this was June, the northern springtime. The humming-
birds were busy in the blossom—and there were other heralds of
spring besides these. This was the day of the new hatch of mosquitoes, and several thousand of these keen young sap-suckers
were actively on the job, experimenting with human blood and
evidently enjoying it. The big, old mosquitoes that Nature so
wrong-headedly nurses through the winter to prevent the extinc-
tion of the race are deliberate even to the point of fussiness. One
can deal with them as they stroll about on the back of the hand,
searching for some dainty titbit. But the illimitable hordes of June
are in a hurry: they land with all the fury of youth, and where
they land they drill, in a second, through the toughest hide: death
means nothing to them—it merely makes room for more. The im-
minence of rain excites these pests to a frenzy, and on this occasion the daily thunderstorm was working up; above the canyon
ranges black clouds were climbing up into the blue with a yellow,
angry sunset beneath them—and soon the storm broke with a
crash of thunder; flash after flash struck the Twisted Mountain,
and I lay inside my net listening contentedly to the maddened
hum of the mosquitoes and the roar of the torrential rain.

The morning was cool and sunny. I decided to take one day
and climb the mountain and then to drop down to Gordon's
camp, perhaps with a moose, pick up another load and try to
repeat the performance up to the Twisted Mountain cache again:
any advance, however slow, was better than none, and the Safety
First programme was already forgotten.

The Twisted Mountain has two almost sheer sides and one gentle slope where the south-west dipping strata make a highway to
the summit. This face had been cleared of most of the old forest by
fire, and now it had a bit of everything—bare rock, grassy slopes,

beautiful stretches of natural rock garden bright with small, delicate flowers, and areas of jungle-like second growth—poplar, spruce, alder and jackpine. The first of the wild roses were out, and there were bluebells and great yellow daisies, small purple orchids and the little flowers of the rocks. And in the hollows and crannies of the mountain the white fruit blossom shone like small stars—gooseberries, saskatoons, strawberries, choke-cherries and blueberries, they were all there with swarms of gaily painted butterflies among them, small blues, swallowtails, every shade of sulphur, and then the more sober colours from red and purple to the darkest brown. There were the currants, too, red and black, dwarf raspberries and high-bush cranberries: down to the lowly kini-kinik and the low-bush cranberry there was no plant missing from all the multitude of the northern fruits that blossom in June and ripen in August under the blazing, day-long sunshine. The mountain was a garden.

Just below the summit, 3,000 feet above the river, in a slope of broken stone, was a thick, green cushion of *pentstemon fruticosus* covered with its gorgeous purple flowers. And on the very peak, of all the unlikely things to find in that place, there was one single moose track in a patch of sandy soil. The precipice fell away sheer on two sides: either this was a winged moose and consequently a new species, or else it had toiled up the long slope by which I had come—perhaps to get away from the mosquitoes. In either case it must have been a magnificient sight, standing there outlined against the sky, on the topmost point of the Twisted Mountain.

I sat down and pulled out the glass. Straight opposite lay the valley and the jagged mountains of Jackfish River and a great marshy lake over against the Outpost Hills. To the left one could see the Liard and the last calm reaches of the Nahanni and, in the west, the gateway to the Lower Canyon and the snow-clad mountains of the Tlogotsho. The black masses of thunderstorms were wandering over the immense country, and every detail was utterly clear and sharp in the rain-washed air. Below lay the maze of The Splits with their snyes and winding channels—and I began to map out my course through the islands back to Gordon's camp. Away down the main channel something caught my eye—an unnatural-looking object, and it seemed to be moving upstream. It was a scow, and it came up to the head of an island and then careered wildly across the river to the far side, disappearing behind some trees. It remained invisible for a long time and then reappeared creeping up under the bank, and this time there was a small black figure on shore moving slowly and painfully in advance of the scow—a man tracking, no doubt. The scow came to the head of an island where a fast snye ran off into the woods; the little figure clambered on board, and the scow tried to cross the head of the snye, failed and was swept backwards down it and into the bush: this was all most interesting: this would be Starke and Stevens, and they were quite obviously having no fun; Jack LaFlair had sized up that scow of theirs pretty accurately.

Half an hour or so later two little figures appeared, and they seemed to be working up the bank with axes, cutting off the sweepers and overhanging trees. Then they went back again, and some time later the scow reappeared and was slowly tracked to the head of the snye. But there was a chute there—one could see that by the way the sunlight flashed from the water—and they couldn't get up it into the main channel though they tried for a long time with their engine presumably running all out and one man poling. They tied up, and the two black dots were next seen wading deep into the main channel and back to shore, and doing this again and again, going always to exactly the same spot in the water. This new manoeuvre was beyond me completely, and it was too far away to see what they were up to. Perched on my mountain top I was pretty nearly frantic with curiosity—and when they both went on board and I saw the scow crawl slowly up the chute and into the main channel again, with one man poling and one steering and no other visible means of support, I was utterly defeated. The scow crept slowly on towards the Twisted Mountain and, muttering things about ''wizards,'' I hit the trail for camp. Late that evening the scow pulled in to the bank about a mile below me, and the smoke of a fire drifted out onto the river.

Next morning Starke and Stevens seemed to be in difficulties right from the start, so I went down and gave them a pull on the trackline, and between us we struggled the scow up to my camp.

That made one mile for a hard morning's work; and as we sat down to lunch the daily thunderstorm broke loose, and the rain fell in blinding torrents, continuing throughout the after-noon—and we made no move.

They made me an offer: if I would come with them and help on the trackline and in cutting the tracking path along the wooded banks, they would put my canoe and half my load on board, and we would try to make the Hot Springs. I knew the river and that would help, Starke said, and with one extra man on the line he thought they could do it: and when they reached the Springs they would unload and haul their scow out of the water and cut a couple of feet off the beam of her—from what I told them of the canyons they could see that that was going to be necessary if they were ever to see the Flat River before the snow flew. So that was settled, and we sat through the storm in the shelter of a huge lean-to that they had set up, idly prodding the fire and talking in the drifting, eddy-ing alder smoke into which the mosquitoes could not come.

Starke was tall and powerful and somewhere in his early fifties. He came from a farm near Stirling in Scotland and was the chosen one of the family to enter the ministry. But the news of the Klondike strike penetrated to Stirling just in time to rescue Starke, and the spring of '98 found him camped at Lake Bennett, waiting for open water "along with a few hundred other damnfool greenhorns," all headed for the golden river. Since then he had ranged the whole wide northland from east to west, and the grass had never had time to grow beneath his moccasins. He had only seen one country, in all those thirty years of wandering, in which he had felt he could ever settle down—a country of open, bunch-grass hills tucked away in northern B.C., set with little bluffs of poplar and pine and watered with good springs and clear flowing streams; "as sweet a country as a man could wish to see." And he told me where it was—but he never went back to it, for there was too much elsewhere to see and do. . . .

Stevens was a much younger man, tall and clear-skinned and tremendously strong. He came from West Kensington in London and, Gordon told me later, had been a prize-fighter at one stage of his career. Both were men of very even temper and great patience, and together they made a formidable combination that was known and respected from the Barren Lands far into the western mountains. They operated on a definite system: if they made a strike of gold and cleaned up anything worthwhile they would go out, up the Mackenzie and through the Great Slave Lake to Fort Smith, and from there to Edmonton. When they had disposed of their gold and furs they would make arrangements in Edmonton for a fresh, two-year outfit—the best of everything— and for their return passage to Fort Smith. And when that had been seen to and paid for they would make the rest of their "stake" fly as if wings had suddenly sprouted on every dollar: their last combined effort that I heard of was when they took a house in Vancouver for race week and wrote a splendidly crimson page in the annals of the coast city. They had dropped on to a pocket of gold, that time, and cleaned it out clean as a whistle— and they saw it on its way with a zest that even Swiftwater Bill, of Klondike fame, might have envied them.

Next morning, hitching on to trees with block and tackle, we worked the scow up the Twisted Mountain Riffle, and then for nine days we crawled at a snail's pace up the river, beset by hordes of frenzied mosquitoes, drenched by thunderstorms, sweating under the blazing sun in heavy clothes, leather gloves and headnets or scarves of mosquito netting. A moose fell before us under a wild barrage of rifle fire and we lived on moose meat, porridge and tea—and throve, putting in a twelve-hour day. We would cut trail along the bank for perhaps half a mile and then go back to bring up the scow. Stevens and I would adjust over our shoulders the loops of moosehide that attached us to the trackline while Starke warmed up the engine; and then off we would go once more with the "Black Pirate" standing motionless in the stern, pipe in mouth and hand on the tiller, peering ahead at the boiling surface of the flooded river, while the two trackers at times literally crawled upstream on the taut, vibrating line, grabbing with gloved hands at willows, wild roses, even at clumps of fireweed—anything that would give a pound or two's extra pull on the scow. The language flew as we slipped and staggered along, and we encouraged each other and called out rudely to

Starke for more power from his old teakettle—and it was in those days that he got and accepted the nickname of the Black Pirate; and a very fitting one it was for him standing there, his face blackened by sun, smoke and beard, a black pipe upside down in his mouth and the whole beauteous vision topped off by an old black sombrero on which there was never standing room for even one more mosquito. They loved that hat, those mosquitoes, and they were happy there, and Stevens was sure it was the only thing that kept us sane. "Lose that hat," he said, "and we'll have another four thousand after us—and the bunch that's loose *now* has got us crazy enough. They don't need any helpers. . . ."

And there was the time when the trackline snapped and Stevens and I fell flat on our faces while Starke whirled downstream and out of sight. We found him, by the grace of God, a mile below, tied up in an eddy and with the trackline snarled round the propeller. Stevens stripped and went down into the ice-cold water and worked there on and off for half an hour, straightening out the tangles: and we fished him out blue and put him in his eiderdown, and then we made camp and fed him moose soup scalding hot—and the Black Pirate and I sat alone by the fire that evening with me listening to tales of the Trail of '98, of the Fairbanks rush and the Omineca country, and the golden beaches of Nome. . . .

The end came when we were within sight of the Hot Springs and a mile and half downriver from them. We came to the point of an island and ran into the usual trouble there, eventually being carried down the snye and under the cliff on the north shore. We got out of that mess by building a series of deadmen out into the main river on a submerged bar and then windlassing the scow up the chute from one deadman to another out into the stream. The deadmen were constructed of heavy poplar logs held down in the water by boulders and slabs of rock as large as we could carry—a "deadman" being some solid object from which a pull can be taken. This was the manoeuvre which had so puzzled me when I watched it from the Twisted Mountain.

We then charged up the river in an eddy, hit the full force of the current as we came out from behind a rocky point and hurtled across the Nahanni. We failed to make the point we were aiming at on the mainland, escaped going down another snye, crashed into a driftpile at the head of an island with a shock that threw us all off our feet and slid back downstream on to a gently sloping beach of shingle. And the period of scow navigation was at an end.

Starke landed first and let rip with a highly coloured oration which would most certainly have gained him no advancement in the ministry had he decided, in his youth, to plump for the kirk and not the Klondike. Here he was, he said with embellishments, and here he was going to stay until the river had dropped and he had made the adjectival scow into a smaller and a sweeter craft. And damn him if he ever tackled the Nahanni again with any engine of any kind: a two-man Yukon poling boat was the only thing, and nobody but a lunatic—and at this point his voice tailed off, the speech came to an end, and he turned to us with a smile on his face.

"Come and look at this," he said.

We walked quietly forward over the stones and there, in a little clump of cottonwoods lay a two-month-old moose calf. His mother's tracks were fresh on the sand: she had left him there where the wolves were not likely to come, and he lay quite still, except for his anxious eyes, until we were within five yards of him. Then he could stand it no longer and jumped up and ran to the edge of the snye. But the snye was a young river in itself and too strong for him, and he turned back and clattered past us towards the lower end of the island. . . .

That slope of shingle was to be the careenage, and the Black Pirate and his partner set up a good camp on the point of the island, emptied the scow and built a capstan on the beach while I, gloved, veiled and sweating quarts, built a cache back in the bush and carried my load up into it. That took a day, and we met again at suppertime on the point, in the breeze and the fire smoke and away from the mosquitoes, and there we sat, cracking the great shin bones of a moose to get at the marrow, talking and watching through the glass a number of moose that were milling around in the shallows below the mouth of the Lower Canyon, and one

solitary bear that was capering about on the shingle a mile or so
downstream. Right after breakfast next morning we cut two long,
straight aspen poplars and dragged them down to the beach. This
was June when the bark of trees slips off as easily as taking off a
glove, and in a few minutes the big trees were peeled and white
and glistening in the sun with the wet, slippery sap. We slipped
the peeled skids under the empty scow, from each end of which
heavy ropes ran to the capstan—and then we began to turn on the
crowbars. Gently and sweetly the scow slid up the skids until she
was safe above high-water mark. There they blocked her, and I
left them drawing lines on her with charcoal and arguing. It was
June 18th, and I knew that in each of their minds, as also in my
own, was the firm conviction of historical accuracy. On what date
was the battle of Waterloo fought? The argument had started at
suppertime and continued at breakfast: the 16th, 17th and 18th of
June had each one been backed by its proposer in no uncertain
terms—and as I ran down the river towards the Twisted Mountain on this gay morning of early summer, scaring moose and
moose calves right and left, the thing bothered me. There was $10
apiece on it now, and if Starke was right about Ney at Quatre
Bras I could kiss my ten good-bye. . . .

In two hours and twenty minutes I undid the work of nine toiling days with the scow and landed at the Twisted Mountain
cache. All was in order, and I loaded up and hit the river again
with the bottled-up energy of a couple of weeks' frustration. This
landed me at Starke's camp just forty-eight hours after I had left
it: Stevens was still in bed, but Starke was sitting on a log,
breakfasting on beaver tail and bacon. One side was out of the
scow, and the reconstruction had begun.

"You've made good time," Starke said. "Sit down and try
some of this—it's good." And then, as we ate, "We've been
unable to settle that Waterloo date yet. But Stevens is entirely
wrong—and so are you. . . ."

I tied up at Gordon's camp that evening. Nobody was at home,
but presently Gordon appeared poling up the snye with the dogs
following through the bush; he had been down to South Nahanni

and was full of news: Faille had gone down to Fort Simpson with
a sack of what he thought was gold in his canoe—we must have
missed him somewhere in The Splits. Father Gouet's cattle for the
Mission had been wrecked on an island in the Liard: their scow
had slid up high and dry on to a driftpile, and the cattle had swum
ashore and camped, like sensible beasts, on the nearest patch of
green grass. The R.C.M.P. was going to send a patrol under
Harrington to the Flat River next winter—and so forth. After
supper we walked up to the head of the island and looked out on
to the main river. The Nahanni had suddenly risen a foot, and it
was still rising fast. It was muddier again and sending down drift
logs and great floating trees. Now what? Another flood? Gloomily
we started to load the canoes.

Faille appeared next day, struggling up the snye when the new
flood was at its height. He had been a month on the way from
Fort Simpson, working his canoe with a ton load in it up the
rapids of the Liard, and now he was going on to find new country
above the Falls. He camped with us till the river began to drop
again, and bit by bit we heard the story of his winter on the Flat
River.

His trapline there was too much hemmed in by the mountains,
and on it he had had nothing but bad luck. Early snow and ice
caught him barely ready, and then a wolverine broke into his
shack and stole three wolf pelts and so much of his grub that he
nearly starved. In order to get in, the wolverine tore out the stove
pipe and enlarged the chimney hole and, once inside, proceeded
to raise hell with the whole outfit. One dog was drowned, and
another ran away to the wolves. Faille himself slipped on a mountainside and was laid up for three weeks, during which time many
of his traps were frozen into the overflow ice and he lost much fur.
The game left the country and, being laid up, he was unable to
follow or tell where the animals had gone: wolves and wolverine
ate the fur from his traps: he fired at caribou, needing meat, and
missed, not knowing that his fall on the mountainside had jig-
gered his sights till they stood permanently at a thousand yards:
he had some narrow shaves on a raft amongst the running ice,
was wind-whipped by savage squalls and whirlwinds in the can-

yons on the way down—and his "gold" proved to be copper pyrites. A full winter. And now, cheery as ever and talking hard, he was stirring Norwegian Logging Cake over the fire for his last meal with us before hitting the trail. We were putting on a banquet to speed him on his way—and soon afterwards, to the tinny whine of his little outboard, he shot out of the snye and turned upstream.

A confused couple of weeks followed during which we sometimes travelled and sometimes sat by the fire and stared gloomily through the pouring rain at yet one more high water. But we got our main camp shifted up to the Hot Springs, and while Gordon fished and hunted I dropped down to the foot of The Splits for the last time and brought up the rest of the outfit. I made the round trip in two and a half days: it was my ninth time through The Splits, and by now I considered myself something of an expert on that bit of the river: I knew, at any stage of water, which channels were passable and which were not, and by means of a maze of short cuts I could double my original speed. I landed at Gordon's camp dog-weary, having been eleven and a half hours on the river that day.

In the morning we redistributed the heavy load between the two canoes and poled on into the Canyon. At the foot of Lafferty's Riffle we found the reconstructed scow but no sign of its owners. Their camp came into view as we hauled the canoes up the riffle, a tiny oasis of humanity on the great flow of rock and broken stone that comes down from the gorge of Lafferty Creek, and there we found the two partners asleep in the sun: they had been hung up there for eight days, unable to get up the rapid, and they had portaged half their outfit up to this camp to lighten the scow. Now they were waiting for a drop in the river, but, instead of that, the Nahanni was rising again after the torrential thunderstorms of the last few days—and as we ate our midday meal and lazed on the sun-warmed rocks we all cursed the turbulent river and the everlasting storms and watched the new flood as it crept up on the little cairns we had built as markers down by the canoes.

Gordon and I pushed on and camped late, after a hard struggle, near my "Last Man Camp" of the previous summer. Far above the river the topmost cliffs were lit with the wild, yellow light of the setting sun, but down by the water's edge there was only the puny flame of the evening fire. The canyon walls were cold and grey in the creeping shadows: the rising Nahanni swirled and clashed, with a threatening note in its many voices, against the tremendous cliffs: the dogs lay close by the fire, and the two pygmies who were moving so busily between the camp and the canoes knew that they were there only on sufferance and for a little while: the great, fantastic place was meant for loneliness and not for men.

The winds blew, and we struggled onwards with an icy rain falling and dark, cheerless clouds driving low down between the canyon walls. There were stretches of sheer cliff, with no poling bottom, where we could make our way up the river only by poling horizontally against the rock—and in these places we had to carry the dogs in the canoes. And there were points and buttresses where no efforts would get us by; and there I would have to climb away up the cliffs, taking with me all the trackline that we had, and then drop down again to some small ledge or beach. I would tie one end of the two-hundred-and-fifty-foot line to a piece of drift and so float it back to Gordon who would fasten it to the forward thwart of his canoe. The signal for me to haul was two tugs on the line, and presently the nose of his canoe would heave in sight with its occupant ramming against the canyon wall with his iron-shod pole, struggling to keep the canoe from sheering out—for if that happened no power on earth could hold it against the Nahanni current, and the work would be to do again. And then one of us would climb back over the point to the remaining canoe and the performance would be repeated. A mile of canyon was won only with difficulty and danger, but we crept forward. And there was no sign of Starke.

There came a sunny afternoon of bellowing west wind with great, white, cumulus clouds climbing up into the summer sky. The full fury of the wind caught us on the moraine of a creek that broke out of the canyon wall on the left bank: spray was blowing off the river, and it was impossible to go on. We dropped back to a sandy beach and made camp high up on the shore: down came the inevitable deluge, heavier even than usual and lasting for several hours; the river began to rise, and the canyon walls vanished into the driving rain and the scudding streamers of mist and cloud. The monotonous roar of the downpour on the tent was soporific, and we fell asleep.

It cleared about six: Gordon went up to the creek mouth to fish, and I took my rifle and climbed up over the moraine and into the gorge of the creek which I followed for an hour or so. It was a valley—almost a canyon—of tremendous stones, wooded at the sides and rising to the great limestone cliffs and the high pastures of the wild sheep. It was cool in there in the evening shadow, shut off from the world and lonely. Across one end and far below, the brown flood of the Nahanni swirled past: upstream, and infinitely remote, a green upland country stood out against the rain-washed blue. The sun was shining up there, and the last wisps of storm cloud were rising from the valley. In the creek bed were masses of beautiful quartz, gay with the blue and green stains of copper. An interesting valley and a pity, I thought, that we had no time to give to it. . . .

There were a few mosquitoes about that evening—not many, for the June heyday of that pest was over—and we ate supper inside the tent with the mosquito screen down over the doorway. Outside, in the murmurous dusk, a harsher note was coming from the river, and the new rise was spewing down incredible quantities of drift. Inside the tent we were busy with fish and conversation was sporadic.

"It's an odd thing, Gordon, the way that mosquito screen distorts things. Look at those canoes—you could swear they were closer. . . ."

And a few minutes later:

"From where I sit, George, you'd think the canoes were trying to climb in at the door. It's looking through the screen on an angle that does it, I suppose."

And then, after a very brief pause, confusion reigns and all the characters speak hastily and at once:

"By God's truth they *are* trying to climb in at the door! Out of here, quick, and into the bush! Rifles and cameras first! Mind that rice pudding! Roll up that————mosquito screen before somebody puts his great flat foot through it. . . ."

That was the quickest rise we ever saw: unfortunately we didn't measure it from the start, but it must have been six or seven feet in under an hour—a terrific quantity of water in a big river like the Nahanni. That was July 13th, and it effectively settled any idea of travelling on the morrow. Now for that upland country and perhaps a sheep.

Breakfast was eaten while camp lay deep in the morning shadow: then I gathered my outfit and joyously hit the trail. I climbed quickly up the creek bed in sunshine, mist and rain, and at 3,000 feet above the Nahanni I came to the last of the trees—a little wood of stunted firs. The creek valley ran on up into the bald hills and the blue sky, walled in by grey screes and grassy, rock-strewn hillsides running up to the naked rimrock. There was a cold wind blowing and here and there a patch of snow; and fluttering around the snowdrifts, flashing in the sun, were gaily coloured butterflies—sulphurs and the gaudy black-white-and-reds. I began to climb, and at 4,000 feet I came over the rim of the valley and on to the plateau, the grazing lands of the wild white sheep. Miles and miles of close-cropped alpine turf, still bright with flowers though many were already over, streaked with beds of gravel in which quartz crystals flashed like diamonds, rent with creek canyons and deep valleys out of which came the noise of water and the boiling cloud vapours—God, there was no end to it, and a man could go on for ever over that great, green upland country that lay before me with the sunlight and the cloud shadows and the wind sweeping over it.

I went on for about four miles, searching the valleys and the prairies with my glass for game, sheltering now and then behind the great, solitary blocks of stone that lay upon the grass like farmhouses in their fields. There was sheep sign everywhere, but never a sheep; and then, as I topped a gentle rise, I saw them, fifty-four head as near as I could count them, ewes, lambs and young rams—a splendid sight to see as they grazed and lay there, white and shining against the green, straight into the eye of the afternoon sun. And as useless to me as if they had been on the moon, for the plateau between them and me was slashed by the deep cleft of a creek canyon, and the afternoon was on its way. So I perched on a block of stone that crowned a little round grass hill, 4,500 feet above the river, and watched the movements of the sheep and tried to set in my memory the whole amazing view from Nahanni Butte to Deadmen Valley so that I might have something of it to look back on in the years to come. Time slipped easily by on that flower-starred plateau: the sun slid down the tremendous sky, the shadows lengthened, and the wind grew cold—and I went down again into the valley of the great stones and back to camp on the Nahanni in the gentle twilight of a perfect summer's day.

"Somebody," Starke said, "had better get some fresh meat soon, before our jaws come unhinged chewing at this stuff," and he glared sourly at a piece of dried moose meat that sat stiffly on his plate, surrounded by a mess of dried potatoes and wild onions. Then he turned to me.

"Was the river as high as this when you and Faille went up last year?" he asked.

"No," I said. "But I think Gordon and I can get the canoes up somehow—by wiggling around amongst the rocks."

"You *might*. But Steve and I won't tackle it: I'm going to wait till it drops at least a foot. And I doubt if you'll make it against this water. . . ."

We were having supper at the foot of the Cache Rapid where we had fetched up together once more in our progress upstream. The waves from the foot of the big riffle were washing up and down on the black sand of the little bay, and from beyond the point of rocks came the steady roar of white water. After supper, when the others were all in bed, I walked up over the point and sat for a while on a sun-warmed rock watching the furious rush of the rapid in the rose-coloured twilight. In the background, through the upper gateway of the canyon, the Bald Mountain in Deadmen Valley stood up black and sharp against the evening sky. It looked like home.

After breakfast Gordon and I set to work. He went ahead, over the point and up the river to the head of the eddy, which was so strong that a heavily loaded canoe travelling upstream in it could drive on to the rocks at the upper end hard enough to damage itself. I snugged everything down in the little canoe and then raced upstream, round the point, in the eddy to Gordon who caught the canoe and cushioned the shock. Then with Gordon on the line and myself in the canoe we worked our way carefully to the head of the rapid, tied the canoe to a rock under the cliff and clambered back along the boulder-strewn shore to camp, wet and battered but triumphant. The day was turning grey and cold, and rain was in the offing.

During lunch Gordon spotted a sheep on a ledge high up on the canyon wall, across the river and behind the island on the far side of the rapid.

"That sheep's nearly five hundred yards away," he said. "Now's the time to use that telescope sight of yours. . . ."

I had bought the telescope sight, rather as an afterthought, in London the winter before. I had had it fitted in Edmonton, and it was badly fitted, set too far back—and practice at the Hot Springs had made it clear that, while it certainly produced meat at long ranges for the camp, it was equally certain to produce for its owner a perfect jewel of a black eye. With a feeling of resignation I put down my plate and went down to fish the cursed thing out of the canoe, well aware that Gordon would be outlining to the others the probable course of the coming action.

I sat down on the moss, sighted carefully and fired, receiving a slam above the right eye that would have flattened a gorilla. The sheep started violently, ran a few paces along the ledge and then stood stock still.

"Did you get a black eye that time, old man?"

"Yes, blast you!"

"Well, have another go—he's still waiting."

As I sighted for the second time I could feel, behind my suffering head, three grins of anticipation: this was brightening an otherwise gloomy day for the assembled ghouls of our little party.

I fired, and the ram crashed down in a shower of stones and dust to fall, stone dead, on the beach at the foot of the canyon wall.

"Well shot, George!" Gordon called out. And then, as I came back to the fire and picked up my plate and mug, he looked closely at my eye.

"Good work!" he said. "Both shots took effect, I see. On you, I mean. I shall recommend you for a bar to your Black Eye!"

"I've got one already, you perfect idiot. . . ."

The next thing to do was to get the second canoe up the rapid and somehow get across to that sheep: Stevens volunteered to give Gordon a hand on the line, and the two of them disappeared over the point while I loaded the big canoe and made ready.

All went well for a time until Stevens, more accustomed to hauling on a scow than on a canoe, gave a tremendous yank on the line at the wrong moment. The effect was that of a sheer: out I flew from the eddy behind a rock into the worst of the fast water: Stevens hung on with all his great strength, the water started to boil up over the gunwale, and the noise of the river was too great for any of us to shout out and be heard. If Stevens hung on I would be pulled under: if he let go there would be a trailing line following me, and it might snag and draw me under. I drew my hunting knife and started to run forward over the load to cut the line: then I would try to run the rapid backwards, forwards, sideways—any way so long as I got the canoe safely down into the big eddy again.

Suddenly I felt the canoe gripped by some invisible force and propelled upstream. The change of direction almost threw me off my balance—and then the canoe's nose slammed violently against a rock and I sat down heavily on the load.

I had been picked up by the eddy below a great rock, away out from shore and in the fastest of the white water. The whole force of the Nahanni drove past this rock, roaring over it at times, and the big freight canoe in the eddy behind the rock was almost two feet below the level of the river: the eddy was literally a hole in the water. The noise of the rapid was terrific: on shore Gordon and Stevens were evidently shouting something, but not a word of it reached me. Stevens still held the line: it had burnt his hands as

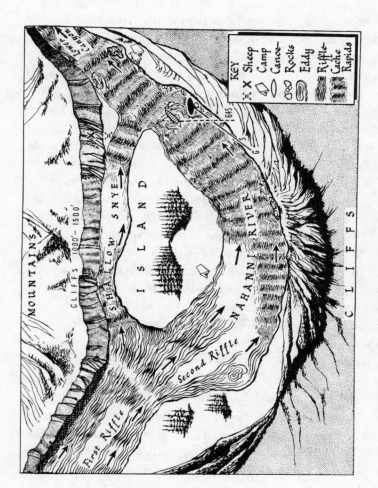

DIAGRAM OF THE OPERATIONS AT THE CACHE RAPIDS

(size of canoe, length of trackline and distance of central rock
from shore all greatly exaggerated in order to show detail)

the river whirled the canoe out to the rock.

I made a sign for them to hold everything—no action of any kind. Then I did some work with the pole and got the canoe lined up at the proper angle to get back to shore; and then I signalled to Stevens to pull. That was one thing he thoroughly understood—pull—and I came out from behind that rock with a surge and a rush, going like a destroyer, only sideways, hurtling across the tearing water and smashing broadside on into one of the shore rocks with a wallop that stove in one of the ribs of the crazy old ruin that I was nominally handling. But I was still above water and, after holding a brief post mortem on the shore on this last effort, we carried on and reached the head of the rapid.

Dividing the dogs between us we made a frantic crossing to the island, beached the canoes there and started out to bring in the sheep. To get to him we had to wade the snye between the island and the canyon wall, and that took us in over our waists and almost swept us off our feet. A cold, miserable rain was starting to fall, and by the time we had skinned the sheep, fed some to the dogs and waded the snye once more with the rest of the meat, we were two pretty wretched-looking objects. The next good camping place was up on Ram Creek in Deadmen Valley, and it was too late now to start up the Cache Riffles; so we made camp where we were, put on dry things and warmed our innards with mountain mutton and strong tea. "He was a yearling ram, and never was meat so tender or so well tasting—practically lamb."

The canoes were on a poor sort of a beach, and my old ruin was leaking badly after its rough handling in the rapid, so I went down at intervals in the night to bail and see that all was well. On the last of these expeditions a lovely, rain-washed dawn was breaking, and I lit the fire and roused Gordon with a great mug of mutton broth—odds and ends of sheep with barley and plenty of pepper in it. He sat up and stared at the fire in a morose sort of way; then he caught sight of my eye and that cheered him up a little; and then, muttering something about "a beautiful sunset," he started to lap up his soup. Presently, as I stirred the porridge and turned the mutton chops, I heard a muffled curse followed by

obscure mumblings: "Mutht be the other blathted bullet," he
was saying with a look of pained surprise on this face and half his
fist jammed into his mouth. "Ah—got him!" and he held out for
my inspection the butt end of a mushroomed bullet and a sharp
splinter of nickel. One bullet had turned up already, when we
were skinning the sheep, and now both shots were accounted
for—and from that time forward I heard no more rude comments
on my honourably gained black eye and bar.

We started early up the two big riffles. I was ahead with the big
canoe and I lost track of Gordon: I had my own troubles, and the
uproar of the river drowned out all other sounds. I spent the
morning hauling the canoe up hills of water, poling a little but
mostly in the water, out of my depth twice and soused to the neck.
I had on a pair of khaki drill trousers: both knees had a tear in
them, and the force of the water was so great that it got inside and
tore the lower part of the trouser legs so that they trailed behind
me, flapping in the river: in a fit of fury I took my hunting knife
and did some swift work with it and travelled on in shorts. And
after four hours of illimitable damnation I came out from the
shadow of the Little Butte into the calm water and beached the
canoe at the mouth of Ram Creek.

I strolled across the creek and into the spruce where there was
an old trapping camp and cache, and there, wading in the tall
goldenrod, I fell on great fat raspberries, luscious and sweet,
gooseberries and red and black currants. Soon Gordon joined me,
and we both stuffed ourselves with the fruit while I listened to his
tale of the woes of Starke and Stevens.

Just as I was getting well stuck into the first riffle the Black
Pirate had foamed into view, going all out and doing remarkably
well with his clumsy old winkle barge. The river had dropped six
inches in the night—not the foot that he was waiting for, but the
sight of us going on had been too much for his patience. He got
level with Gordon who was still loading his canoe, and he shouted
out to know if there was any more strong water ahead. Gordon
told him yes, there were two big riffles—and Starke went on.
Then he crossed the river; and something must have happened

there, in the shadow of the canyon wall, for the scow was swept backwards and over a big rock.[1] Stevens jumped for the shore with the line and tried to hold the scow, but couldn't and was pulled into the river. Starke swung the scow at an angle and charged across the worst of the water towards the island, with Stevens towing behind him like some monstrous fish. Gordon suddenly realised that Starke's point of impact was going to be exactly where he was standing, and he jerked his canoe into deep water and floundered upstream with it—and just in time, for the Black Pirate fetched up against the shingle with a crash that threw him off his feet and would have made matchwood out of our little canoe. A beat late Stevens crawled out from beneath the waves, and the two part-ners held a spirited interchange of views on the advisability or otherwise of this novel method of crossing a river. When they had got that all ironed out to their own satisfaction they went on, un-daunted and undefeated, and Gordon had left them damning and swearing in the middle of the lower riffle, with their propeller dinging on the stones.

And now the raspberries were all finished and a gale of wind was roaring out of the south-west, bending the trees, drifting the poplar seed before it like driven snow. It was impossible to travel, and in any case the big canoe had to be repaired before we could go on: we unloaded it and spread the stuff out in the sun to dry: Gordon cut some meat, and I lit the fire and took over the cooking of lunch—and Gordon lay down on the warm sand with a sack of flour as a pillow and his hat over his face and slept.

I moved busily round the fire, barefooted, warm and dry in the hot sunshine and the wind. The Cache Rapid lay below us: we had arrived, and I would make Logging Cake à la Faille to celebrate: one would have to be careful of the batter, for fierce gusts were driving small whirls and eddies of ash out of the fire on the leeward side. . . .

Suddenly a piercing yell shattered the peace of the summer afternoon. Gordon sat up: the hat fell off his face, and he blinked wildly at the sun. A gust of wind had whirled a piece of glowing

[1]Which we came to know as Starke's Rock.

charcoal out of the fire and lodged it neatly between my toes: swearing with pain I gallantly set down the panful of precious batter and the ladle that I held in my other hand: a lesser man would have flung them down, in the grub box, on Gordon, anywhere. . . . Thank God the river was near, and I rushed into its cooling waters with a hiss.

The wind blew for two more days—no unusual thing for Deadmen Valley. We dried the outfit and patched and mended the old freight canoe: Gordon fished and went back up Ram Creek towards the mountains: I went up the Little Butte and looked over the far side of it to see if I could get a sight of Starke. The Cache Rapid and the island lay almost at my feet and far below, but there was no sign of the scow or of any camp. Yet they must be there somewhere: shortly after we had landed at Ram Creek a tremendous column of smoke had risen from behind the Little Butte. They must have fired a driftpile, an old trick of theirs, in order to thaw Stevens out after his submarine trip across the Nahanni.

Sheep were always in sight from this camp, across the river, down by the water's edge or grazing along the rocky ledges. We fired one or two very long shots, but without effect, as we worked on the canoe. Then, very early on the second morning, one of the dogs barked. We sat up in bed, wide awake in a second—and there, visible through the tent door and right down by the river on the far shore, were three young rams. We were out of bed in a flash and out of the tent without a word—two men, pyjama-trousered and carrying rifles. We sat down on the rocks and fired simultaneously: two sheep fell, mine apparently dead and Gordon's wounded and struggling up the hill. Gordon jumped up and ran for the little canoe: he threw it into the water, hurled himself, rifle and paddle into it and skimmed away across the river. The wounded ram disappeared into some poplar brush with Gordon after it but well below: presently the ram came out on to a rocky bluff, and there was no sign of the pursuit: probably I had better shoot—and I was just pressing the trigger when the ram tumbled down the cliff, and a fraction later I heard the sound of Gordon's shot. Down rolled the ram in a cascade of loose rock, to fall dead on the beach within a few feet of mine. Down came his rock avalanche, too, and one of the larger stones struck my ram which was lying close to the water's edge. The blow must have aroused some last flicker of life, for the ram gave one kick and rolled over into the river, apparently stone dead. He drifted gently down the calm water, and then, gathering speed, he slid past a huge rock[1] and bounced away down the Cache Riffles. That's what you get, I thought, for being too cocksure: I should have gone with Gordon in that canoe.

Two or three days later we were poling up a quiet, dreamy snye of the right bank, somewhere above the mouth of the Meilleur River. The water was deep and fast, and the hot afternoon sunshine poured down in shafts and columns of golden light through the branches of the cottonwoods which met and interlaced overhead. Not a breath of air was moving, and we were weary: ramming the canoes upstream in that green, sun-dappled, shadowy place we sweated prodigiously.

We had looked at every possible building site in the valley and had found only one that pleased us; the rest all lacked something—either there was no good building timber, or else the site and landing were poor. This was the last throw: and it was a washout, one could see that now, for we were coming out of the snye and back into the main river; only one long reach separated us from the entrance to the Second Canyon, and the mountains were closing in on us again. There was no sense in going further—and so we made camp and cooked supper and sat on the soft cushion of the dryas, eating and watching the red light of the sunset on the face of the Second Canyon Mountain. In the morning we would drop downstream to the mouth of a little creek in the centre of the valley and build a cache: we had come to our journey's end.

The valley lay in the shadow of the western range: the evening was warm and soft, and there were no mosquitoes bothering—the

[1]Known as Starke's Rock today, with a garbled legend attached to it. The original and proper one, over which Starke's scow was swept, was down below in the rapid.

days of that pest were practically over, and we sat there utterly contented. A bull moose came out of the bush and swam to a shingle island in the middle of the river: that was exactly what we needed; feeding this dog team was like feeding a bunch of wolves, and feeding them mountain mutton was a crime. We laid down our plates and picked up our rifles: Gordon fired first and dropped him, and my shot finished him. Then we picked up our plates again and went on with supper. And next morning we dropped gingerly down the river with about two inches of freeboard apiece. Gordon had three dogs and all the load he could cram into the little canoe, while mine carried Poilu, our lead dog, all the moose and the rest of the outfit. The aged bateau, sunk deep in the water and with her soggy old canvas hide, was hard to handle—but no wind blew, and in less than an hour we swung into the eddy below the little creek and beached the canoes on the sand.

The site was a good one. It was on the south bank of the Nahanni, a little above the mouth of Prairie Creek and on the opposite shore. Just above the cabin site a stream of clear water flowed into the Nahanni, chattering over the stones; it came down from the Bald Mountain, and we named it Wheatsheaf Creek in memory of a friendly house that lay beyond the seas. The landing was good, and the building timber was plentiful and of all sizes: wind-twisted it was true, but what else could one expect in that windswept valley? And there was game: in the first hour, as we unloaded the canoes, we saw five moose either swimming or coming down to drink, and in the afternoon, two more. And it went on like that. Then there was Prairie Creek with its fish and sheep and a vast berry patch which supported more bears to the acre than any place I have ever seen. And up the little Wheatsheaf Creek the partridges and the blue grouse scratted in the gravel and roosted in the trees—it was a land of plenty where a man could hunt and live well and be happy with never a worry in the world. . . .

Starke and Stevens turned up that first evening: they had damaged their scow on the rock in the rapid and again in the big riffles and had had to unload and portage all their outfit once again and make repairs. They camped overnight with us, shot themselves a moose and passed on.

A week's work followed, during which we cleared and levelled a site for the cabin, cut spruce for building timber, taking the trees from the south to let in the sunlight, and painted the canoes. Gordon built a shelter and a meat-drying rack and smoked and dried the moose meat, and I built an enormous cache, set on four big trees which I cut off twelve feet above the ground: these were peeled and then ringed round, each one, with a couple of feet of tin just under the cache floor. This floor was a platform of spruce poles built with an overhang; above it was stretched a big tarpaulin on a frame, and inside this shelter there was room for all the food and perishables that we had—safe from marauders.

When all this was done we took the big canoe, the floating ruin, and ran down through the Lower Canyon to pick up the stuff we had left in my cache on Starke's Island: and by evening we had it all loaded and tracked up to camp at the Hot Springs. Then the canyon walls blacked out under the dark wings of the storm that had been gathering all day over the Tlogotsho, the lightning flashed, and down came the rain in torrents. And with a perfect sense of timing the river began to rise. . . .

In sunshine and in rain we struggled up through the Lower Canyon for the last time, cursing ourselves for not having brought both canoes, for the leaky old sieve of a freight canoe was dangerously overloaded and had to be bailed at every stop. We wondered how we should manage to cross to the island at the head of the Cache Rapid with it, for in that place the dogs could not be left to swim and we would have to carry them.

We found out on a chill, grey, sunless morning of early August. As the canoe drove out of the eddy at the head of the rapid it hit the current with a plunge, and a boiling surge of water foamed up along the gunwale. The frightened dogs all shifted to the downside, and the canoe lurched and almost filled with water. I managed to swing it back to the shore we had just left, and Gordon jumped with the line. But he was pulled into the river, as Stevens had been, and down we went. The canoe slid backwards over a rock that was just awash: the tail went clean under water while the nose hung in mid-air with the river driving past on both sides. I could just see Gordon: he had fetched up against a rock with a smack that almost stove his chest in, and there he stayed hanging on to the line very stoutly with both hands. His arms must have been pretty nearly wrenched out of their sockets.

The water swept over his shoulders, and every now and then, with the rising and falling rhythm of the river, he would be completely submerged. He seemed to be trying to speak, but in the rush and tumult of the Nahanni all that came to me was a faint croaking sound as of distant frogs.

"Can you hang on there for a bit?" I bawled at him.

His mouth opened—but at the same moment a green wave cascaded over him, and nothing reached me but a half-drowned splutter.

We were close to shore: hoping to God that Gordon meant yes, he could hold on, I got out, steadied the canoe and hurled all the heavy stuff, traps and suchlike, that I could easily reach out on to the rocks. Slowly we bailed and raised the lightened canoe, and reloaded and tracked up into the eddy once more: there we made coffee and fried some moose steaks with which to warm our sodden selves; and then we went at it again, with awful caution and after thoroughly intimidating the dogs; and this time we succeeded.

In this fashion we came home to Deadmen Valley—and two days later I left, with the little canoe and a light outfit, for the Flat River.

I unloaded the canoe at Faille's old camp at the foot of the Box Canyon portage. Then I kicked out from shore and struck across the Nahanni for the ledge on the far side from which Faille and I had tracked the canoes the year before. Again the river raced past the skittering canoe, and again I just caught the tail end of the shelf where it sloped off into the water: all was well now, and I shoved the canoe out into the current and shook out the trackline.

But all was not well: a wind was blowing downstream through the Box Canyon[1] and, when I was about half-way along the ledge and about twelve or fifteen feet above the water, a sudden gust

---

[1]A canyon with sheer walls on each side and no beaches is called a box canyon.

spun the canoe on its tail and it vanished from sight. I jerked on
the trackline, but there was no give to it; then I lay down flat on
the wide shelf and looked over. The tail end of the canoe was
visible, but that was all: evidently the ledge overhung and the
wind had driven the canoe under it and jammed it there between
the shelving rock and the water. I tugged at the line this way and
that way, and not one inch of movement could I get out of that
canoe: this was a sweet mess to be in—on a ledge with the sheer
canyon wall at the back of it, the canoe stuck underneath it and
the complete outfit on the far side of the Nahanni. And at
breakfast time the river had been rising a little: if it was still rising
it was a case of get that canoe out now or never. . . .

I lay there looking longingly at the tail of the canoe and thinking hard. The trouble was that I was pulling more or less vertically on the line: if I could get a downstream pull on it I might be
able to do something: and if that didn't work the only chance left
would be to chuck myself off the ledge into the river holding the
line and trust to my weight pulling the canoe out of its jam: if it
came out we would be swept down the river together, and there
would be a good sporting chance of getting somehow into an eddy
and to shore.

In the meantime there was the downstream pull to be considered. I crawled upstream along the edge of the shelf as far as
the line would let me go: it was tied, as usual, to the nose and to
the back seat with the bight passing through my hands. Taking
the bight in my teeth I lay absolutely flat, reached over as far as
possible and cut the forward section of the trackline with my hunting knife. Then I backed up, put my knee on the line to hold it
and tied the cut end to my wrist—for if I dropped it I could call it
a day and write finis to the Nahanni story right then and there.
And then I went down the ledge as far as the line would let me go
and started to wiggle at the canoe. . . .

An hour later I was still hanging over the edge and wiggling.
Every now and then one got half an inch or so—it depended on
the pull coming exactly in time with the little, rhythmic drop of
the water as it rose and fell. But the drop was hard to predict and
the river was undoubtedly rising: I was just keeping level with the

rise on the sloping roof of the cavern in which the canoe was jammed. Both arms were ready to drop off, for with my left hand I had to hang on to a knob of rock and my right hand was busy with the trackline. A great black and yellow pine bug kept circling around me in an offensive sort of way—a thing about the size of three hornets. It seemed to be interested in my nose. . . . But, thank God, the canoe was on the move at last: inch by inch it was coming, tapping against the roof of the overhang as it rose and fell on the waves. Suddenly it spun out into the open river, circled and fetched up with a jerk on the end of the line. I eased it back downstream to the foot of the ledge and bent down to examine it: the nose of the canoe was battered and scraped from its long contact with the rock, but no real damage had been done. The trackline, however, had another story to tell: about four feet from where it was tied to the canoe it had been working on the rock and was frayed about two thirds through. A little more wiggling and it would have parted, and why it had held the canoe on that jerk was a mystery—born to be hanged was Gordon's theory when he came to hear of this afternoon's manoeuvres. . . .

Every day on this river one took risks—calculated risks, most of them, with a few extras thrown in for good measure. But it never did to push the luck too far: only a fool would make a trial of fortune right after getting out of a jam like that. So, while the wind blew, no more tracking here—and I yanked the canoe out of the water, put my arm round the centre thwart, hitched the gunwale on to my shoulder and walked up the ledge with my burden. I had had enough fun for one afternoon.

The little cone-shaped mountain was not very high but it was isolated, and from its peak there was a tremendous view. On all sides there were mountains: a great granite range faded away into the north-west; and a rough-looking proposition it was, pitted with cirques and shadowy coulees, and with its peaks powdered with new snow. In the west a jagged rampart rose up, blue and unsubstantial in the faint smoke haze of some distant fire; it was hard to see distinctly against the afternoon sun, but there seemed to be small glaciers shining in the deep clefts of the range. That range, too, ran into the north-west, becoming fainter and finally vanishing into the dim blue distance; it ran parallel with the granite range, and it had to be the Yukon-Northwest Territories divide. Divide to what? I wondered, peering through the glass—for neither of these ranges was marked on the map, and the map itself was a beautiful blank with the Flat River represented by a dotted line in the wrong place. That was the charm of that map: one might chance upon almost anything in those empty, un-crowded spaces.

It looked as if the Flat River must flow down between those two mountain ranges: it was a wild little river here; one could see it here and there, 3,000 feet below, glittering in the sunlight. Right on the point of its southernmost bend, where it swung round the end of the granite range, it dived into a little canyon, foaming round great boulders in a series of wild cascades. That would be the "Cascades of the Thirteen Drops" of the McLeods, where they had upset and lost their gold twenty-odd years ago. I looked down at what I could see of the white water in the canyon: not for me, with a canoe at this late season, I decided: I would build a cache and go ahead on foot; it would be easier and a lot safer—and I picked out a possible line of travel towards the western range.

To the south the view was shut off by higher mountains, but to the south-east a wide valley ran away over an alpine summit: the faint blue of lakes showed through the haze far down the valley. Two miles away another cone mountain rose out of the little plateau, the twin of the mountain that I was on: between the two was a little alpine lake from which a small stream flowed down to the Flat River. A couple of caribou, grazing and running, had just passed by the lake and vanished behind the other cone; they always seemed to be in a hurry, those animals; could it be on ac-count of wolves?

I pivoted around and looked to the north. From the bend the Flat River ran almost due north to Irvine Creek, a green river streaked with white; all very calm and peaceful looking from here but a dirty piece of water to haul a canoe up—just one little boulder rapid after another. If the water dropped much lower

with the coming of September and the first hard frosts it was not
going to be at all easy to run that canoe back down to Irvine
Creek. . . .

Further north the eye followed the great trough of Irvine Creek
till it vanished behind the outposts of the granite range: a pass
back to the upper Nahanni above the Falls, that must be; and
somewhere up there, perhaps thirty or forty miles away, Faille
was probably building his cabin and blazing his trapline. I had
looked in at his old cabin at the mouth of the Flat to pick up a gold
pan and a prospector's pick that I had left there in his care: the
place was deserted, and the cabin in which we had passed such
pleasant evenings was dark and chill; there was a pencilled note
on the door: "A. Faille left here for the Falls, July 8."

I had passed Starke and Stevens some seventy miles down the
Flat River from this point. They were almost out of gas, and their
remaining propeller was badly dinged upon the rocks. They were
windlassing up a riffle when I passed by, and they had asked me
how much further it was to Caribou Creek. They brightened up
visibly when I told them it was only another two or three miles.

"Then we'll make it," Starke said, "if we have to rack the guts
out of the old engine and portage the scow. But no further: that's
the trail's end for us."

With Gordon away down in Deadmen Valley that accounted
for all of us—five men scattered over this huge country and all living like fighting cocks on the very best of fish and game. At least, I
hoped the others were: I certainly was. My last meat—and I
would soon be ready for some more—had come to me in the form
of a moose. I was sitting on a log having my weekly shave when I
heard a stone rattle: I looked up, and there was a bull moose by
the water's edge a couple of hundred yards up the Flat. Very
quietly I put down my shaving brush and picked up my rifle and
fired. Down came the moose, and I wiped the lather off the stock
of the rifle and set the weapon back against the log. Then I finished
my shave.

And fish—arctic grayling and Dolly Varden in every pool!
There had been one pool that I had found at the foot of a waterfall
where it was not a question so much of catching your fish as of

choosing the one you wanted and avoiding the one you didn't
want: the surface of that pool literally boiled with fish the moment
the line hit it. And there had been that time at Irvine Creek when,
landing completely tired out after a long day's travel, I had not
bothered to cut and trim a green willow but had picked up a light,
dry spruce pole, a relic of some Indian's camp, and tied my line to
that. With it I dragged ashore a monstrous fish—a Dolly Varden
about the size of a young porpoise. It flapped wildly on the shingle
and, before I could get to it, it broke the gut and bounded back
towards the river with my favourite Indiana spinner in its mouth.
There was only one thing I could do, and I did it with all the fury
of the hungry man who sees his supper departing—I brought
down the spruce pole with a terrific two-handed swat on the fish's
back.

"That'll fix you, you——!" I shouted as I struck. But it wasn't
the fish that was fixed: the rod, which was old but by no means
rotten, broke in two, and the fish capered gaily off taking with it
my best spinner and my most earnest benediction. . . .

The shadow of the little cone mountain was creeping out
towards the lake. A long line of fleecy clouds had appeared over
the jagged peaks in the west, and the sun was sinking towards
them, touching the tops with gold: one sweep of the glass over the
stony, barren-looking mountains to the east and then I would go:
I knew now all I wished of the lay of the country.

Two or three days earlier a sudden night frost had struck, and
now all the lower summits, wherever there was alpine vegetation
above timberline, had turned completely and dramatically
scarlet. This was due to the sudden turning of a particular kind of
moss, of a host of small alpine plants, and of the blueberries and
the dwarf wild roses. It was one of those things that a man may
see once or twice in a lifetime and no more: in other years the hills
might be snow-covered, or the leaves might wither and fall before
a hard frost came—or any one of a dozen things might happen.

But on this autumn day, from this small peak, the flaming hills
rolled away to the eastward in a savage blaze of colour against the
cloudless sky. The dark forest, itself splashed with red and gold,
climbed from the small, green river to die out in straggling out-

post trees against the scarlet alpine country which, in its turn, faded gently into the grey limestone summits. This redness was no modest rose or blushing pink; the frost had worked with stronger colours, vermilion and ruby, carmine and crimson, and the result was a picture that no artist would dare to paint and no words can ever properly describe. . . .

That evening, after supper, I cleared a space around three chosen spruce, made a ladder and began to build a cache. I worked till I could see no longer in the shadow of the trees, then, last thing of all, I went down to the river to bring up water for a wash and for the morning. The scarlet-topped mountains were fading and, one by one, the stars were coming out; the crisp sharpness of frost was in the air, for this country lay high: since leaving Deadmen Valley I had poled the canoe up a hill of water that was anything from a thousand to fourteen hundred feet in height, judging by the aneroid readings—an average drop of ten feet to the mile, I figured, from here down to Gordon a hundred and forty river miles away.

Three days later I was far to the westward, ramming my way through the bush. The afternoon was still and sweaty: thunder was rumbling in the western mountains like the echo of distant drums, and the peaks, the little one could see of them through the trees, had vanished into the lowering canopy of cloud: my landmarks were gone. Early in the morning I had waded a small river, then, after crossing a low pine ridge, I had followed a creek valley running from the west. And now this creek divided into two equal streams with a little flat between them set with big, old spruce. I had been aiming at a great bay in the mountains, and one of these streams, I thought, must come from there—but which one? Right-hand or left?

One last shaft of sunlight, pouring down through a window in the cloud, came stalking over the country: it rested on the flat for a moment or two and then passed on. The gloom deepened; lightning flickered and struck on a spur of the range; the grey skirts of rain trailed along the foothills and a weird blue shadow crept forward over the forest beneath the inky clouds. I dropped down into the valley, waded the stream and cut out my shelter under the biggest of the spruce. The storm broke with a flash and a crash and a deluge of rain, but it found me dry and comfortable beneath the umbrella of the old tree.

In the morning a dripping blanket of cloud lay heavy on the tree tops. I stared at the two streams; then I picked up a nice, flat, well-rounded pebble and scratched a cross on one side of it. That would be heads—and I would have it heads for the north-west stream and tails for the south-west stream. I flipped, and the pebble came down with a thud in the sand: I bent over it; it was heads, and I took the right-hand stream. . . .

The caribou stood like a statue on the rocky spur, silhouetted against the sky: the late afternoon sunshine was almost straight into my eyes, and my position on a steep, mossy slope was a poor one: hoping for the best I steadied myself against a stout old birch and fired. The caribou staggered and then disappeared over the ridge, in the wrong direction of course, and I sweated up and after him.

From the top of the ridge I could see him travelling very slowly down the opposite slope with one hip knocked down and a hind leg useless. He was heading down into a wide alpine valley between two low spurs of the dividing range. A stream wound across the floor of the valley, fringed with willow and thickets of fir; if the caribou got down into that stuff I would probably lose him. I dumped the heavy pack on the ridge and clattered down the stony slope, thanking God that I was wearing hobnailed boots and not moccasins. The caribou hobbled along and I ran: but I was gaining very little on him so I sat down and fired again, twice. A lucky bullet knocked him flying into a thicket of willows, and a neck shot from close range finished him. Camp that night was down in the old firs by the creek, and it was full of pleasant smells: a bed of sweet scented balsam fir was laid down, soft and deep, by the fire, and the pungent, aromatic fir smoke blended with the heaven-sent odours that came from the frying pan where caribou meat was sizzling noisily along with strips of fat and liver. I wished that Gordon had been with me to share the feast—he had no caribou in Deadmen Valley and, had the kicker not smashed on that snag down by Nahanni Butte, we should have been here together.

I don't think that either Gordon or myself ever felt lonely in the generally accepted sense of the word, though we were often alone and far apart: there was so much to see and do in this strange new country that we were always far too much occupied and interested to have time for any mawkish feelings of loneliness. Neither of us had any brothers or sisters and that may have had something to do with it—we had never been accustomed to rely on the support of others. But there was also this, that we both took a certain pride in our ability to travel alone into places where most men would hesitate to go in couples.

The dawning of a perfect day flooded the valley with light, and, after breakfast, I took my rifle and headed up the creek towards the mountain wall. The creek puzzled me: it was deep and strong, and yet the precipice was less than two miles away; it ran sheer between two peaks, and somewhere at the foot of it the creek must well up in a tremendous spring. And I was going to see it: owing to the storm and a day's dripping fog I was well to the north-west along the Yukon Territory divide from my original target, and now I was going to take potluck and see what was here instead. I went up the creek lightly and easily: walking without that ton-weight pack one floated along like the fairy in the pantomime.

But there was no big spring. The creek came through the mountain wall in a narrow cleft,[1] a gorge that was completely invisible, except at close quarters, at this early hour of the day—for the morning sun struck the range direct and threw no shadows. The canyon was dog-legged, and the bellowing waters raged through it in a wild cataract: nothing grew in that sunless place, the sky was hidden by the overlapping cliffs, and every rock dripped and glistened in the drifting spray. On the left bank, on the talus slope and jammed against the canyon wall, there was a game trail like a road. I got across the creek on the boulders and followed it, thinking what a remarkably poor place it would be in which to run into a grizzly: in this thunderous din and with the

[1]Not unlike Sinclair Canyon near Radium Hot Springs in the Southern Rockies.

breeze drifting downstream through the cleft he would never hear
you or wind you, and the two of you would meet head on, perhaps
right at the dog-leg corner. And then the race would be to the
swift—and I wondered if the detonation of the Mannlicher would
not fetch down a sizable chunk of the roof and so settle the hash of
both contestants. There was an overhang just here that looked
decidedly unsafe. . . .

But the canyon was opening out to the west: blue sky was showing and a far-off line of cliffs streaked with snow. I climbed up
alongside a cascade and into a dark wood of firs. From there I
went up an open slope to the right, and I kept on climbing till I
could see the whole of this new basin. Then I sat down on the
warm, springy turf and took the glass out of my pocket to see what
I could see.

In past ages the basin had been a lake. It had been contained by
the snow-streaked cliffs on the west, by two great buttresses of the
range on the north and south, and finally by a natural dam of
some different kind of rock on the east side. The dam rose some
four or five hundred feet from the floor of the basin, sloping gently
and dotted with scattered clumps of alpine fir. Its outer face, the
one that looked towards my camp, was sheer and rose about seven
hundred feet from the exit of the stream.

Down this face, at one time, had come the overflow of the lake
in the form of a waterfall. Then, as the millenniums rolled by, the
water had cut into the dam on the line of some fracture or
weakness, down and down, lowering the level of the lake until
finally it had made the canyon by which I had entered, leaving the
basin drained and dry.

The floor of the basin was level. It was about two miles across
from the north wall where I was sitting to the wall on the south,
and from the dam back to the snowdrifts under the western wall
must have been about three miles. The sun was high by this time,
and at the head of the basin one could see the sparkle of innumerable springs. The creek gathered on some meadows that
stretched from the snow half-way down to the dam: then the trees
began, and the creek meandered through clumps of willow and
dark thickets of fir until it cascaded down a rocky slope and disap-

peared with a dull roar into the canyon. Here and there birches, alone or in small groups, shone in the full blaze of their autumn glory against the sombre background of the firs.

The strata dipped to the west, down towards the drifts of old snow and, except for the dam, the walls were sheer with a slope of talus and turf running down to the level floor of the basin. Sheer, that is, with one exception: across the valley on the south wall I could see a long, sloping ledge above a dark-coloured stratum of rock. It was wide like the tracking ledge in the Box Canyon: it dipped down in the west into the meadows, and it seemed to break off at its eastern end and peter out high up against the mountain side. No doubt there would be a corresponding ledge above me on the north wall, but from where I was sitting it was hidden from view.

The place was what the old mountain men used to call a hole or a park—it was a little country all on its own. Luck and nothing but luck had brought me to it: on a dull day, or with the sun anywhere except in the south, one might pass a dozen times within a mile or two of the canyon mouth and never see that anything might lie behind the wall. And it was worth a visit, this hidden pocket: never before and never since have I seen anything quite like it as it lay there on that autumn morning in all its wild alpine beauty of soft greys and greens, with its black firs and golden birches, and with the blue cloud shadows sweeping over the valley floor on the warm west wind. The caribou had led me to this place over the last ridge: I would call it the Caribou's Hole.

I dropped down the slope and went on up the floor of the basin, keeping outside the trees that fringed the stream. The trees thinned out and gave place to open flats, and the stream broke up into its various heads, each one winding swiftly and silently through the meadows over beds of clear, sparkling gravel; and it was then that I first noticed the queer pebbles—for the rocks in the gorge had all been uniformly discoloured with a yellowish deposit. They were heavy, these pebbles, and they evidently fancied themselves in strong colours—bronze, dark green and peacock hues: there must be copper here. But there were other things as well: there were heavy rounded pebbles of iron grey, speckled with some dark minerals and with flat crystal surfaces that gave off a bluish lustre—and the sand on the points of the streams had a bit of everything in it: I should have brought a lunch and the gold pan and the prospector's pick with me instead of going off at half-cock out of camp this morning with nothing but a rifle. And I looked up and around to see where all this stuff could have come from.

Something was moving through a thicket of willows about a quarter of a mile to the east—something big and brown. A grizzly walked out into the open, purposefully and sedately, but the willows still remained in a state of agitation—and then out capered a cub. It rushed after its mother and fell in behind her, imitating her solemn gait for a few paces. Then it sat down suddenly and scratched. And then it pranced off at a tangent—and back again in just as much of a hurry. But the old lady never hesitated or turned her head. She was heading west up the green, gentle slope towards the foot of the ledge that ran, as I had expected it would, up and across the northern wall. When she reached it she swung around on to it and started to climb, upwards and eastwards, across the face of the precipice: the cub followed, and the two bears climbed higher and higher, disappearing from view at times, for the ledge seemed to be wide like a broad highway: finally they vanished from sight round the shoulder of the mountain. They must have been somewhere down in the trees by the creek when I passed by, and then the west wind would have carried my scent back to them and disturbed them. It was nice to see them, and it was nicer still to see them go: that she-bear and cub combination would have been the worst possible thing to run into in the dog-leg gorge by which the stream escaped.

The dark bands of rock that formed the ledges on each side of the Hole seemed to be the first thing to look at: halfway up on the north wall, the way the bears had gone, a good slice of the ledge had recently fallen away and scattered down the hillside: the newly fractured rocks would probably tell the story. But first I would go on, right up to the western wall, close under the snowdrifts: then I would come back up the ledge and down to the rockfall—and I slung my rifle and moved forward across the flower-starred meadows. . . .

The hours slipped by. The afternoon shadow was creeping out across the floor of the Hole, and still I sat there on the sunny slope by the rockfall. My seat was a great broken slab, lobed with dark green and white, and spread out on it beside me was an array of mineral specimens that would have done credit to a museum. Bronze and green, peacock and blue, iron grey, granular and blue lustred, and one heavy chunk of rock, to which I could find no twin, with a grey sheen to it and queer, eight-sided crystals, they sat there and glittered and winked at me—wealth untold if you had them in the right place, and as far as I could see, not worth one solitary, continental damn in these far-off mountains. A treasure house and useless. . . . And suddenly I realised that I was as empty as a drum, nine strenuous hours had gone by since breakfast, and I hit the trail for camp and caribou steaks with all the hunger of the high hills hounding me on.

After I had eaten I moved camp a mile upstream to a little gravelly flat, ringed round with sheltering firs. There I made the perfect camp, and out on the gravel by the stream I built a rack for the caribou meat. I thatched it with fir branches against the rain and the sun, and underneath it I built a stone fireplace in which I lit a smudge of alder and dwarf willow. The work was finished in the twilight; then I made tea and fried up more of the caribou meat, and when supper was over and all was done I lay rolled in my blanket on the balsam mat by the fire, watching the green glow of the aurora over the granite range and thinking of the Caribou's Hole.

A few days later I stood on the top of the old dam—the east wall of the Hole. Far down below, from my camp among the firs, a blue wisp of smoke curled up and drifted away from the creek— the alder smoke from the rack of caribou meat. Away to the east lay the granite range in the full glare of the evening sun, and somewhere beyond it, hidden by its spurs, lay my two landmarks, the little cone mountains. I mapped out a route for the morrow through the bush towards them—I would keep up in the alpine country longer this time before diving down into that blue-green jungle of the trees: then I walked along the crest of the dam to where the waterfall had once been and peered over into the canyon of the stream. But one could not see to the bottom of it; projecting ledges made that impossible, and only a muffled roar from the depths proclaimed the furious passage of the water.

I went down the gentle inner slope of the dam towards the floor of the Hole. I knew now all that I needed to know about the place: I had taken samples of the rocks, and I had panned the stream gravels and, what was more important, the gravel and sand from the great potholes and "kettles" worn in the walls of the canyon, scratting it out with my two hands and using the frying pan as a scoop. There was a bit of everything here in the Hole; and with the nearest railroad at Skagway, four or five hundred miles away to the south-west, there wasn't a thing that we could do with it that I could see. Later on, perhaps, in the years to come. . . .

I looked over towards the Bear's Ledge—it would make a good name for a mine, I thought. From it a wide and well-worn game trail, a sort of rough stairway, led to an open, stony plateau that offered an easy passage westwards. It had been hard to resist going on, but the year was too far spent, and it was a long, tough trail back to Deadmen Valley.

I went down through the scattered clumps of fir. The evening shadows were lengthening, swallowing up the wild beauty of the Hole, but it was still daylight and summertime on this sunny eastern slope. A myriad of bugs danced their delirious, care-free fandango in the sun, tracing silver patterns of light against the black shadow of the western wall.

But I turned my face to the east and ran down by the cascade into the dripping cavern of the stream.

The canoe shot like a live thing down the boulder rapids towards Irvine Creek, touching twice: the Flat River was very low. Snow drifted over, powdering the red-topped hills with white, and the miles rolled by. At the two islands, which make the Three Channels Rapid, a moose stood bang in the fairway, dead centre in the only good channel: shouts, curses and a shot in the air—nothing would shift him, and down the wrong channel I had to go, milling around amongst the rocks and getting through by the skin of my teeth. Further on a young bull caribou swam the river in front of me, just above a riffle. I steadied the canoe till the last moment, then dropped the paddle and shot the caribou as he landed—to find myself bumping and crashing down the riffle broadside on and in grave danger of holing the canoe. That evening I came to Starke's camp at Caribou Creek, splashing up the shallow stream, tracking the canoe. Stevens ran out with a rifle at the ready.

"Gosh, it's you!" he said. "It sounded just like a moose. . . ."

They were still living in their tent, but a cache and a smoke-house were up and a cabin was well on the way. We had the first meal in it that night, off the caribou together with unaccustomed luxuries from the cache. My tongue, I found, was still working properly, and we exchanged news and drew maps of the country (but the Hole was not on any of these), and made plans to go out together in the spring, down to Fort Simpson and up the Mackenzie.

I left them at noon the next day. It was "Good-bye and good luck for the winter" this time: we would meet in Deadmen Valley in May. The mists were clearing, and the mountains were showing through, white against the cloudless sky, and on a many-coloured afternoon of Indian summer I ran on down the Flat. A little black bear was the last wild thing that I saw on that river: he was standing upright, within a foot or two of the bank and with his back to the river, reaching for high-bush cranberries. I slid silently down till I was within five yards of him, and then I rattled the paddle. He whipped round with a grunt of surprise, tried to back away and fell backwards over a log into the cranberry bushes. The last thing I saw of him was the soles of his hind feet kicking in the air over the log: the memory of that and of the look of astonishment on his face kept me happy for many a mile.

Two more camps were made, and then, in the sunlit peace of a perfect afternoon, I ran down the last riffle and slipped into the home eddy. The sound of an axe could be heard back in the bush: I whistled, and was almost torn and eaten by a savage onrush of startled dogs.

4

Fall of the Leaf

"Then came the autumn. . . . The air grew thin and sharp, the days thin and short. The river ran sluggishly, and skin ice formed in the quiet eddies. All migratory life departed south, and silence fell upon the land. The first snow flurries came . . . and the running mush ice. Then came the hard ice, solid cakes and sheets, till the Yukon ran level with its banks. And when all this ceased the river stood still and the days lost themselves in the darkness."

The Story of Jees Uck, Jack London

We supped off the caribou, sitting by the rock fireplace that Gordon had built outside the tent, and then in the dusk, after supper, we took a look around the clearing.

Gordon had been busy. The walls of the cabin were partly up, and the rest of the logs were cut and lying in the bush: any trees that threatened the safety of the cache and cabin had been cut down, and all the tops and useless timber had been sawed up and split and now made the foundation of our winter woodpile. The clearing was a more open and orderly place than when I had last seen it—and, in addition to this, a lot of trapline had been cut out. We decided to put in a week's straight work on the cabin in case of an early snow, and then, after that, we should be able to take days off alternately and do some hunting. Gordon had been living on a sheep he had shot over on Prairie Creek and on fish: there was just about enough sheep and caribou left to do us for the week's combined effort on the cabin.

The soft autumn darkness shut down on the valley: we chained the dogs up to their trees and went into the tent and lay and talked and drew sketch maps there for hours by candle light. I told Gordon what I had found up beyond the canyon of the Flat River, and I listened to all he had to tell of Deadmen Valley, its high

133

alpine basins and its queer side canyons. It looked as though we
might be on to a pretty good thing in the way of trapping: the best
thing we could do now, we decided, was to concentrate on that
and make all we could out of it. The knowledge we had gained
about the Flat River country we would keep under our hats, and
hope to make use of it later. We had tried to cram too much into
this one trip, we could see that now. What we should have done
was to go all out for the Flat River part of the plan, with only a
few traps and either no dogs at all or perhaps just one big one
trained to carry a pack. However, it was no use crying over spilt
milk: we had seen some wonderful sights, a lot of game and a lot
of new country—now for a successful winter! I blew the candle
out and in a few minutes we were fast asleep.

After breakfast we spat on our hands and went at it, and for a
week the little clearing echoed to the rhythmic clicking of the axes
and the monotonous swish of the crosscut saw which, away down
south in the Peace River country, I had come to know as "the
homesteader's fiddle." These were not the only sounds: ten to
one I would be whistling, with my axe striking in time with the
refrain of the moment—and then there would come a call from
one or the other, "Give me a shove on this log, will you . . ." or
"Steady this end for me while I cut the notch," and occasionally a
cry of "Timber!" and the crash of a falling spruce.

Being naturally indolent, and so having a horror of working
with anything but the sharpest of tools, I set to on the first morning with a file and a stone and sharpened to a razor edge the crosscut and all the axes. Then I rolled up out of the bush a huge ten-
foot-long butt that Gordon had discarded as being too heavy for
the walls. This we heaved up on to a couple of four-foot cross-
pieces sawn from the same log and notched to receive the ten-
footer. Then I went along the length of this big log with a wood
auger and set in eight stout pegs at various intervals, four leaning
to the south and four to the north. This gave us a sawhorse on
which we could cut up our wood supply and also a rigid base on
which we could hew a log into a half-round or a plank. The first
thing to come from it was a large half-round hewed log which I
pegged down on to a couple of stumps to form a work bench.

These few additions to the amenities considerably speeded up the work of cabin building for us.

The cabin was fourteen feet by thirteen, inside measurement. To save extra building, and to give more warmth we dug down a foot or so below the moss into the silty, sandy soil of the little flat: this would obviously soon be bone dry, and we did not intend to put a pole floor in the cabin—there was no time to fool around with luxuries of that kind with all Deadmen Valley luring us away. We built the cabin high enough to be able to stand upright in the corners (and we are both six-footers) without fear of whanging our heads on the roof poles. The corner notches were saddle notches—that is to say that the upper log was notched underneath and so sat astride the log below, which was shaped to receive it, in the same way that a rider sits astride a horse. The door was in the middle of the south wall: contrary to the usual practice, we built the door frame first and braced it in position; then we cut the south side logs to the requisite length and ran them up to the door frame and spiked them there: this saved cutting half a dozen or more of full length sixteen-foot logs, and hauling them up to the shack and building them in, sawing the doorway out later from the completed wall. The gable ends were pegged into position with pegs of birch driven down through augered holes: they were then tied firmly into place by the roof stringers and finally by the ridgepole.

We took a very practical view of this cabin: to us there was nothing romantic about the building of it: it was simply a necessary chore that used up time which could have been more profitably, and much more pleasantly, spent in exploring Deadmen Valley and the valley of the Meilleur River, and in hunting and cutting trail. This point of view is the only explanation that I can find for the tremendous appetites that we developed during this week of construction work. We were not doing any harder work than we had done all this summer of constant travel—climbing mountains, hauling canoes up rapids, portaging, hunting, back-packing in the bush and packing meat in to camp. But we were now doing, to a certain extent, routine work, and routine work gives you time to think about other things—about what you're going to do, for instance, to that caribou mulligan or to those collops of mountain sheep in the noon hour. The result was that the caribou and the sheep caught hell, and we began to see that, before the cabin could be finished, somebody would have to go out and re-stock the larder.

At this camp and in good weather we always lit our fire and ate our noonday meal down on the beach, sitting on the upturned canoes with a rifle and a field glass handy in case anything eatable showed up; since from there we could see far down the Nahanni, and a long way upstream over the big sand bars. But nothing came within range: we only saw one moose—it swam the river a mile downstream—and a couple of timber wolves playing, running in short circles and then rolling each other over and over, down by the mouths of Prairie Creek. The geese and ducks were starting to fly south now: they came mostly too high, but we got a right and left at some mallard during one of these noon hours, and a frenzied pursuit in the big canoe retrieved the birds from the swift-flowing river.

About the fifth day of the struggle Gordon laid what had been a nice haunch of mountain mutton on the bottom of his canoe and rose and stretched himself.

"It's time we had some more meat around here," he said. "I'll take the big canoe and Poilu and Sammy and try my luck over the river. We'll be turning green if we hack about in the shade of these spruce much longer."

He was right about turning green. The cabin stood on the south bank of the Nahanni, and the tall, thin spruce that grew south of the cabin reached far above the level skyline of the Bald Mountain, which one could just make out through gaps in the wall of the trees. We were well into September now, and already the midday sun barely cleared the spruce; in a few days it would not clear them at all, and it was not so far ahead to the dark winter days when only the rim of the sun would show for a few minutes around noon above the crest of the mountain. A sudden longing for the Flat River with all its gay colour, and its great rolling, sunlit uplands, came over me as I walked back into the shadow of the trees. But there were high alpine valleys here, too, that led

The Pulpit Rock, looking upstream.

Bay of Black Sand, Nahanni.

Camp by the Big Spring, Lower Canyon.

Evening on Falls Creek.

Nahanni Butte from Faille's canoe.

Early morning in the Lower Canyon.

Old Timers at the Sikanni Crossing.

The author at Twisted Mountain. *(photo by Faille)*

Canoes by the Little Butte.

The Falls of the Nahanni.

The Gate of the Nahanni.

A thirty-foot boat driving upstream through Hell's Gate.

The cabin in Deadmen Valley; 44° below zero.

Indians from S. Nahanni River, at Wheatsheaf Creek in Deadmen Valley.

Gordon Mathews at South Nahanni.

The head of Deadmen Valley.

The Pulpit Rock in mist.

The Falls of the Nahanni.
(inset photo: R.C.A.F.)

Falls Canyon.

Sunset by Nahanni Butte.

towards the sun. Behind the Bald Mountain, now . . . what would one find there? And, with my mind far away in strange, new valleys, I set to cutting and trimming spruce poles for the cabin roof.

The hours went by, and the pile of roof poles grew. They would be laid and spiked as close together as possible, running from the ridgepole down to the top logs of the north and south walls, overhanging sufficiently to form the wide eaves that would shelter a small outdoor larder and all the odds and ends of tools, snare wire and the like that we might hang from pegs driven into the wall. I laid a few poles in place and spiked them down (we spiked about one in three, since spikes were none too plentiful), in order to get some idea how many I needed. I was well over half-way apparently, and I headed back into the bush again.

The sound of a single shot and then its echo, rolling amongst the hills, drifted up the valley: it sounded as though Gordon was somewhere near the Dry Canyon. I listened: no second shot came. That was good; he had probably got it, whatever it was, and we could finish off the sheep tonight without worrying about tomorrow. I went on cutting and laying poles until I could see no longer; then I lit the fire by the tent, put on the tea pail and went and looked down the river. In the evening stillness I could hear the clatter of an iron-shod canoe pole about half a mile downstream. Then Sammy and Poilu appeared suddenly like shadows out of the trees; they looked distended and rather smug and pleased with themselves, and came down to be welcomed home. Finally Gordon became visible, walking up the shore and tracking the canoe.

"A black bear," he said. "A young one, medium size and nice and fat. I've got everything with me—hide and all."

Two days later we roasted a haunch of that bear, spinning it suspended on a wire from an overhanging branch above a slow fire. It was tender and altogether delicious, rather like good mutton. The liver had gone in a couple of breakfasts, and the hide was fleshed and stretched on the cabin wall. And things were looking up in the carpentry line: the roof was on, with the stovepipe hole cut in it and the roofjack in place: over the roof poles we had a thick layer of moss, and on top of that a heavy covering of earth and clay overlaid with a few spruce boughs to prevent it from drying and blowing in the wind before it had a chance to freeze. Now let it snow—it could do us no harm. I was off next day up Ram Creek while Gordon, who had cut his leg the day before with an axe, was going to stay and carry on with the chinking of the cabin, driving moss in between the logs with a big wooden chisel and a mallet. The heavy work was done; and we sat by the fire eating till we could eat no more of the rich, tender meat. Late that night, while I was busy packing up my camp for Ram Creek, we talked again of the strange outcroppings that I had seen in those lonely hills of the Yukon divide, and made our plans to return to them.

A couple of evenings later I sat in camp on a pile of sweet smelling balsam fir branches in a lonely country at the head of God-Knows-What Creek—at least that is the name that I see in my diary, which was written up that night by the light of the fire. The water ran southeastwards, falling away in a wild valley into a tangle of mountains and high hills: where it went to I didn't know, for there were no maps of that country then, but I thought it might be a head of Jackfish River, or even of some river running south directly to the Liard. I wasn't even certain whether I was still in the Northwest Territories, or whether I had crossed the divide into the Yukon Territory. I did know that it was a lonely spot—one of the loneliest-looking places I had ever seen, I had decided, earlier that evening, as I worked my way down from the head of the valley, across the screes towards the only trees in sight, this little clump of dwarf alpine firs. I had stopped for a moment on a shelf of rock to rest and look around me: the jagged, snow-powdered ridges of the Ram Mountains shut me off from Deadmen Valley, and the mountains themselves disappeared into a low, grey ceiling of cloud from which a fine rain was falling. An early twilight was closing in, and with the increasing darkness the roar of the torrent came up more clearly from below. A small, cold breeze with a threat of snow in it was rustling the dead leaves of the dwarf willows, and I had wondered then if I would find enough dry wood for the night fire down in these trees by the valley stream.

The going had been dangerous for a man carrying rifle, axe and heavy pack, for in one of the heads of Ram Creek, and again in the head of this creek, I had run into something that I never saw before or since. Tumbled from the mountains, and piled in wild confusion on the lower slopes, were acres of huge boulders and great blocks of limestone, and over these was spread, resting only on the high points and surfaces and not following the contours of the rocks, a loose carpet of moss so thick that dwarf alder and willow were growing in it—even in those sections which bridged the gaps and had beneath them only empty space. It was as if somebody had laid this carpet in one piece over the chaos of the slides and then planted in it these small, alpine growths and bushes. It sagged and swayed as one walked over it, and more than once I had put a leg clean through it into the void beneath and touched nothing. A fine place in which to break a leg, falling heavily through the moss into one of these rocky crevasses with all the impedimenta of camp on one's back: and it would be no use hoping for Gordon and the dogs to come; Gordon had no idea that I would head this way. We usually outlined our plans to each other before leaving camp, in case of accident, and he would think that I had taken a westward-heading fork of Ram Creek up into the Ram Mountains, as we called them then. So I had, and it had wasted a day for me, landing me into a cirque of precipices from which there was no way out. From there I had returned to camp at the forks of Ram Creek, preceded, at about a thousand yards' range over an open slope of heather, by a large grizzly who seemed to be heading towards the Nahanni and stopping only to lift the odd slab of rock in search of grubs or rock rabbits.[1]

And now I was here, wherever "here" was, comfortable enough, jammed in between two boulders on my pile of balsam and with a drift of light rain pattering on the tarpaulin lean-to. The fire was burning brightly, giving out the black, oily smoke of this alpine wood: a thick coating of unaccustomed soot from it now covered the tea pail and the frying pan. I had a good pile of

[1]The pika (*Ochotoma collaris*).

this tough, twisted, thick-based fir beside me: one would have thought that here was a hidden place in the hills were no man had ever been, but one of my pieces of fir bore the diagonal cut of an axe: some lone hunter must have camped here before me, about twenty years ago, I thought, from the look of the axe cut. I finished my diary, put the morning's wood shavings and kindling under the lean-to, sharpened my axe with a pocket hone and rolled in and slept soundly.

No snow fell in the night on the little thicket of fir, and that was odd in weather like this and at this season, because the aneroid showed this camp to be 3,000 feet above the Nahanni, and the Nahanni in Deadmen Valley was about 1,000 feet above the sea. But by morning the clouds had come still lower down the mountains, and a light powdering of snow reached down to within a few hundred feet of camp. At the head of the valley the glass showed a single ram grazing his way up towards the Ram Creek divide: he moved higher and very soon vanished into the clouds. This was great weather that I had picked to go and see what lay behind the Bald Mountain.

The creek that I was camped on ran south-east, following the strike of the mountains. That was no use to me: I wanted to see what lay *behind* this range, so my trail led south-west up a long draw on the far side of the valley. Full of tea, bear meat and ambition I rammed my way up the draw, through the dwarf willows and black birch scrub, up into the clouds and the wet snow. The morning was spent in outflanking cliffs that were barely visible in the driving mist, in backing up, searching for weak spots and again pressing forward. Midday found me travelling across a high plateau about 5,000 feet above sea level: the north-east wind was at my back, and the cold, grey mists rolled along with me as I walked. The going was first-rate; small patches of fine gravel and then stretches of short yellow grass—sheep country. A powdering of snow lay on the grass, and there were small snow-drifts in the hollows: half-left, the noonday sun was making a rainbow-coloured glory in the mist. Visibility came and went in this illusive radiance of the sun: stray rocks and erratics appeared dimly in the form of monsters, loomed up close and then were gone.

There was no fatigue in walking, but one felt incredibly isolated and alone: the plateau, it seemed, was the world, and the whole world was the plateau—so it had always been, and there could be no end to it.

Once there sounded a rattling of stones and a quick thudding of hoofs away off to the right. Rams probably—for I knew from the Indians that this was a ram range. I found out later that they called these mountains the Tlogotsho, the Big Prairie Mountains, because of these high grass plateaux, and that is the name of the range on the map today.

The mists seemed to be clearing. The sun appeared for a moment as a golden ball, was blotted out again by a driving bank of fog and then suddenly blazed forth out of a deep blue sky in which grey, smoking wreaths of mist were being whirled aloft and driven back by a warmer wind. Just in time, too, for I had come to the south-western edge of the plateau. The ground fell away in a sheer precipice which ran around the head of another south-east flowing stream. I walked to the edge and took off my pack and sat down to examine the country with the glass.

The plateau that I had crossed ran away to the south-east for miles in a long spur. The same kind of country was continued to the north-west and to the west around the head of this new basin, and then faded and became lost in a maze of valleys and canyons from which the mists were rising and being driven back by the Chinook, the warm south-west wind that comes through the mountain passes from the Pacific Ocean, bringing warmth in wintertime to the valleys of the cordillera. The enemy of the Chinook, the cold north-east wind, had not been driven very far away, however, and a writhing mass of grey cloud half a mile back on the plateau showed where the two winds met, head-on.

Away to the south-west, with white, bumbly summer clouds lying along their summits, was a range of not very spectacular mountains: that must be the Yukon boundary, I thought, for the stream below me in the basin flowed south-east for miles and then seemed to swing to the left—it had to be Jackfish River, there was nothing else it could be. Everything stood out very clearly in the warm afternoon sunshine, and there was no sound, not even from

the stream that flashed and glittered down there in the basin—
only, now and then, a gentle murmur from the Chinook as it explored some new cranny in the cliffs below, or rustled the dead
herbage of pentstemons and saxifrages on the edge of the drop.

I munched away at bannock and a handful of raisins and considered the situation. Camp would have to be in this basin somewhere. A mile or so to the right there seemed to be an easy way
down, a break in the five- and six-hundred-foot wall that rimmed
the basin—and I picked up the glass to see what sort of a campsite
there might be down below. Something moved in the field of vision, and two Dall rams came grazing into view on the grass and
talus slopes along the foot of the precipice, beyond the break in
the wall. How unusually convenient! Camp and supper within
half a mile of each other! And one of the rams seemed to have a
remarkably good head. I would have that head and take it out
with me; and a cache of mountain mutton here would enable me
to travel on another day over the plateau to the west towards . . .
towards what? I wondered—some fork of the Meilleur, probably.
I picked up my pack and rifle and got going.

A mile further west along the rim I made a small cairn of stones
to mark the way down into the basin, for the fogbank had never
rolled back very far. I went on for another four hundred yards or
so and looked carefully over the edge: there were the rams grazing
away from me along the foot of the cliff. That big head seemed to
be quite unusual, and I pulled out the glass and looked and then
began to pray, quietly and fervently. All thoughts of meat had
vanished now: this head was bigger and better than the one I had
got a year ago at the Falls. Just let me get him, and I'd willingly
pay for it all the rest of my life—grow cabbages, work in an office,
anything! I went back from the edge to a safe distance and quietly
took the bolt out of the Mannlicher and looked up the spout. It
was clear, and I replaced the bolt, put a cartridge in the breech
and flipped the safety catch over. Now then. . . .

The rams were moving, and from the next place where I hit the
cliff edge I couldn't see them at all. I made a quick half circle to
get ahead of them: they were about five hundred feet almost vertically below, and by getting well ahead I would be able to get a

shot back at them off the right shoulder with some chance of success. I settled myself against a rock on the edge of the drop and
looked over. The smaller ram grazed into view around a rocky
point: this couldn't be better, and I raised the rifle and waited for
the big ram: the Chinook had dropped, and an utter silence lay on
the basin. It seemed to be getting colder—and where the devil was
that fool of a ram? Couldn't he hurry? A grey wreath of mist slid
past me—and then the north-east wind was back, and the basin
vanished from view as the fog bank rolled over me and poured like
water down the precipice—carrying my scent with it, too, I
thought bitterly. And that was that.

Without the cairn that I had built it would have been hard to
find the trail down. I let myself down easily and quickly, dislodg-
ing no rocks and using the rubber-shod carbine to steady myself.
Very soon I was down on the grass slopes and below the level of
the cloud, but the rams had vanished and the basin, which had
looked so gay in the bright autumn sunshine, now looked cold and
forbidding. I looked round for a camping place: a well-beaten
trail ran to the left, wide and cut deep in the grass. It seemed to
lead to a little, level plateau where, judging from the growth of
willow and stunted firs, there ought to be a spring. I followed it
and found a clear stream of ice-cold water breaking from the foot
of the cliff and chattering down over the rocks. There was enough
dead wood in the dwarfish growth along its banks to make a good
fire, but there was no shelter from any but the north wind and no
good trees to hold a lean-to. Across the spring the little flat continued, vanishing behind a buttress of limestone. I walked round
to see if any sheltered corner lay beyond, and found myself looking into the mouth of a cave in the rock wall. The entrance was
nine or ten feet high, and the cave was about twelve feet across
and ran back between twenty and thirty feet. One went up a
three-foot step into it, and the entrance was protected by twin buttresses of rock. A hard trail led to the door of the cave, and the
cave itself was evidently used by bears and wolves as a refuge in
times of storm.

A couple of paces into the cave and on the left-hand side there
was a fireplace—a rough semi-circle of big, flat stones enclosing a

little space against the wall in which lay a pile of old charcoal and
butt ends, greyed over with a thick layer of dust and grit through
long years of eddying winds. The wall and roof of the cave just
there were blackened and scarred with the smoke and flames of
many fires, and soon the latest one of all in the cave's long history
was flickering there, sending up a warm glow of welcome as one
came again and again round the buttress from the spring with
armfuls of wood and fir branches. The cold fog seemed to thicken
after nightfall—and then, later on, as I was dividing what remained of the bear meat and making the evening tea, I noticed
that the mists had cleared again and the stars were shining. I set
the tea pail back a little from the fire and went and looked out: a
warm breath of Chinook greeted me and now, from far below in
the darkness of the basin, I could just hear a faint noise of water.
By walking round the corner of the west buttress one could hear
the smaller babble of the spring, but that was all—there was no
other sound. There was no moon, but in the faint radiance of a
dim aurora one could just make out, from this cave in the mountainside, the black rim of the basin enclosing the dark valley and
cutting across the glittering cohorts of the stars.

The step of the cave, I noticed was well worn. An idea struck
me, and I got the little axe from beside the fire and started a small
excavation with the back of it in the mossy slope below the step
and away from the trail. It was as I had expected—bones and
then more bones, the midden of the cave. After supper I came
back to it, lighting a small fire on the edge of the step in order to
see better. But there was nothing, only bones in all stages of
decay—gnawed bones, bones smashed for the sake of the marrow
in them, feeble old powdery bones, splinters and chips of bones. I
was on the point of giving up and was scratting idly amongst the
fragments when I came on one piece that seemed harder and
sharper than the rest. There were curious toothmarks on it, and I
held it up to the firelight and examined it more closely—it was a
stone arrowhead. I dropped off to sleep that night by the fire, very
snug with the warm rocks of the cave around and above me—and
behind me a long line of copper-coloured hunters reaching far

back into the darkness of forgotten centuries. . . .

Three or four days later Gordon and I were working on the cabin. We had levelled off the last of the floor that morning, carried the excavated material out and banked the cabin with it. Then we had set up the cookstove, shoved the pipes up through the roof jack and completed the roof around it, strengthening it till even the wolverine, that pest of the North, would have to back down before those massive cross braces. We had put a fire in the stove to dry the place out thoroughly, and I was busy putting in the windows: these we had cut out, one in the east and one in the west wall, and the filling was to be of cello-glass, a roll of which was warming behind the stove so that it could be fully stretched without cracking. It was a compound of a fine wire netting and some celluloid type of material: semi-opaque, it gave no view, but let in most of the light, which was all that mattered. The window battens had to be hewed out of birch, and I was busy with this job at the workbench when two shots sounded from upriver. We stared at each other. Faille was above the Falls, and Starke and Stevens were up on the Flat River—and there were no other men on the river. Had some accident occurred to one of those three? or could it be some Indian hunters coming downstream in a skin-boat? We downed tools as one man and hit for the landing.

Round the bend and down the home riffle came two canoes with two men in each. They saw us and pulled in to the eddy, but didn't land, and a little, dark, clean-shaven man with black hair and Indian features said, "I'm McLeod from Providence," and then introduced the other three—a man called Wrigley, a big fellow known as Grizzly Simmonds and a third man whose name escaped us. They had been dropped by plane on August 4th, with their outfit and canoes, on calm water above the canyon of the Flat River, and they had been prospecting. That was the reason for the plane we had seen in the summertime, and it fitted in with rumours I had heard in Edmonton before we started. This must be Charlie McLeod, the surviving brother of the McLeods who were supposed to have been murdered in this valley in the winter

of 1905-6, and whose death gave it its name. Charlie had been
with his brothers when they found their gold in 1904, but did not
come back in with them on their second and fatal trip. Why had
he waited almost a quarter of a century before returning?

The canoes they were using were sectional canoes. They could
be shipped, broken down in sections, in a plane, to be fitted and
bolted together when they arrived at their destination. I was interested and asked how they had found them in rough water, but
nobody seemed to love them at all. They had had a rough time of
it, they said, coming down the Flat River in these stubby little
canoes with two men and all their gear in each. They had drawn
more water than I had, alone in my sixteen-footer, and had been
forced to portage or line all the canyon and then to portage again
in places where I could just slip through. One of the men—and I
think it was Simmonds—was decidedly on the heavy side: his
canoe, perhaps as a result of this, had struck and holed, and he
was sitting with his feet in the ice-cold water, bailing with a tin
mug.

"Flat River, hell!" he said. "It's name should be the White
Water," and they all seemed thoroughly cold, weary and fed up:
The day was doing nothing to help—it was grey and cold and still,
and it had rained in the night.

Charlie McLeod wanted to know who was on the river, and we
told him. He hadn't seen any sign of Starke and Stevens—
hadn't known there was anybody up Caribou Creek. But what
did seem to be interesting him was the track of a hobnailed
boot—a right foot with nine nails,[1] he had counted them—that he
had seen on a patch of sand by the Flat River, and, in another
place, moccasin tracks and the ashes of a fire on a sandy beach.

"Whereabouts on the river?" I asked him.

"Above the canyon," he said.

I walked slowly up to the tent, without saying a word, and
returned with my battered old mountain boot. That would probably shake him a bit.

"Anything like this?" I asked. His face was a study.

[1] See Chapter 1, p. 20.

"You?" he said. "How much further did you get?"

"Oh—quite a little way," I said. "And you—were you very far up from there?" It was none of my business but, since we were asking rude questions, I might as well try my luck, too.

"Oh-h, ye-es," he said. "Quite a ways—quite a ways."

That settled that, and we were neither of us a bit the wiser, though all square.

"Well, you'd better unload and stay the night," Gordon said. "The cabin's warm, and you can hang a tarp over the door and sleep in there. It'll be a lot better than camping."

Three weary-looking faces lit up at that, but not Charlie's. The affair of the boot was worrying him, and he kept looking at me. I knew what he was thinking: he was wondering how far I had gone beyond those tracks, how near I had come to his party and how much I knew, just as I was wondering exactly where he had been and what, if anything, he had found. He began to talk rapidly: they had to be getting on, they were trying to catch the last boat out from Fort Simpson before freeze-up, and anyway they had planned to camp that night at the Hot Springs and all have a good bath. They sure needed one, and they—

"But you can't make the Hot Springs tonight," I broke in. "The day'll be shot before you get to the Lower Canyon, and you can't run that in the dark. Better camp with us—"

But Charlie was off again. Oh, no, not those hot springs but the ones in this valley. Hadn't we known? Just a few miles down, up that little creek—yes, the creek this side of the Little Butte, that's where he was heading: just a few miles down from here. And, maintaining a vague but incessant chatter, he shepherded his once more doleful-looking party out of camp, and we watched them paddle sadly away downstream.

Now, what was all that about? we wondered. What had they found up on the Flat, and why was McLeod so anxious to get them away from us? Had they really found something, or had it been just a nice summer's picnic? Anyway, if a stampede came we were in a good spot for it—and, in the meantime, there was still that last cabin window to fix before dark.

A month or so later I took half a day and hunted high and low at the head of the Lower Canyon for Charlie McLeod's hot springs. They may be there all right, but devil a smell of them could I find—nor has anybody that I have ever questioned so much as heard of them. I was the one, of course, that "bought" the yarn and followed it up in my own simple fashion. Gordon just scoffed at it.

On the night of September 20th came the first severe frost, and the morning of the 21st was cloudless and still. The valley was very beautiful in those autumn days: the night frosts had ended the runoff of the glaciers and tightened up a myriad of mountain streamlets and small springs, and the Nahanni was dropping fast; it was carrying hardly any silt now, and its water ran clear and green. The leaves were falling with every wind, but still the hillsides glowed with belts and clumps of poplars in full golden leaf. The cottonwoods still held their duller, richer gold: the alders were bare, but the willows clung tenaciously to their yellow leaves. Cranberries, choke-cherries and the tall wild roses strewed their reds and scarlets in amongst the gold and green, and on all this patchwork of gay colour the deep blue sky and the grey snow-powdered mountains looked down.

The camp needed meat as usual: the dogs ate like wolves and we were as ravenous as the dogs, and Gordon's bear was fading fast. Another bear would be the thing, we thought; this last one, with all its autumn fat on it, had slicked up the dogs' coats far more than moose meat ever could, and they were right on their toes: Mam'selle was busy digging out a den in a sandy bank under an old spruce where, she had decided, her puppies were to be born: Quiz spent his spare time up the creek hunting partridges where they came to scrat in the grit by the water's edge, and now and then we would notice him returning to camp in his sly, coyote way, with a satisfied look on his face and a feather sticking out of a corner of his mouth. Poilu and Sammy lay in the sun, shining and beautiful and dreaming of fights to come. Occasionally they hunted squirrels which chattered and swore at them from the safety of the trees; Poilu would get there first while Sammy brought up the rear, thundering over the ground with all the grace and agility of a baby elephant; he tipped the scales at Fort Simpson at ninety-two pounds the following January when Gordon weighed him there.

It was my turn to go and hunt up some meat, so after breakfast I threw the little canoe into the water and put my stuff into it—an old packsack with a light axe and a coil of line in it, and a tea pail and a small frying pan. Against the thwart in front of the rear seat I laid the shotgun and the Mannlicher, both loaded and set at safe, and then I kicked out from shore and slid down the river.

I was heading east into the sun which was climbing into the sky above the Lower Canyon: as it rose it touched with fire and lit, one by one, the cottonwoods along the river and the clumps and belts of golden aspen poplar on the benches and the mountain slopes, till the valley shone with the flaring magnificence of the trees. The air was clear and keen like a fine dry wine, and the deep blue shadows of early morning filled the clefts and canyons of the hills. On the banks the tall green spruce marched by, with a low, scarlet fringe of wild roses and blueberry bush between the forest and the grey waste of the river stones. Something, I noticed, was moving in an eddy over there in the shadow of the trees; and suddenly, with a trail of flashing spray, two mallard rose— straight into the sun of course, it would have to be like that! Down clattered the paddle, and the twelve bore slammed twice, rather wildly, as the canoe swung broadside on and bounced light- heartedly down a riffle. I retrieved one mallard from under a lean- ing spruce in a deep eddy, while the other flew on unharmed towards the canyon. The little grey canoe drifted on downstream: the uproar on the left came from the many mouths of Prairie Creek, where its clear, blue water came chattering in over the stones. I dropped down below the lowest mouth and stepped ashore, pulling the canoe up on to a soft bed of kini-kinik and ty- ing it to a young fir.

I hunted down the flats and through the gaily painted woods towards the head of the Lower Canyon. A bull moose was calling somewhere on the far side of the Nahanni, a sign of fall and the rutting season. The beaches and the sandy places were covered with tracks—moose, sheep, bears and wolves, and at least one wolverine, possibly two—never had I seen so many tracks of game. But no living thing, except for a partridge or two, and I didn't want to wake the echoes by shooting the heads off them with the .375. There was nothing at the lower salt lick and nothing that I could see on the sheep's favourite ledges opposite Ram Creek. I followed a single sheep track for a while into the Dry Canyon; but the track vanished as the watercourse began to climb, and I roused only a couple of ravens who flew out, croaking and swearing, towards the valley and the sun. The south-west wind was rising now, and blowing up the canyon so it was useless to go further in that direction: I turned back to the canyon mouth and worked my way from there along the foot of the mountain and the Bear Garden slope towards the lick on Prairie Creek. And there I found them, two dry ewes and a young ram on a steep, stony slope, feeding on the hips and haws of the wild roses.

They were not in a good place. They were browsing with their backs to me on a slide of rock and earth that ended abruptly in a sixty-foot cliff. Below was a long, deep pool in a branch of Prairie Creek, spilling out into a foaming rapid. There were plenty of small trees and bushes well placed to deflect a bullet, and to get a chance at the sheep I would have to make a stalk over this unpromising hillside, winding up by shooting half off my back and adhering to the slope by means of faith, friction and the seat of my pants. But the wind was in my favour, and there in full view was the meat that the camp needed, so I slipped out of my pack and started to crawl forward. . . .

The roar of the carbine rumbled and echoed in the gate of Prairie Creek, and one of the ewes rolled down the slope and disappeared over the cliff edge. A faint splash seemed to indicate that the body had committed itself to the deep. Now for number two before they woke up to what was happening—and I jerked at the bolt lever. Seven great big crimson damns to the useless thing—it had jammed!

That had fixed it, I thought. One sheep out of three—truly my luck was out! Half-lying, half-sitting, and with the edge of the drop just below me, I felt gingerly around for a rock: my hand closed on a thing like a heavy scythe stone, and I started hammering at the bolt lever with it, thinking what a beautiful fix I'd have been in if the target had been a grizzly or an infuriated bull moose. The fact that the Mannlicher was a carbine wasn't helping me now: I had bought it to use from a saddle horse, and the bolt lever of a carbine is streamlined almost flush with the wood so that the weapon will slip easily into its leather scabbard and carry comfortably under the flaps of a saddle. So there wasn't much to hammer at, but nevertheless I bashed away at the lever, and in a few seconds the bolt flew open and the empty cartridge tinkled on to the stones and down over the drop into the pool. I jerked another shell into the breech and looked up—and there, to my amazement, were the two sheep still in the same place, about two hundred yards away, and regarding me with interest! I squirmed around and fired again, and the second ewe rolled down over the cliff and disappeared, and I very nearly followed it: the slight shock of the recoil had upset my delicate balance, and I skidded on the loose rocks a few feet down towards the cliff edge, fetching up with my feet against a tough old piece of buck brush.[1] By the time the noise of the splash reached me I had made the pleasant discovery that the bolt had jammed again, and I fell once more to blacksmithing, certain this time that the remaining sheep would be gone. But this was the Nahanni, and that ram had probably never seen a man: he certainly wasn't at all disturbed by the strange antics of his companions and, as for noise, he had heard many a thunderous rockfall in this land of canyons. Soon the bolt sprang open, and the empty shell tinkled gently down the slope and over the edge to join the growing collection of bric-a-brac in the pool. That left two remaining candidates for admission, myself and the ram, and the chances were about even which of us would get there first.

I pivoted delicately to the right on my tail end, keeping my left foot firmly on the buck brush, and raised the rifle. The ram had moved a little: now and then I could see his head; he was once more busy with the hips and haws, but the main view was of his rump. It seemed a pity to hit him there, but there was no help for

[1]Shrubby cinquefoil (*Dasyphora fruticosa*).

it—this business of shooting practically round the back of one's neck and uphill, while perching insecurely on loose rock, left little choice of aim. I fired and slipped simultaneously, and the result was a clean miss. But the ram didn't move, and this time the bolt didn't jam, and the next shot dropped him in among the wild roses. He didn't roll down the slope as the ewes had done—and then I saw a hind foot kick. He went on kicking: perhaps he would kick himself down and end the matter. But no, he was tangled up in some briars, and I would have to get up to him.

The only thing that kept me from cascading down the slope and over the edge in a shower of earth and stones was the stout little tussock of buck brush with its woody stems and golden flowers. Very carefully I slung my rifle and turned over till I lay flat on my face. Then with toes and finger nails and friction I began to hitch myself up the treacherous earth slide. It took me about twenty minutes to reach a place of safety, and that included one failure, with a sickly slither of some five or six feet back to the buck brush—fortunately a deep-rooted, tenacious plant, trustworthy and dependable.

I laid my rifle down and climbed high up above the sheep which was still kicking, descending on it in a wild run down and across the slide. I tripped over the ram and measured my length in the briar patch, getting a flying kick in the wind from one of those sharp feet; then I grabbed my sheep, knifed him and threw him down the slide. Over he went, and the customary splash indicated that his journey was ended. But not mine, and not until another staggering run across the steep hillside had landed me with an avalanche of rocks and dust into a thicket of choke-cherry, just above the cliff edge—not until then did I dismiss the possibility of a quick, unrehearsed trip down into the pool.

I went down and dragged the three sheep out of the water and gutted them: one hindquarter of the ram was badly knocked about by the heavy bullet, but the two ewes were neck shots and nothing was wasted on them. I left the sheep on the shingle by the pool, covered with poplar branches to shade them from the sun and with a couple of fires smoking alongside of them to keep away the flies; I was hungry and the rest of the day was mine, and I was going to spend it in the Hermitage, frying trout, drinking tea and lazing in the sun.

Prairie Creek issues from the range by a narrow cleft, or gate, between the mountain and the Needle Rock: I followed the sheep trail up and over the neck of land behind the Needle Rock and dropped down the other side into the little basin. Only the north wind can blow into that sheltered pocket, and this was a day of Indian summer and Chinook. Prairie Creek comes down out of the high, stony mountains to the north where the Dall sheep trails run, and flows deep, strong and clear through the Hermitage. The sun poured down, the golden leaves of the poplars glowed against the black wall of the spruce, and a warm autumnal smell rose from the ground cedar, the kini-kinik and the fallen leaves. I cut myself a willow rod and went down to the pool by the Needle Rock to see what I could coax out of it with a spinner: very soon trout and arctic grayling were sizzling in the pan and the tea water was bubbling merrily. Well-filled contentment was then the order of the day, and I lay there on the little flat and loafed in the warm autumn sunshine, regardless of time, for there would not be many more of these perfect days to come. The afternoon slipped by: the shadows lengthened, and a sudden shaft of light shot through the cleft by which the stream escaped: all too soon it was time to go—time to leave that hidden, scented place and head back to camp beyond the Nahanni.

As I poled back upstream in the dusk, the campfire smoke drifted out of the trees on to the river and then swung down to meet me on some faint evening air. I beached the canoe and walked up into camp with half the largest sheep on my shoulder and the packsack full of all those coy titbits that we most enjoyed. There was a welcome waiting for me, and hot water and clean clothes—and we had sheep's kidneys for supper, with the wavering light of the aurora showing through the trees.

Bright and early in the morning, we went back up Prairie Creek for the rest of the sheep. On the way across the gravelly flats of the delta I spotted something moving on the Bear Garden slope. The glass showed it to be a very large grizzly navigating uphill towards timberline as if his life depended on it. I handed the glass to Gordon.

"Oh, yes," he said, after a brief look at the bear, "that's Slim Jim. He spends his days there cleaning up on what's left of the berries. An enormous beast—about the size of a box car and timid as a deer. I got within half a mile of him once, but usually he runs as soon as he spots you coming, and that's anything up to two miles away on this open flat. A pity—there's a lot of dog feed in that bear."

We got the sheep meat down to the canoe in one load, carrying all we could manage ourselves and packing the dogs with the rest; and very disgusted they looked, staggering along each with a heavy load of meat in his little canvas panniers. Lunch that day was an enormous frying of mutton chops, and the afternoon was devoted to hanging the meat under the cache, safe from the weather and in the shade, and to more work on the cabin. This was interrupted, towards evening, by a visitation of whiskey jacks who certainly seemed to be excellent judges of meat, for they ate only the very best cuts and knew exactly where to look for the best pieces of suet. That couldn't be allowed to go on, and we couldn't cover the stuff up completely since the weather was too warm, so I had to shoot a couple of the raiders with the .22; that and the two small bodies dangling on moccasin strings beside the sheep meat seemed to serve as a warning to the rest.

The perfect weather continued. Gordon took all the dogs and the little canoe and shoved off upstream to the Meilleur River for a two or three days' hunt and a look around, while I kept an eye on the camp and carried on with the work on the cabin. I first of all made a tight, solid door, hewing out the braces and using them and two or three planks which I had brought down from Scow Creek. I hung the door and made a wooden bolt for it; then I went inside and shut the door—and then opened and shut it several times in succession. Then I went out and shut the door and admired it from the outside, and then I came in again, shutting the door behind me. I looked around: the windows were finished, and there was a fire burning in the stove: obviously the cabin was going to be light and warm—and it was roomy, just what we needed. Then I threw the door open and forgot about it—the new toy had lost its novelty.

The next thing on the list was a bed. We had brought with us very few spikes and nails so whatever I made would have to be pegged. I took down the crosscut and sawed four large blocks, each about two feet long, from a big spruce log. I peeled these, set them in the corner to the right of the door and levelled them off in the sandy floor: they would act as legs, and on them I built a frame of peeled spruce poles, securely pegged down to the big blocks. In this frame I laid a deck of light, peeled poles, about seven foot by three foot six, and on that, held in by the side poles of the frame, I laid a deep mattress of the softest spruce tips I could find. Over that I threw a tarpaulin, a stout, stiff affair that had once served as cover on a packhorse load—and the bed was complete. I got my eiderdown out of the tent and threw it out on the tarp; all it needed now was a sackful of spruce tips as a pillow, so I gave it that, and then, feeling struck all of a heap at the sight of so much luxury, I hastily rolled the eiderdown up to the head of the bed and went to stir the mulligan on the stove. It was late, and I was getting hungry.

Lunch was eaten down on the beach, in the sun, and then I returned to the cabin to deal with a problem that had been puzzling me more than a little—the jamming of the Mannlicher. The tarpaulin-covered mattress made a wide window seat and an ideal place to work, with the afternoon sunlight filtering down through the trees and tracing its shifting patterns on the cabin floor. Very soon I had the bolt action taken down and lying in pieces on the tarp—and not a fleck of copper or brass nor one single granule of sand or grit could I find. The only thing to do was to clean and oil the thing to the nth degree and then assemble it and try a shot. I had the bolt together in a minute or two: it slipped into its groove with the old familiar click, picked up a cartridge from the magazine and was locked home. The cabin was light, and there was a knot in the log wall behind the stove that made a beautiful target—why waste time going outside? Sitting on my bed I raised the rifle to my shoulder. . . .

Take my tip, gentle reader, and never loose off a .375 Mannlicher carbine in a small room when your ears are tuned for silence. A shattering explosion rent the air: the four steel lids of the stove leapt up and settled again with a tinny clatter, while down from between the roof poles and up from the powdery floor there drifted a grey mist of dry silt. I shambled out into the quiet autumn afternoon and sat myself down on the sawhorse, my head singing, the rifle across my knees: the local squirrels, I noticed, were all high in the tree tops, swearing with fright. I just sat there and brooded in a dull sort of way on the advantages of soft, shock-absorbing silt as a floor material: with anything harder and more resonant I'd have been looking for a spare set of eardrums. . . .

I tried the bolt: it hadn't jammed. But it would be better to test it once more; and so I walked to the river bank and sat down and fired at a white stone on the far side of the Nahanni. The stone flew into fragments, and the bolt was jammed again, solid. I fooled around with it for another hour or so, testing it, taking it to pieces, cleaning it and cleaning out the firing chamber. But, though there seemed to be no rhyme or reason to it, that bolt never jammed again: probably it had been something to do with the firing pin and the ammunition, I thought, and I left it at that—though I remained a little distrustful of the rifle for some time to come, and this must explain the queer ape-like tactics that I employed towards a certain moose a few weeks later.

The next item was a table. I hewed five wind-twisted spruce logs into half-rounds. Then I turned them face downwards on a level surface and mortised cross braces of birch into the round surfaces and spiked them there. I then added a diagonal brace and the thing was complete—a nice, handy little table top weighing about a hundred and forty pounds. I manoeuvred it into the cabin and across to the north-west corner by the stove: there I spiked two pieces of hewed birch horizontally, one on the west and one on the north wall, to take the weight of the table. And then the fun began: to make more room and easier sitting at the table I wasn't going to have an upright leg at its south-east corner. I planned instead to have two angle supports running from the east edge of the table to the west wall of the cabin—and all I needed to get things exactly the way I wanted them was a cast iron head and shoulders, three hands and a monkey's tail. Logs are not exact things; they have small curves in them and uneven surfaces. That table had its share, and I couldn't both hold it in position and reach over at the same time to see what the trouble was. I nearly went mad over that table, in addition to getting just about flattened by it when the first two efforts collapsed on top of me—but I got it into place in the end and sat on it in triumph, swinging my legs and mopping my head. It was solid as the Rock of Ages, and I took my revenge by having supper off it that same evening, sitting on a log stool with backrests of birch driven into it and feeling very civilised after six months of rocks, moss and upturned canoes.

One day of golden Indian summer followed another. Into the valley crept a thin, blue smoke haze from some far distant forest fire, and through it the mountains looked dreamlike and unreal. I turned my back on all this beauty and hewed out shelves and set them in place in the cabin, made a wash bench in a corner by the stove and set up empty raisin and prune boxes, with their lids on leather hinges, as cupboards. Then I started to make the window shutters—strong grids of hewed and squared spruce that could be clamped over the windows as a safeguard against the wolverine when we should both be away from home. That proved to be a fiddling, precise job, and irksome to one of my nomadic temperament, so once or twice I prescribed for myself ''a complete change of scene'' as an antidote. The wild fowl were coming south now in ever increasing numbers, and I dropped down the river a couple of times in the freight canoe to the calm water by the Little Butte that Starke had christened Patterson's Lake, returning each time with half a dozen birds on the floor of the canoe—mallard and butterballs mostly, and the odd golden-eye. On the evening of the 26th I walked down the river to a little clearing where there was an old grave with a rough wooden cross over it, much overgrown by a tangle of wild roses and high-bush cranberries: from there I had a good view of the Prairie Creek delta where we so often saw game, and I sat there for an hour or so, waiting. But nothing came within range, not even a wolf; one moose crossed the flats about a couple of miles up towards the sheep lick, and that was all. It was almost dark when I got home: a light was burning in the cabin, and Gordon was back from the Meilleur with no game, but with a fine string of trout and half a dozen partridges. He had been up into some interesting places on the western wall of Deadmen Valley and had some good rock samples taken away above timberline: in another place he had found petrified trees, and everywhere signs of mink, lynx, marten and wolves. Quite near home, and hidden away in big old spruce by a snye of the Nahanni, he had stumbled on some weird old cabins, built of upright logs and with a stone and clay fireplace in the centre of each one. About thirty years old Gordon said they might be, which would place them back in the year of the great Klondike rush of 1898. I saw these cabins later on, and passed by them often. There was an eerie, uncanny feel to them that could not be wholly accounted for by the silence of the place, hidden away up this snye and removed from all the rush and turmoil of fast water; or by the dark, old trees with their long, grey-green streamers of moss that swayed in such ghostly fashion at the faintest whisper of a breeze. There was something *wrong* about these old cabins; something happened there to the men who built them. We both sensed it and often wondered what it could have been. Scurvy? Starvation? Indian attack? Oddly enough, years later, I heard of a party that planned to go that way, by the Nahanni and then by some westward flowing river, to the Klondike. They disappeared into the wilderness of the Nahanni and were never seen or heard of again—and they had planned to build exactly this type of cabin.

Wolves were howling over by Prairie Creek at sunrise. We breakfasted off trout with a duck apiece to follow and then set to work on the dog house. The day was dead still again, but the smoke pall was thicker: the bitter smell of wood smoke lay heavy on the air, and the ramparts of the valley had almost vanished into the haze. Clouds crept slowly down out of the north blotting out the sun, and, with that, summer—though we did not know it yet—was over. We finished the dog house, a solid little log affair with a sloping roof of poles and sod, well chinked with moss: later on we would make it warmer still by banking it with snow. That evening there came to us from somewhere downriver a curious wailing sound, like the cry of a man in danger—probably the call of a lynx.

The next day it rained all day, a cold, driving rain, and then, on September 29th, we woke up to the first snow—the usual wet, slushy snow of the fall. Mist hung over the valley and hid the mountains, the sun never shone, and a raw east wind whimpered over a sodden desolation. All day it slopped and thawed and snowed again; and for the next ten days we hardly saw the sun, and it snowed and melted, and then snowed and stayed—and then a fine snow came, and it got colder, and ice formed in the eddies. And on October 12th the Nahanni was running ice for the first time—hurrying, jostling cakes of thin ice, hissing and tinkling, and sometimes lodging in the eddies and freezing solidly there to the shore ice, narrowing still further the channel of open water.

We were rarely at home. Now that it was cold enough to keep meat in the cache we needed meat in bulk, and that meant moose or bear. So we ranged the valley, on foot and by canoe, and with singularly little luck. We cut more trail into the basins and high valleys and packed our rifles with us—and saw nothing, only tracks. Gordon even saw a bull moose swim the Nahanni close behind me as I dropped downriver in a canoe: I was travelling into a head wind and never heard a sound nor looked behind. The canoe trip down to the Little Butte always produced about half a dozen ducks of various kinds. I camped down there by the mouth of Ram Creek for a few days and shot ducks from the canoe morning and evening, travelling over the country during the days in search of moose; and all I got was a long, optimistic shot at a running bull—a miss. I poled back to the home cabin that same evening, the 6th of October, with an east wind driving me upriver, ice-forming in the slack water and ice on the pole and the paddle. Mallard and butterballs were coming down from the north, low over the river under the grey snow clouds, and the shooting was good.

Gordon specialised in the country across the Nahanni and west of Prairie Creek. He kept running on to fresh tracks of moose, but it was the rutting season now, and they were on the move, and his luck was out. He seemed to have struck an Eldorado of partridges, however, and the living was good in those days—arctic grayling and Dolly Varden, partridges, wild duck and cranberry sauce and mountain mutton. But no moose. Gordon camped across the river a good deal—he said it saved smashing a way in and out of the shore ice morning and evening with the canoe and gave him more time to spend in hunting. He found a beaver dam over there on a creek that we came to know as Trowel Tail's Creek: out of that dam he shot a nice fat beaver one moonlit night, and the camp feasted next day on beaver mulligan and on beaver tail, that fatty delicacy of the North. We were not without something to celebrate, for Mam'selle had had her puppies that evening in the den she had dug under the spruce roots: how many she had produced we didn't know, and nobody volunteered to try and find out. Any enticing noises that we might make at the mouth of the den met only with a savage snarl. . . .

Any spare time that we had we put in on the woodpile for it looked—as it always does with the first snow—as if winter had come to stay. The beavers in the dam up Trowel Tail's Creek evidently thought so, too: anyway, they were taking no chances on a Chinook and were working overtime felling the aspen poplars, cutting them into lengths and trimming off the branches, and finally skidding the chosen pieces with the juiciest, tenderest bark on them down their small logging roads and into the dam, where they would be staked securely down in the deep water as winter feed. Trowel Tail's Creek was partly fed, in its lower course, by water from the Nahanni filtering under a big shingle bar and becoming warmed in the process. The water foamed over the main dam into a series of basins formed by subsidiary dams, each one lower than the last: these the beavers had built to take the pressure off the main dam. There was barely any current in those basins or on the creek below them: a leaf, urged by the faintest breeze, could float back upstream. And yet this water never froze—fifty below zero, which is eighty-two degrees of frost, could not put even the faintest skin of ice on the edges of the creek. But the main dam froze, and evidently the Trowel Tail outfit knew that it would for, on the night of October 11th-12th when there was a real crackling frost, Gordon was camped over the river and watched the beaver working parties hard at it in relays, some cutting and others swimming, breaking the ice as it formed in their dam and keeping the channels open.

We woke, on the 13th, to the roar of a Chinook. It was in full strength; the tree tops were bending before it, and sunrise showed us blue skies, melting snow and the running ice almost gone from the Nahanni. I spent the day crippled by a savage onslaught of lumbago, pottering around camp and doing all the odd jobs. Gordon left early for a high alpine basin that I had found up against the Bald Mountain: it had looked as if it might be good moose country. He came home about dark and pottered about for a bit, and later, while he was changing into dry moccasins, I asked him if he'd had any luck.

"Three bulls," he replied in a bored, offhand mutter—and I take my hat off to him now, all over again, for complete self-control and concealment of any jubilation. It was exactly the sour tone of voice in which he would have said "Three partridges."

He had come on two of the bull moose when they were fighting, and dropped them close to one another. The third, an enormous old bull, had been browsing on the stunted alder brush, about a mile away by a lick, and taking wild side swipes with his horns at the small firs and anything else within range, obviously not in the best of tempers. He had charged straight at Gordon on sight, and Gordon had wounded him with his first shot and dropped him with his second.

Breakfast next morning was porridge with raisins in it, cold wild duck and smoking hot moose kidneys. When that was over I did the camp chores, cut more wood and shot a blue grouse, while Gordon made ready the dog toboggan, taking off the canvas cariole. There was over half a ton of moose meat lying up there in the hills, and the problem now was how to get it home before the wolves got it. Soon we had the dogs hitched up and were threading our way through the timber down the river flats.

It was a perfect Chinook morning, warm and soft with deep blue sky and a strong sun. It was so perfect that, at the top of the first ridge, we ran into bare ground and no sledding, so we unhitched the dogs, put the toboggan up on skids and walked on up to the kill. We tackled the two smaller moose first, skinning, cutting up and putting the meat up on to a cache of poles in a nearby clump of firs, and around 4:00 I set off for home, leaving Gordon hard at it and taking with me a pack of meat and liver for myself and Mam'selle. The sun was setting behind the Bald Mountain, and the blue evening shadows were lengthening out over the snow: the timberline country was looking very wild and beautiful in the red light of the sunset. Far below, one could just see a bend of the Nahanni, and then the blue channels of Prairie Creek and all the greens and drabs of the flats, backed everywhere by the snow mountains, rose-coloured now against the cold northeastern sky. The Chinook had dropped, and a dead silence lay on all the upland country. . . .

Suddenly some damned thing went "Pa-aaf!"

I was well out in the open, crossing a patch of ling. I stopped and looked in the direction of the sound. About six hundred yards away a very big bull moose was coming down out of the big basin, following the stream. The two moose we had been working on were most of a mile up the other fork, the stream that drained the little basin. Where the two streams met was a natural salt lick and that was where Gordon's third moose, the big bull, was lying. This new moose smelt the dead one and went into the lick, and I could plainly hear him thrashing about, snorting and pawing. Then he came out into the open and completely demolished an inoffensive young fir, horning at it and twisting it until there was nothing left but a stump of yellow, shredded wood. I moved towards some higher ground to get into position for a shot, and as I moved the bull saw me. His head shot up, and he let a snort of rage out of him that a locomotive would have been proud of: then he headed towards me, swinging his great head from side to side and snorting with fury. I slipped the pack of meat off my shoulders and straightened up—and then hastily unstraightened myself again with a grunt of pain: lumbago brooks no disrespect. The moose had disappeared into some alder that ran up a long draw towards me from the lick. If he stayed in that I wouldn't see him again till he was fifty yards away—far too close, I thought, for lumbago and a rifle that might jam. But this lone spruce, now—if

I climbed to the top of it I could probably get the moose with a long shot; or the Mannlicher could jam to its heart's content if that was what it wanted to do—or I could even miss the moose, and it wouldn't matter a bit. I slung the rifle and reached for the lowest branch. A frightful twinge shot through me, but a perfect volley of snorts and a clattering noise spurred me on. What could he be up to now? Swearing with pain at every heave, I rammed my way through the thick branches until, at last, I was perched in the very top of the old tree, comfortably seated with my left arm round the trunk. There was the moose down near the lick and behaving like a demented thing: he seemed bent on flattening every alder in the country, he had made a sizable clearing already. I turned the safety catch over—it must be a good quarter of a mile down to the moose, I thought. If he would just stand still for a moment. . . . Now. . . .

The crash of the old cannon was followed by an instant of silence as the heavy, low velocity bullet arched towards the moose. Then "Whuck!" and I was sure from the sound that I had hit him, and the rolling thunder of the echoes sounded from the cliffs and screes of the Bald Mountain. But I had been mistaken: the moose stood for a fraction of a second and then ran easily into the trees by the lick and disappeared from view. I waited, and he didn't reappear: he must have gone back up into the big basin, keeping within the trees that fringed the stream—he could never have run like that if I had wounded him. Disgustedly I climbed down the tree, picked up my pack and hit for home. It was dark when I came up the river flats: Mam'selle seemed pleased to see me—and doubly so when she found what I was carrying. . . .

Gordon came home next evening carrying a heavy load of meat himself, and with the three dogs packed as well.

"What happened when you fired that single shot?" he asked. I told him the tale, adding that it was very odd my missing the moose completely when my bullet had made a sound like that—it must have smacked into a bank of wet clay or something.

"You didn't miss," he said. "You got him: he ran a short distance and then fell dead among the trees, within a hundred yards of my big one. Sammy found him.

So now, through luck in this last instance more than good management, we had almost a ton of meat up there on the heather and no snow to haul it home on. We decided to cut a good trail up into those two basins: all the ridges and all that timberline country looked like pretty good trapping ground, and we could extend the trail along the mountain and over to Ram Creek if need be: very soon more snow would fall and the dogs could haul the moose meat home on the sled.

So we cut the new trails and packed the two smaller moose home as we cut. And it didn't snow; the Chinook came back to the valley, after a day or two's frost, and blew like fury for seven days, and the snow vanished from the flats and from the heather; and the Nahanni rose and broke its ice, and the partridges began to drum, thinking that this was spring. But they were mistaken, and on the 24th the Chinook died away, and the south-east wind came whining into the valley and snuffling up the river, bringing with it grey, racing clouds and snow. I passed through the Hermitage that day: it was only a month ago that I had lazed away a sunlit autumn afternoon in there, stretched out on the kini-kinik and full of trout. When I came back to the Nahanni in the evening I had to cut the newly formed ice out of the eddy with my axe in order to launch the canoe. All the way across, the cakes of mush ice came hissing and shoving against the canoe, pushing me downriver: then, on the home side of the Nahanni, I smashed my way with pole and axe through to solid ice, skidded the canoe out on to it and so to shore; and that ended the year's canoeing, unless we include one brief, spectacular performance by Gordon, of which more anon.

We were now able to haul the two big moose home, and this was done with only two casualties—a floor board of the toboggan which got broken on a snag when the restraining rope that Gordon was holding broke, and the liberated sled, with a heavy load of meat on it, careered wildly downhill in hot pursuit of three terrified dogs—and the stock of Gordon's rifle, which was shattered when he slipped and fell on some icy slabs of rock. How he managed to walk as he always did—upright, like a grenadier on parade—across glare ice, sloping ice and ice-coated rocks was a mystery to me: I always tackled them at the crouch and with bent knees. On this occasion the system broke down: his feet flew into the air, and the first thing to hit the rock was the back of his head; I thought he had killed himself.

We got that meat home just in time: the wolves were coming daily closer to the lick where the two big moose had been killed. Never expecting such a long Chinook, we had put the meat, to save time, up on comparatively low platforms of poles. It was not above the reach of the wolves, huge beasts whose tracks in a dusting of snow over ice or rock measured five to six inches in diameter, and the smell of campfires and the flutterings of a gaily coloured blanket were scaring them no longer. So I went up there and camped for the last two or three days of October by the kill while Gordon did the hauling with the dogs. I helped him to load up on those trips and saw him part way down the mountain, and then went my own way, hunting for yet another moose. Coming back to camp one evening I stepped out the distance from the big spruce that I had climbed to the place where my moose had been standing. It was four hundred and twenty yards; my estimate of a quarter of a mile had not been too far out. The moose himself had a very odd head: one horn was very like that of an elk (wapiti), while the other was the ordinary palmated moose antler.

The morning of October 27th was the first morning of winter. The sun came up with a blaze of light into a frozen, shining world: the snow squealed and squeaked underfoot, my nose stung in the frosty air, and the moose steaks that I had cut overnight for breakfast were frozen like bricks. I was away hunting in the morning, but I met Gordon at the camp by the moose at midday. I had tea ready for him, and he had brought up a freshly made bannock and two cold roast mallard so we did rather well, as usual. With us, as with the Indians, it was always a feast or a famine. When I parted from him that afternoon I made a long circle round towards Ram Creek, coming back to camp by way of the little basin and the remains of the first two moose. As I topped the last rise half a dozen great ravens rose croaking into the air and I saw a huge timber wolf start up from the kill: seen through the fine mist of snow that was falling he seemed to be much the colour of an Airedale. I froze: the wolf didn't see me, but the ravens had given him the alarm and, as soon as I began gently to raise my rifle, he ran, disappearing into the alder brush. Three hundred yards away he breasted a little snowy knoll, and I got in three quick shots—the spurts of flame stabbing sharply into the fading light of the October afternoon, and the echoes rolling up the little basin and dying under the outpost spurs of the Bald Mountain. The first shot I never saw: the second fluffed up the snow under his nose and made him tack sharply: the third one landed right where it would do most good and stretched him dead in the snow. This wolf, and a coyote that Gordon shot, laid the foundations for our winter's catch of fur.

On the last day of October the Nahanni jammed solid with ice for the first time, remaining so for four days until another tearing Chinook came along and broke it up again.

November was on us now with its dark mornings and early sunsets. We had counted on having the river as a highway by this time, solid, dependable and frozen like iron. But the Chinook was playing odd tricks: the ice of the early freeze-up was piled high on the banks and well out into the current while, in the centre, there ran a channel of swift black water, "smoking" on cold mornings and running mush ice that hissed and tinkled as it jostled its way downstream. Down this dark waterway would come, bumping and thudding, great blocks and cakes of the October ice; and these blocks would jam and pile up at some riffle or narrow gut, building temporary dams behind which the water would back up, submerging the old ice of the shore lines, climbing up on to the beaches. Then the jam would burst with a rush and a surge of water, and the whole mass would go grinding and crashing down towards the canyon mouth again; and, if the day was cold, there would come from the shore ice minute explosions and a faint crackling sound—the fresh coating of water was cementing together the older ice into a solid mass that would remain until the hot sun of May would send it tinkling down on to the shingle in long, dripping, crystalline "pencils," shattering as they fell like the fragments of a chandelier in which the candles have been forgotten and allowed to burn too low.

So the river was useless to us, and over there on the north bank and up Trowel Tail's Creek, the beavers could proceed with their logging in peace, and the white sheep could come down to their licks unmolested. And on November 1st we abandoned our hazardous dodging of the running ice for good, and "carried up the little canoe and laid it by for the winter."

If the river was no highway the creeks were almost equally obstacles to the hunter. Like the river they were solidly frozen at the edges, but often with an open channel of rushing water in the centre. You did the best you could with this—teetering across on a fallen tree, jumping, snowshoeing lightly over some bridge of wind-drifted snow—or just travelling along the banks in search of a place that offered some chance of getting across. The penalties for a slip into these miniature ice canyons were at best a wetting in cold weather, and at worst a broken leg. And, until they froze solidly across in the cold that was yet to come, the creeks remained a terrible nuisance.

There were two more little obstacles to travel that we had to cope with which are not usually included in the popular conception of a Canadian winter in the Northwest Territories—overflow and lack of snow.

In these western mountains the streams tend, in cold weather, to freeze solid right down to the gravel, or nearly so. But still the water comes down from innumerable springs, and it *must* go somewhere. So it preserves a channel for itself under its own ice; and then, where the creek fans out over shallow riffles, or where the water becomes too much for its channel, the overflow spreads stickily out over the surface of the ice, a moving, gelatinous flood that is neither ice nor water, varying in depth from half an inch on the glare ice to a foot or more under deep snow, where it lurks invisible over the ice of a river. Overflow can *appear* solid—so solid that it is possible to tread on it in all good faith and yet be deceived: a residue of moisture is still there. If a man is travelling in moccasins and the day is really cold the results can be quite spectacular. Anxious to avoid wet feet he steps hastily ashore, and, if his feet find a landing place on some mossy bank all is well. But rocks may be awaiting him and these, at low temperatures, freeze instantly to the wet moccasins with the grip of a fiend. With a wrench that tears half the nap off the moose-hide sole he flounders forward or measures his length on the stones according to the nature of the going—and yet one more desperate oath goes spiralling up into the copper-coloured winter sky. As for snow-shoes, they can come slopping out of the deeper kinds of overflow coated with a weight of slush which will make further travel impossible unless it is swiftly removed before it can freeze solid.

And then there were those Chinooks. For days on end the warm south-west wind would come roaring through the passes in Deadmen Valley, licking up the snow, keeping the river open, sending great white summer clouds spinning across the crest of the Bald Mountain. For it is the habit of the Chinook, that when it blows strongly the sky changes from the pale, cold blue of the north-east wind to a blue that puts new heart into a man, a deep, warm, almost African blue, broken only by clouds like those of summertime carrying with them no threat of storm.

This was unexpected, and it was not doing so much good, since, while it was pleasant enough, it made it hard to locate the fur-bearing animals and harder still to trap them. The snow was disappearing again except in the thick bush and in the hollows and on the north slopes. The valley, viewed from some rock out-crop up at timberline, lay spread out below in all its soft fall colouring of grey, brown and green, broken here and there by the scarlet of a thicket of high-bush cranberry, or by a belt of red willow. And over it incessantly sang the south-west wind: by day it blew down in the valley bringing warmth, laying bare even the little low-bush cranberries, sweeter than ever now for their sojourn beneath the snow, and a sure bait, along with the hips and haws, for partridges and blue grouse: by night it retreated up into the crags and clefts of the Bald Mountain, and you could hear it roaring and raging up there in the loneliness of the timberline country. If you looked carefully in the morning you might find a little hoar frost on some hard surface—on the oak handles, for example, of the dog toboggan, which was leading a useless existence, amid all this bare ground, propped against the cabin wall. But the

Chinook would be back again an hour or so after dawn, and the hoar frost would vanish with the first puff of warm air that came stealing across the flats, feathering the tips of the tall spruce by the cabin. We would discuss this phenomenon at length, usually at suppertime, and we came to the conclusion that Deadmen Valley must be a "Chinook trap" into which the Chinook is concentrated and funnelled from the south-west by the lay of the mountains and the passes. This, we decided, together with the hot springs and a little quite natural drawing of the long bow for the benefit of the always hopefully credulous townsman, could easily have given rise to the legend of the "tropical valley" that was supposed to be cached away in these boreal solitudes. We reached a few more conclusions regarding these, to us, untimely Chinooks, but they found expression in terms so violent and with an imagery so picturesque that I hesitate to set them down here in this sober chronicle.

I was partly out of action in the first part of November. I had twisted a knee carrying home a load of moose meat from our kill up in the basin; it was painful, and all I could manage was to hobble around on short trips and to do the carpentry and camp chores for the two of us.

There was plenty to do. By now we had trails radiating out in various directions and traps set along these trails, and a little fur was starting to come in—weasels mostly, a couple of foxes, mink, one lone coyote and the first of the marten. These last, though we did not know it then, were to be the largest single item of our catch, and for marten alone we received $1,980 at Fort Simpson in the following May, over and above the rest of the fur—and a dollar was still a dollar in 1929.

Since the fur was coming in we needed fur stretchers, and I set to work with a light 2 lb. Hudson's Bay axe to hew these out of the surrounding spruce. These gave me just as little help as possible: Deadmen Valley is a windy spot, and the spruce on that point by Wheatsheaf Creek were so wind-twisted that it would have broken a snake's back to follow the grain. It was impossible to split them and get a surface that was even remotely in the same plane; and so every stretcher had to be hewed separately from its parent log—scored and hewed, and scored and hewed again, until at last the fine lines of the finished product began to appear. Slowly, however, stretcher after stretcher was laid by—small narrow ones for the ermine, those cream-coloured, black-tipped aristocrats which, when all is said and done, are only weasel in their winter jackets; three-part, adjustable stretchers for the foxes, hinged at the nose with copper snare wire, pegged at the rump so that they can be spread to an exact fit; one-piece stretchers for the marten, in varying sizes and with wedge-shaped slivers of wood to slip in along the belly and take up any slack; squat looking one-piece stretchers for the mink. Wolverine we would skin open and stretch in a frame; and, as for beaver, no stretcher, thank God, was needed for him: his shapeless hide would be laced into the stout circle of a bent willow hoop.

Since a man, working in natural materials with his hands, must have some rhythm to work by, the axe rose and fell to the tune of a song that Jack Hulbert was, perhaps, still singing at the Ambassadors' Theatre in the Strand. London had been whistling it in the spring: I had it badly on the brain, and so Deadmen Valley had to listen to it in November.

Gordon had to listen, too, when he was home, which was not often—and here he showed not only an appreciation of good music, but a kindly tolerance, remarking only that it was a wonderful thing how the tempo of "The Calinda" could be varied to suit any type of axe work. So "The Calinda" became merely part of the general scene, though it could have been a serious danger: I had read of a man who was shot by his partner for no greater crime than the persistent singing of a simple little ditty entitled "I wisht I was a little bird. . . ."

There were other things to do besides making stretchers during these days of my lameness. There were traps to be boiled in the big boiler, with the bark of the aspen poplar in the water. This treatment removed the man smell from them, and they were not touched again with bare hands, but were lifted out on a forked willow and hung outside, ready for use, on one of the trees of the clearing.

Then Gordon shot, at the foot of the great berry patch on

Prairie Creek, a medium-sized black bear, tender to eat as the best of mutton and fat as a pig. I built a fire close to my work bench and fed it with spruce and alder till I had a mass of glowing coals. This was maintained for several days: over it, at a height of about eighteen inches, I hung an aluminum bucket with a lid on it, and into this I would slice the surplus bear fat with just enough water to cover the bottom of the bucket. No flame was ever allowed to touch the bucket, and it would simmer and sizzle away all day, replenished now and then after the purest and whitest of lard had been poured off through a strainer cloth into old jam tins, lard pails and so forth that we had saved for this purpose. This was stored away in the cache; and supper now became roast bear with cranberry sauce, followed by pancakes fried in bear's fat, with maple syrup—a meal calculated to hold any zero temperature at bay.

The Chinook broke down in mid-November for several days, and we had a little cold weather. It was on one of these days, "a day of cloudless sky and a cold, whistling N.W. wind, sweeping the snow in long plumes from the mountain tops and drifting it like sand down the frozen Nahanni and across the bars," and after one of these staggering suppers, that we discovered that Poilu and Quiz were missing. Gordon had been up around timberline all day in the basins of the Bald Mountain and had come home latish carrying a No. 1. prime red fox—a real beauty—and a good marten. On the way down he had passed my old camp and moose kill, and the dogs had tried to hang back there.

"They'll have gone back to that moose of yours," he said. "I'll have to be quick: they're probably into our traps by now, and they'll be frozen before morning, to say nothing of wolves."

He slipped on a sweater, mitts and a woollen hat, looked for an instant at his parka, threw it down again and was gone. I limped out just in time to see him disappearing into the darkness at that easy jog trot that ate up distance and which he could maintain all day. Only that morning he had seen two wolves, "the size of calves," he had said.

But he found the dogs—Poilu first, in a trail set in a No. 3 trap, silent and badly scared. He gave him a good basting with a whippy willow and kicked him down the homeward trail—and that would explain the screaming uproar that I heard from the dog house after an interval of some two hours: it was Bloody Poilu returning home, with the black mood on him, and bent on handing on his licking to somebody smaller than himself. Quiz returned towards midnight with Gordon. He was found in another No. 3, away up at the salt lick in the moose meadows, yelling his soul out for any wandering wolf to hear. Both dogs were thoroughly scared and had their feet badly nipped and partly frozen, but no bones broken—and from now on they stayed home.

By November 18th, I was able to travel. It was a raw, blustery day of half-Chinook, and we set out before daylight with a collection of tools and weapons wrapped in a tarpaulin and lashed to the dog sled. We were headed for a dry, sunny spot, a mile or two south, on a sandy ridge where the dogs had discovered a bear's den. Gordon had noticed them excitedly sniffing around a day or two ago. As he was coming up he had seen a large black paw reach out from amongst the wild rose briars that obscured the entrance: the paw had taken a sleepy sort of half-hearted swipe at Sammy and had then withdrawn into the den. Gordon had hastily called off the dogs and let sleeping bears lie—the idea being that, with a bit of luck, we could get the bear when we needed it and that, in the meantime, it was just as good as in the cache.

There was a little snow on the ground—just enough for the dog sled. And, where the snow overhung at the entrance to the den, the underneath side was faintly discoloured—a reassuring sign. We trimmed the undergrowth a bit and the branches of the surrounding trees to allow for sudden action, and then we started operations on the entrance with pick and shovel. The rifles hung ready for use on the tree branches—and, as the dogs were frantic and all piled in, plus the toboggan, to help with the digging, we unhitched them and tied them out of harm's way.

Gingerly we enlarged the entrance. Then we prodded around inside with a long pole, but the den was very big and ran away back and we could touch nothing, nor could we feel the end of it. And we could see nothing: the sun was up now, and the contrast between the snow-powdered, sunlit hillside and the black void of

the den was too much for human eyes. Something had to be done
about it, so finally I shut my eyes for a minute or so to accustom
them to the darkness and then crawled rapidly into the den armed
with matches and a 9mm Luger automatic. There were no plans
made, except that Gordon was to pull me out of the hole by the
hind legs if any fracas that might break out inside seemed to him
to be going the wrong way: he was then to shoot, fast and often.
The first match flared up, and I looked around for bears sleeping
or aroused. But there was only a nice dry cavern in the sand,
floored with twigs and moss, clean and warm. This den lay round
a corner to the right: straight back was a sort of long cave in the
sandstone, and that explained why we hadn't been able to touch
bottom, as it were, with the pole.

Well, it was lucky that no bear had been at home, or I'd have
crawled right in on top of it, instead of having at least a pole's
length between it and me, as I had expected. I lit another
match—the feeling of tremendous alertness was dying down now,
and the thought of Gordon standing out there, Mauser in hand,
tense and waiting for the sound of mortal combat, was affording
me some pleasure.

"Gordon."

"Yes, old man? What's in there?"

"I've got a nice, motherly old bitch-bear in here, and I won't
have her touched. It'd be a damned shame—"

"Nice old *what?*"

"Bitch-bear, I said. Are you deaf? And another thing—I'm
wintering in here, along with her. To hell with our cabin, this is
warmer—better in every way. Go down and fetch up a load of
grub. . . ."

"Bitch-bear! Who ever heard of a . . . ? Here, come out, you
fool, and let me have a look. . . ."

It was a bit cramped in there, and I was not sorry to back out
into the sunshine again. The bear never came back: the dogs must
have scared her—for we decided that it had probably been a she-
bear's den, it was so warm and so carefully lined. We loaded up
and moved on up towards the Bald Mountain to cut more trail,
coming, that afternoon, across the tracks of a fisher which we

were never able to catch.

It was good to get around again. There was much in the valley that we had not seen, and it was high time we knew something more about its outlets as well. So we were away on foot all day, travelling the various lines that radiated out from the cabin and pushing always on a little further. This was necessary especially in this alternating warm and cold weather: the Chinook would come along one day and drive the temperature up to 50°—60°, melt the snow and run moisture all over the traps. The next day it might be blowing from the north-east and down to zero, and a whole series of traps would be frozen solid, waiting to be lifted and reset. Fur, especially marten and weasel, was coming in, and we could not leave any part of our lines unvisited for too long.

I was interested in the valley of the Meilleur River which came into Deadmen Valley from the south-west. It looked as if it broke through, or flowed round the end of the Tlogotsho Range, and it seemed to me that it might lead to a sunnier, more open country towards the Yukon border—and that, I thought, was probably where the game had gone. For there was no doubt that the moose, and the sheep, too, were leaving the valley. The last moose we had seen was the one I shot from the top of the old spruce. A moose track was a rarity now: a big bull had crashed away from me recently in a tangle of willow and alder too dense for me to shoot, but otherwise no game. Deadmen Valley lay too much in the shadow of the Bald Mountain and the Tlogotsho Range at this season; nor, probably, did the wild game enjoy, any more than we did, the fierce winds that swept the valley floor. So I explored the Meilleur River valley, which later on we found was the Nahanni Indian trail to the Beaver River in the Yukon Territory.

The first venture was a queer one. I was new to mountain country then and so, instead of looking for an easy way round, away from the bed of the Meilleur River, my first idea was the direct attack—through the "gate" of the Meilleur and straight up the ice of its canyon. I left the cabin in the afternoon with a night camp in my packsack and headed over the bars of the Nahanni towards the mouth of the Meilleur. Thirty-eight below zero it said on the cabin thermometer, and Second Canyon Mountain glittered against a cloudless sky with the unearthly clarity and precision of extreme cold. It was dead still for once: I was hot, and every hair on my fur hat, every thread on my mackinaw, was picked out in hoar frost from the steam of my breath. Two miles up the Meilleur I made camp amongst some scattered firs on a big flat of kini-kinik. During supper, and for hours afterwards, a magnificent aurora performed for my benefit, lighting up the high snows of the Prairie Creek mountains with its ghostly fires.

Only the stars were shining when I woke: a few prods from a long poker made the fire leap into flame, and the tea pail was set beside it in the hot ashes. This was done without getting out of bed, and not until the tea pail began to sing did I crawl out of my eiderdown and tackle the business of breakfast. It was very cold, and from somewhere up the Meilleur came a dull, roaring noise that I hadn't noticed the evening before. A waterfall? And, if so, why wasn't it sheathed in ice and silenced? From the river ice came a series of reports like pistol shots: the overflow was at work and, with water from below, was seeping into cracks and splitting the older ice. From a tree nearby came a crack like that of a rifle—it, too, was feeling a little chilly. It must be somewhere between forty and fifty below now, judging from the groans and cracks of protesting wood and water. Shadows began to shape themselves into trees, and the stars grew paler in the east. I rolled up the eiderdown and shoved it well back under the lean-to, turned the frying pan upside down on the snow, picked up my rifle and hit the trail.

A mile or so from the Meilleur Gap, or "gate"—the cleft through which it issues from the mountains—a breeze hit me. Even the faintest breeze at forty-five below is a burning, searing thing, and this one was getting stronger at every step—and the roar from the gate was getting louder. I backed away from the open river a bit and went up the flats, taking cover where I could from the scattered firs. The roaring noise was wind, I could tell that now—wind howling through that black cleft and over the pearl-coloured ice at almost eighty degrees of frost in the cold light of dawn. It didn't seem to penetrate far into Deadmen Valley; it just blew here by some freak of mountain conformation—down the Meilleur Canyon, exactly where I wanted to go.

I wasn't going to back up in a hurry: not for nothing had I carried a camp and two days' grub up here. I had on good winter clothes: over these I had pulled a pair of khaki ''bib'' overalls as a windbreak, and on top of all came a heavy mackinaw stag jacket with double shoulders. To the devil with backing up, and I edged along in the lee of the cliff towards the gate.

Three times I tried it, slinging my rifle and covering my face with my mitted hands, and three times I was driven back, the last time by a gust of such fury that it blew me, standing on my moccasined feet, like a helpless dummy, down the wind-polished ice. That wind cut through everything; I never felt anything like it before or since: I had been warm before I hit the gate, and now I was chilled right through and shivering: I ducked into the lee of the cliffs outside the gate and swung and banged my arms furiously and stamped my feet. There was a dead fir hard by: I tore it down and made a pile of tiny twigs in a stamped-out hollow in the snow and built a fire. I warmed my mitts and then swung my arms again: this was better, and now what about melting snow and making a mug of tea? Soon the tea was going down, black, scalding hot, heavy with sugar and tasting of spruce needles— when suddenly there was a kind of a giant sigh from the gate, a hundred yards away: the screaming wind died away, and a silence that could be felt landed on the place almost with a thud.

I set down the tea by the fire and ran to the gate and looked through. It led into a great, rock-walled amphitheatre with a wooded beach on the left: the ice was the same as in the gate, glare (that is, free of snow) and full of tiny air bubbles, pearl grey and solid. Beyond lay a narrow canyon from which issued the Meilleur, and from that canyon came the mutter of the retreating wind. Then an utter silence. . . .

All day long I went nosing on up into that fantastic canyon, prying into the secrets of its sunless reaches. No trail ever came this way—that was plain now—but still the wild rock formations, to which only the pencil of a Doré could have done justice, lured me on. There was a fascination in these dark places into which man could only penetrate in the depths of winter, walking on the frozen river. From time to time a little question posed itself, "What if that wind starts up again?" For it was still around forty below, and one would be caught in what amounted to a wind tunnel—a trap. But these doubts were pushed aside: there was so much to see, and one would never come this way again.

I found small showings of copper in the canyon walls and knocked out, with the back of my axe, fossils which a learned man told me, years afterwards, were trilobites. In two places I had to jump an open channel of deep, fast water: rifle and axe were left behind as a concession to reason—and now, looking back a quarter of a century from the depths of an armchair, I think I should make one further concession and leave myself behind with them!

I came back to the amphitheatre in the dusk to find an unexpected barrier cutting me off from the outer world—half an inch of treacly overflow oozing through the gate for a couple of hundred yards from wall to wall. I was hungry and cold: I didn't want to get wet and perhaps have to stop and make a fire; supper was what I wanted, and soon—and, at this point, I spotted a rock ledge some twenty feet above the ice on the left. It vanished behind a point of rock, and I couldn't see if one could get down at the other end, but it might be a way around. A run and a scuffle got me on to the ledge: it was not too bad, about three feet wide or more, narrowing a bit towards the point. I peered cautiously round this; it didn't look so good—there was foothold out on the point but, around it, no ledge till one was back against the canyon wall. There was a good handhold; one might make it—or would it be more sensible to go back and get wet and make a fire? The sudden scream of wind from up the canyon answered that query for me. It had happened: the wind was back, and in another minute it was on me. I figured I had about three minutes to get off that ledge, and I damn well wasn't going back—no puddling about in overflow for me in this wind. I got my left foot into position and swung out and round the point with my right, reaching at the same time for the handhold. Got him: now then—and at this juncture the rifle sling hitched round a point of rock. Devil take the thing—another minute and my left hand would be numbed. I pulled, and the rotten rock broke off: a wild scuffle and I had clawed my way around. I hitched my way along the remainder of the ledge in double quick time and looked down. There was no way down—one could get down six feet or so, and after that it was sheer. A furious gust nearly toppled me over: tears from the wind were running down my cheeks and freezing on them: anywhere, I thought, to hell out of here. I slipped down as far as I could, dropped axe and rifle into a snowdrift and launched myself into the top of an obliging young spruce, cascaded to the ground in a shower of broken branches, picked up the tools of my trade and ran.

To my amazement, I passed out of the wind into dead still air at practically the same point as I had entered it in the morning. Very odd, that—and now, would it reach down in the night and blow me out of house and home? Or would it stay where it was? I decided to risk it and find out; and very soon the fire was blazing cheerfully and snow was melting in the tea pail; the eiderdown was spread out again over the bed of fir tips, and I was reaching back under the lean-to for a flour sack that contained a number of bricks of a reddish-looking material, irregular in shape and with moss and the golden leaves of black birch frozen into them. I selected two of these and threw them into the frying pan with a clang: they were moose steaks, and within about half an hour they were going to be putting warmth and energy into me—warmth so that I might sleep soundly, and energy that would carry me, in the morning, over a spur of the Bald Mountain and into the high valley that I had failed to reach today.

I overslept. The first grey light was outlining the mountains of the Lower Canyon when I was still eating my porridge by the fire. From the Meilleur Gap came the moaning of that zero wind; but from far above on the rock precipices of the Bald Mountain there came a sighing, rising and falling and then rising again till it seemed like the rush of innumerable wings. I looked up. Surely that must be snow drifting from the south-west up there? or was it mist? and was that a west-wind cloud that showed and disappeared again? But it was still too dark to see clearly, and I packed up camp, crossed the Meilleur and dived into the bush, heading for the spur. It was a long climb to the first of the ridges in the cold shadow of the spruce—but a new world was waiting for me up there. I sat down on a log, unbuttoned my stag jacket, took off my fur hat and mopped my head. The Chinook was back. Warm puffs of air were coming from the south-west; snow was falling from the little firs, and their needles were shining with moisture. The sky was a deep, warm, royal blue and, spinning across the Bald Mountain, came flying rags of golden cloud. Summer clouds they were, Chinook clouds, spinning because Chinook clouds always spin, though no man has ever been able to tell me why. And there lay the high valley stretching away towards the Yukon: it looked as though it should be good marten country—and maybe hold other stuff as well. So now we knew how to get into it—and from here I could see how one could improve on the way that I had come. I stuffed my fur hat into my packsack, took off my inner mitts and moved forward a few miles: one might come on a moose, perhaps. But no, the luck was out, so I made tea by a spring, ate some bannock and turned for home—we knew what we wanted to know now, anyway. In the late afternoon I came down the snye that ran past the Klondikers' cabins. The ice of the snye was clear and windswept, the colour of pale green jade. I looked back at one point, and in the mirror of the ice I saw reflected the tall, black sentinel spruce and the belt of red willow that fringed the snye. Adding one last touch of magnificence, there came, floating across the polished surface, the red gold clouds of a flaring Chinook sunset.

Evenings at the cabin—and it was not very often that we were there together—were always full. There would be moccasins to mend and sometimes snowshoes, a rifle or pistol to be cleaned, bannock or sourdough bread to bake and a stew of moose meat and partridges to be tended and seasoned, my diary to be written up, letters written which we hoped to be able to post sometime in January, a torn parka mended and so on. There was always something to fiddle with—knives and axes to sharpen (my job), dog harness to be stitched (Gordon's job), some trap to be filed and adjusted, and always the day's catch of fur to be dealt with.

And outside, in the pail suspended over the bed of glowing embers, the last of the bear fat was being rendered down. Beside that fire, long after the dogs had been shut into the doghouse and a heavy log rolled against their door, and long after Mam'selle had been chained to the spruce roots in the den in the sandy bank which was their home, sat two dumpy little figures—the pups. The fire fascinated them, and they sat there side by side without moving, two black, furry silhouettes against the glowing coals, like a couple of old gossips drawn up to the winter hearth. They were doing well and getting fat on the crackling and on their mother's milk: all of a sudden they would remember that it was milking time, and with one accord they would rise and scamper in their bumbling, half-sideways, puppy gait towards the den. They invariably fell over the vast cliff into which the den was dug, yelping with surprise when this fall of thirty inches knocked the wind out of them. Picking themselves up they would charge into the den where, presumably, the onslaught on Mam'selle began: furious screams from her and yelps of pain from the pups would be heard: finally, we presumed, order had been restored, and Mam'selle and her now bloated family had curled up and were asleep. No sound came from them: their day was over.

After attending this nightly circus we would return to the cabin, perhaps to read for a while before turning in. Our library was not a large one—not nearly large enough, we now thought—but the canoes had been sufficiently overloaded as it was without adding further to the total weight. There was a cookbook, pressed on us at the last moment by Mollie Matthews. It was nice to have it along, but as we had run out of all the more interesting titbits and spices by now, it was mainly of academic interest. There was a large and quite interesting Dominion Government publication dealing with the fur trade and its ramifications, with a foreword by Sir Clifford Sifton. It had some readable stuff on the raising and ranching of white and blue foxes on the Pribiloff Islands: that, we decided, was the life for us when we were through with the Northwest Territories—an interesting and active life, and a fortune for us while we were still young enough to enjoy it in travelling and hunting. There was a *Munsey's Magazine*, picked up at Grizzly Simmonds' Ram Creek camp—and lastly there were our two main stand-bys, *Jorrocks' Jaunts and Jollities* by R. S. Surtees and *Pickwick Papers*—classics of a bygone day which we read in turn till we knew them almost by heart.

5

Winter Trails

"That night the snow fell in such an amazing blizzard of cutting wind that every man feared for his life."

Memoirs of the Emperor Baber

December 1st, 1928, roused us to "a very cold, dirty morning with a bitter south-east wind driving the grey snow powder up the frozen river." The home creek was frozen solid now and overflowing, and the water hole through the river ice had to be cut open both morning and evening on these cold days—a sloppy, cheerless job in the dawn twilight with the splashed water freezing instantly on to one's moccasins and mackinaw pants. Exactly how cold it was from now on we never knew: the thermometer, for some reason, jammed at thirty-two below; shaking and tapping had no effect on it, so, to brisk it up a bit, we put it in the oven. Wolves were almost immediately heard, howling just across the river, and we went out into the bright moonlight with our rifles to see if we could get a shot at them. This diversion took some little time: meanwhile the thermometer, in a vain effort to accommodate itself to its novel surroundings, blew up. However, by certain signs we always knew about where we were: by the feel of the cold on nose and cheeks; by the sharp reports from splitting ice and trees (around forty below and over); by the speed at which water froze, and so on.

We were away up the mountain all day in different directions and came home after dark with one marten and two big No. 1

185

weasel—about $48 for the day's work at the prices of May 1929. Marten were evidently going to be one of the main items of our catch, closely followed by weasels and foxes—it was paying us well to keep hard at it and to get around our queer-shaped line as often as possible, both to retrieve the fur and to keep the marten sets in good order.

A good place for a marten set is up against a well-branched spruce, a foot or more in diameter and right by the snowshoe trail. A bundle of small stakes is first cut; the stakes are cut to about thirty-inch lengths and pointed; they are then driven into the snow or moss, making two semi-circular wings of a small corral that has the tree for its back wall and an open gate towards the trail. Inside this little corral a No. 2 trap is set with the jaws towards the two side wings so that the entering marten is not thrown out of the trap as the jaws spring upwards. The trap is stapled to a toggle—a short, heavy length of birch or whatever wood is handiest, or to the spruce tree itself. We used to slip a piece of very fine birch bark over the pan of the trap and under the jaws to keep the snow from working in under the pan where it would melt in the next Chinook, and then freeze in the following cold spell, thus freezing the trap solid and making it useless. Then one would powder over the trap with spruce dust or fine snow until it became part of its surroundings: some trappers say this is not necessary, but we always did it—a marten in those days was worth plenty of trouble. For bait a bit of partridge liver or meat would be laid on the snow just beyond the trap, and perhaps a partridge wing would be set against the tree at the back of the pen to catch the marten's eye. Then the corral would be roofed over with one or two thick branches of spruce; this would help to keep the next fall of snow off the trap and so give the set a longer life. The final touch was the placing of a short butt of wood across the entrance to the corral—the idea being that the marten, when he entered the corral, would jump over this obstacle and so land with his front feet plumb on the pan of the trap. The corral itself was there for two reasons—firstly to get the marten coming in from the right direction, and secondly because the curious little beast would be instantly attracted by the very novelty of the thing and would go in to see what it was all about. We used corral sets (I found some of them still standing in September 1951, dry and sound, and preserved by the overhanging spruce from the storms of twenty-three years), and we caught marten with them, but there are various other methods: a notch can be cut in a large tree well above the probable snow level, and a pole set up leaning against the tree and leading up to the trap, which is itself set in the notch and stapled to the tree; or the set can be made on the top of an old stump, with the same type of pole runway leaning against it to lead the inquisitive marten up to the trap. These sets are best in deep-snow countries: and there are others still—a cruel business, but one that will endure as long as women wear marten stoles. I have detailed this one set for this one animal in order to make it plain that a day on the trapline is straight hard work and not sport or play in any shape or form. And as the snow gets deeper the work becomes harder as you crouch there on snow-shoes, adjusting the set to new conditions, fiddling with it in sixty or seventy degrees of frost. A dead marten cannot be carelessly yanked out of the trap: he may be frozen down either owing to Chinook conditions or to the warmth that was in his body. You have to cut him out carefully and pack him home, ice and all, to thaw out slowly in the warmth of the cabin. Lastly the trap must be reset and delicately adjusted so that it will catch a marten but will not be sprung by a squirrel or a whiskey jack.

Try this sometime. And then try it all day in zero weather over miles of mountain country, and come home at night to a cold cabin or, better yet, to an open camp such as we had, scattered around Deadmen Valley; for we built no out-cabins. Try it just once—and you will never again look at a marten fur without picturing to yourself the trapper moving silently through the snow-laden bush, covering his line—an anachronism, a piece of the seventeenth century that has lasted over into the warring twentieth.

In the small hours of December 2nd, the wind rose to a gale and swung into the north-west, and from there it blew all day long, a searing blast of cold out of a cloudless sky, drifting the snow down the river with a hissing, scratching sound like that of driven sand. I was at home alone all day, cutting wood, fixing up some fur and sharpening axes and saws. The rim of the sun showed for a while at midday over the Bald Mountain, but its rays gave no warmth and soon camp lay again in the shadow. The raving wind was whipping the tall spruce around like fishing rods; it was somewhere between thirty and forty below, and the dogs, who usually spent their idle hours lying on mats of spruce beneath the overturned canoes, whimpered uneasily and sought the shelter of the doghouse. The wind raged on through the night: in the odd lull one could hear the sharp reports of splitting trees and faintly, for it was across the wind, a fusillade of expanding ice from the delta of Prairie Creek. In the cabin, well-chinked though it was, the alarm clock froze up, and around the latch hole and the door jamb, and on every nail head of the door, there was gathered almost a quarter of an inch of rime.

On the 3rd I was away with daylight on to the ridges to the south-west, and I was surprised to find that ''at the height of a few hundred feet I was above this wind, and could look down from the silence of the frozen woods and hear the roar of the gale and see the tree tops bending in the valley below.'' It was warmer up here, too; truly, this valley was a queer place—and I thought of Gordon and hoped he also had got above the icy wind. He probably had; he had gone off the day before towards the Meilleur with one dog and was most likely somewhere up in the high valley by now. I worked east across the face of the mountain all day and came home by the lick and the old trail to find the wind still howling across the river flats when I got down, and ''nearly got the skin blown off my face as I came up the shore.'' The gale blew itself out in the night.

Faille had told us in June that he had made most of his fur catch, last winter on the Flat River, after New Year. With that in mind, we decided to celebrate our Christmas on December 18th, after which Gordon would hitch up the dogs and drive them down to Fort Simpson for the year's mail and also for certain supplies of which we were short, while I would remain and look after the trapline. It was most of two hundred miles to Fort Simpson but, provided we could get through the Lower Canyon, that didn't seem anything to worry about—and it was, for various reasons, essential that we should get that mail. It was getting to be essential also that we should get another moose: with this long trip in view the dogs had been fed like fighting cocks, and we had not done too badly ourselves: the stock of moose meat was beginning to look a bit sick. However, no doubt the luck would turn—for we had not, even yet, fully realised the completeness of the exodus of game from the valley; there had been so much Chinook and open ground.

So, latish on the 14th, we went down to have a look at the Cache Rapid which we thought might be still open and barring the way into the Lower Canyon. But it was frozen and silent, though the Cache Riffles up above were still partly open, and there was good passage for a dog sled. It was very cold in the head of the canyon, much colder than in the valley; a black, zero wind was moaning between those sombre walls, wailing far aloft in the half-darkness among the snow-capped pinnacles; we were glad to get out of the god-forsaken place into the twilight of the valley and home to a couple of roasted blue grouse in all the snug warmth and cheer of stove and candlelight.

Christmas was a roaring success. We had saved up various good things—maple syrup, butter, coffee, jam, an extra ration of sugar and so forth—and, after a terrific cleaning up of ourselves and the cabin, we brought these down from the cache and laid into them with a will on our officially designated Christmas Eve, December 17th. After a blue grouse apiece, with cranberry sauce, we moved on to the big thing of the evening—hot cakes richly fried in bear's lard, loaded up with as much butter, sugar and maple syrup as they could carry. All records were going to be broken: what we weren't going to do to those delectable pancakes!

But we had left one little item out of our calculations; we had been so long without unlimited sweet stuff that we soon found ourselves stuck. The pancakes were large and of an incredible richness: I downed three and a half, Gordon managed four: we drank a lot of coffee and went out and ran round the shack a few times: we came in and ate one more apiece—and that was that. Bursting, we stared dumbly at each other, and then rose and kicked the cabin door wide open and lay down to talk and smoke. It was a warm night, and the Chinook was roaring on the mountain tops and rustling the big spruce by the cabin with puffs of warm air. One lay there and marvelled at the toughness of the human frame—how a man could eat that much and live! And now for the bedtime story—one more in the long line of unprintable parodies of our Edwardian childhood tales that I used to concoct for our mutual entertainment: it should be that old, well-worn favourite, "The Window Box in the Slum," but with a new twist to it; the way I had it fixed for tonight it was going to be a real humdinger! "Many years ago, my dears," the prim voice began, "in a dark slum of one of our great, smoky cities. . . ."

"Christmas Day" was spent in overeating, in cooking up bannock and biscuits for the trail and in making the most complete preparations for Gordon's departure. Sled and dog harness were ready, mail was bundled up; a savoury stew of beans and moose meat was ladled out on to aluminum plates and set on the cabin roof to freeze solid. When this had been achieved the plates were brought in and set for a moment on the stove: the loosened slabs of stew were then slid off into a flour sack and put outside in the cache to stay frozen; one or two of these could be slipped into a pot, well packed down with snow, while camp was being made, and set by the fire; soon to break down into a warming, heartening soup, made with the minimum of effort. Moose steaks were cut and frozen (the day was, fortunately, colder); Gordon's Mauser was cleaned and returned to its case and his trail axe sharpened to a razor edge; finally another tremendous supper was eaten—and on the 19th Gordon hit the trail for Fort Simpson on the Mackenzie River, with the pups inside the cariole, very placid, and old Poilu in the lead looking like a peasant evicted from his cottage home by an unjust landlord. I went off up the mountain trail, returning late with a nice, well-furred marten; and in the evening I squared away the upheaval and prepared to spend a month or so alone.

A couple of days later, from high on some ridge I heard the sound of a man's voice and the clatter of a dog sled making its way up the river ice. Now what? I climbed a tree, but I could see nothing—and here let us remember that, at this time, the Nahanni River was still largely unknown country, and the Nahanni Legend was still in full flower: this was Deadmen Valley, from which no traveller was confidently expected to return, and men said good-bye to you at Fort Liard or Fort Simpson and wished you the best of luck, much as one might shake the hand of a man about to mount the scaffold, wishing him a pleasant visit and a speedy return.

It was dusk when I got back to the river flats: a light was shining from the cabin window: whoever it was, white man or Indian, he was making himself at home. I came up in the cover of the spruce: about fifty yards from the cabin door there were two big ones, and there I laid down my pack, slipped my rifle off my shoulder and waited. From inside the cabin soon came a faint clatter of dishes but no visible sign of its occupant; the next move was up to me—and, at this juncture, something heavy trod on my foot and nuzzled me. I looked down; it was Sammy, of course, he always trod on your foot. . . .

Gordon had had quite a trip. He had made good time down into the canyon, mostly on glare ice, and was nearly half-way through when his troubles began. He found himself up against the right wall on a wide ledge of very thick, very solid ice with open water on his left. The river was almost at its winter low; it had dropped down from the ledge, which was sheer-sided and about a couple of feet above the water. The ledge vanished round a point of rock: he couldn't leave the dogs, there was nothing to tie them to, so he pushed on, trusting to luck that the ledge would widen out again and the open water come to an end. It didn't. The shelf got narrower and narrower till it tapered out to nothing at all—and by the time he made this pleasant discovery he had gone too far to turn around, and there he was, with a thousand feet of canyon wall towering above him on one side and the dark, cold river on the other, and with about thirty-six inches of polished ice on which to manoeuvre a nine-foot toboggan and four dogs. The river here, he then found, had fallen completely away from the ice, which thus had no water to support it and was adhering to the canyon wall only by its own iron grip: how much extra weight, he wondered, could it carry? He could see no bottom to the river: one way and another it seemed a good idea to be getting out of this mess before darkness fell—and that idea gained considerable support when, from far up above, there came humming down out of the shadows a shower of rock fragments, narrowly missing the dog team and splattering into the river like shrapnel.

The dogs knew nothing about backing up—all they knew was "pull"—so now it was "pull devil, pull baker" for a dangerous quarter of a mile, as Gordon worked the sled backwards to a turning place, dragging the team with it. More rocks came down, and in places the ice shelf sloped outwards to the river, while, to complete the picture of cursing, sweating man and obstinate dogs, the pups were yelling blue murder inside the cariole, for it was long past milking time. They came in the last light to a level beach and a point of trees, and there camp was made—and by the light of the fire Gordon spotted a number of sound, dead trees, killed by the moving ice of some bygone spring.

He got to work on them in the morning and made a raft. God knows what he tied it together with—a long line that he had with him, odd bits of lashing and straps, anything. Somehow he crossed the Nahanni on this thing and tried down the left shore, but the same thing happened again—he fetched up against a sheer wall and open water. The queer thing about these open stretches was that there was ice two or three feet thick right up to the edge of the water and no rim of rotten or part-formed ice at all: we wondered at the time if this might not have been due to the shearing off of the ice in one of the earlier Chinooks; however, be that as it may, these open reaches froze over later on, in the intense cold of January and February, as solid as the rest of the river. From his furthest point Gordon could see that if he had a canoe he could go down the river on the right bank, close under the canyon walls and come to a landing place. From there he might be able to get on: if he couldn't he could come back for the canoe and repeat the performance lower down.

So he turned for home. Luckily it was Chinooking and very warm. He loaded the dog toboggan on to the raft and poled and lugged the clumsy thing upstream to gain height for his crossing.

The river was backed up by ice lower down and had lost its speed, otherwise his crazy argosy could never have made it: as it was, with the dogs on board, he only just made his crossing, working like fury with an improvised paddle—for the wind was rising and blowing down the canyon, and he was in danger of being carried down and sucked into the ice jam that he had seen round the next bend. That was his story—and as he finished his saga it began to rain. Disgustedly we went to bed. Rain, of all things, in Deadmen Valley and on the shortest day of the year!

Next morning I cruised through the bush and cut a couple of young birch. They had exactly the right curve, and I hewed them into twelve-foot sled runners, mortising in two light cross-bunks and two diagonal braces, all of birch. This made a strong, workmanlike sled, light and wide: to it we lashed our sixteen-foot canoe, putting the dog toboggan inside the canoe and adding various equipment, such as pole, line and paddles, for this queer, amphibious journey. Every last detail was attended to—and then, in the dawn light of Christmas Eve, Gordon put his stuff into the canoe and the grunting puppies into the cariole, hitched up the dogs and departed. It was colder, and the wind had dropped to an utter stillness—and that was lucky because it would have been impossible to control a load like this on glare ice in a high wind.

Deadmen Valley then settled down to a dead monotonous level of work and cold weather: it never Chinooked again until early March—that rain was the dying kick. . . .

Considering the queer, unwieldy outfit he was driving, Gordon made good time down to his old camp on the wooded point in the canyon. Nevertheless, the short winter afternoon was on him before he was able to put out on the river, and by this time a chill, gusty wind was blowing upstream, and his paddle became immediately coated with ice. All was going well, however: he had passed the place where he had got stuck with the dog team, and he could see his landing beach ahead—and very glad he would be to get there; the load was bulky and top heavy without having enough weight to set the canoe solidly down in the water, and the dogs were uneasy and would not stay still. And then it happened:

up the canyon came a whirlwind, churning to white the black surface of the river; the dogs cowered all to one side, and over went
the canoe dumping its inmates into the icy water.

Luckily there was just footing. Gordon dragged the canoe
ashore—his axe and rifle were lashed to it, and the toboggan was
jammed under the thwarts: then he wallowed into the river again
and hurled ashore pole and paddles, and his tightly rolled eiderdown which was bobbing gaily downstream. Last of all he retrieved
the grub box, dropping one or two things out of it in the process
and floundering into a deep hole in a vain effort to retrieve a
precious sack of moose meat.

The June flood had built up a huge driftpile on the beach nearby. Sticking out of the driftpile was a birch log with some loose
bark on it, and Gordon's matches were dry: he ran to the wind-
ward end of the driftpile, burrowed into it and jammed some
birch bark into the hole, surrounding it carefully with small twigs
of spruce. His clothes were stiffening on him now: there was need
of haste, and yet he must not hurry and fumble this: very carefully he struck a match and applied it to the birch bark—his
fingers were becoming numbed by the wind: how many more
matches, he wondered, could he light and hold? But the birch
bark flared up, pouring forth its oily, aromatic smoke; he added
more birch bark from the tree in the driftpile, then more twigs,
then larger stuff—and then, fanned by a gust of wind, the fire
licked into the driftpile, shooting forth twisting snakes of flame.

Gordon then got a small campfire going about ten yards away
from the driftpile: it was going to be impossible to get near that
very soon and what he wanted was tea, red hot and lots of it. He
set a frying pan full of water on the little fire—and then he did a
war dance round the flaming driftpile, twisting and turning and
beating his arms as he ran. The wind dropped (it was somewhere
around zero or a little below that night, I gather from my diary),
and from the driftpile there rose a thin, vertical, whining shaft of
flame, some thirty feet in height, or more. Gordon downed a frying pan full of hot, greasy tea—for the tea pail had gone down the
river—and felt the better for it: he started to cook some oatmeal.
His clothes felt hot and wet so he took off the outer layer and hung

them on the great roots of upturned trees, to dry in the heat of the big fire. Then he took all his clothes off—they seemed to dry faster that way—and it was getting pretty damned hot here on this little beach; the canyon wall was throwing the heat back down on the camp—and it then occurred to him that the heat might loosen a bunch of rock and send it crashing down. But there was nothing he could do about that, so he continued his mad dervish dance, capering and twirling round the monstrous fire like some frenzied imp of the lower regions—but stopping now and then, as he passed by, to give the porridge a stir. Round with him went the pups—in their short lives they had known little but snow and ice, and this was the best thing yet. Gordon tripped over them, and they fell over each other, and Mam'selle joined in—round and round went the lunatic circus. Except when he stopped to stir the porridge, inevitably singeing some portion of his anatomy as he did so, he had lots of time to think, he told me afterwards. It must have been a wild-looking scene, he said: down on the beach a devil dance, a revival of ancient sorceries, reflected in the darkly gleaming Nahanni; up aloft the snow-powdered wall, lit by the leaping flames till the shadows of the little firs on the lower ledges danced a wild fandango of their own, then reaching upwards and out of sight into the shadows and the outer darkness.

It gave him, he told me afterwards, some quite revolutionary ideas for the redecoration of the infernal regions.

Such was Gordon's Christmas Eve (Gregorian style)—not entirely, perhaps, "a day to remember," but quite certainly one that he would never be able to forget.

From this camp, without much grub and coping in turn with open water, overflow and drifted snow, he made his way in three camps to Jack LaFlair's trading post by Nahanni Butte. There he re-outfitted and then hit the great highway of the Liard, northwards towards Fort Simpson.

January was cold. The cold was alive, active and hostile like some visitant from outer space. It beat down upon the valley, watching its only human occupant as a cat watches the scurryings of a mouse—waiting patiently to see if he would make a mistake.

It gave one a sense of pressure—of the presence of an enemy who had all the patience and all the time in the world. You could feel it in an open camp as you lay by the fire watching the play of the flames, or looking beyond them into the dark, shadowy world of the trees: and you could feel it in the cabin as the logs "ponged" with the increasing cold, and the rime thickened on the nail heads of the door and around the latch hole.

But only one mistake was made: I was camped, in mid-January, away up the Meilleur; I had followed two fresh moose tracks all day towards the Yukon in the hope of getting in a long shot and had run clean out of all landmarks into country I had never seen—and still no moose. Making my way back to camp by moonlight I cut across the Meilleur on nice, even-looking snow—and suddenly I went through, snowshoes and all, into knee-deep overflow. I came out of that in record time on to wind-swept rock, almost before my feet were wet, and hit the high spots back to camp, two miles away, in long, swinging downhill strides, knocking what ice I could off my snowshoes with the back of my trail axe as I went. Camp was near enough—but, even so, the fire came none too soon.

The snow began to pile up: it was on January 8th that I used my snowshoes for the first time. Marten kept on coming in, and quite a few weasel—and on January 4th I shot our one and only wolverine. I was on my way, on a very cold morning, up the mountain when I heard, coming towards me, a desperate snarling and clattering noise. Round a bend in the trail came a wolverine, clawing into the snow and dragging a No. 3 trap and a big, heavy poplar toggle: he was held, I found afterwards, by only one claw of one hind foot. He saw me and came towards me—and never have I seen on any animal's face such a look of utter ferocity. I stepped to one side and gave him one bullet from my 9mm. Luger automatic pistol, right behind the shoulder. It seemed to act more as a tonic than anything else. He redoubled his efforts to get at me, and I rapidly fired six more shots, alternating hard point and soft nose bullets, and the only effect they had on the wolverine was to make him madder and more active than before. I couldn't understand it; we were in the habit of shooting the heads off blue grouse and partridges with our Lugers, and here I couldn't hit this wolverine ten feet away: there must be something wrong with the gun, I thought—and I had no axe with me. Very carefully I fired the eighth and last shot, and the wolverine dropped dead. I found later, when I skinned him, that the eight bullets had gone practically through the same hole—one further proof of the amazing strength and vitality of this animal. An enduring, indestructible beast he must be, for Michael Mason writes that his remains are found in company with those of the mastodon and the three-toed horse, unchanged from that day to this. Whether, blinded with fury and trapped and cornered, this anachronism would have gone for me if he got loose, I do not know: under normal circumstances a wolverine would not attack a man. Fortunately there did not seem to be many wolverine in Deadmen Valley. They are absolutely fearless and combine the curiosity that killed the cat with the strength of a small bear: apart from the fur that they destroy by following a trapper and dealing themselves a series of free meals out of his traps, they will get to work on a temporarily deserted cabin or cache, and if strength and ingenuity can do it they will get in—frequently by tearing out the stovepipes and roof jack and making their entry through the roof. The ensuing devastation within is even worse than that of a country house in which "the military" have been billeted in wartime: the place looks as if all the fiends of hell have been romping in it, and whatever the wolverine has not been able to carry away is fouled up and rendered useless. An enemy of man—as Faille had found to his cost of the winter before, on the Flat River, when he almost starved to death owing to the depredations of a wolverine. In the afternoon I skinned this relic of the Pleistocene, stretched his hide on a frame and chucked the sinewy body into the boiler; it would make a meal for the dogs when Gordon got back.

The days got colder. On January 21st I went up to the head of the valley, right up to Second Canyon Mountain, and picked up a marten but saw no sign of game. "A cloudless sky and very cold," I wrote, "the coldest day so far. It must have been around 50° below, and the open stretches of river are steaming in the cold air and spreading a raw mist over the floor of the valley." The next day was colder yet: it was about time for Gordon to show up and, on days when I was at home, I began to look down the river towards the canyon mouth, last thing in the evening after opening the water hole. But nobody came, and I began to wonder what could have happened—it was four weeks now since Christmas Eve.

The 23rd was still colder, and I put the ladder up to the cache, got down the boiler and considered the wolverine: the moose meat was finished now, and all I had was tea, salt, beans and rolled oats and no fat of any kind—a poor diet for building up heat and energy against this intense cold, for it must then have been pretty close to sixty below. The flat, almost reptilian head of the wolverine was the most repulsive thing about him: one blow of the axe fetched that off—and then, from his hinder end I chopped a good sizable stew. The head and the rest of the beast I put back in the dog boiler, and, that night, I supped off muscular chunks of wolverine and a thick mess of rolled oats and beans cooked in wolverine soup. The flavour was the trouble with that beast: the wolverine is the biggest of all the weasels, and if anybody wants to know what it was like, let him catch a weasel and cook himself up a nice, appetising weasel stew. The cooking, boiling or simmering is the worst feature of the whole performance: it seems to bring to the surface all the more unpleasant characteristics of the weasel family, and you cook yourself clean out of the shack and into God's clean air no matter what the hour or temperature. I sawed wood to keep warm—sawed wood like mad by the light of the stars till it was safe to go inside again.

Each day now was colder than the last: what it went down to I never knew—somewhere in the sixties probably. Then on the 26th it warmed up to about twenty below and began to snow—and still no sign of Gordon. I began to wonder if his programme of aquatic sports in the Lower Canyon had gone a bit crossways with him: if he had gone through the ice in The Splits: if he had cut his leg with the axe, making camp in the dark: if. . . . But probably he would turn up tonight—and if he didn't come by the 30th I would snowshoe down to Nahanni Butte and find out from Jack LaFlair if he had gone by. In the meantime, powered by the strength of the wolverine which had now become mine, I covered our trapline in that intense cold, picking up a couple of nice marten in those last days, but meeting with no respite from the wolverine stew in the form of partridge or blue grouse—they had all gone under the snow.

Gordon didn't show up on the 30th, and the next day I made my preparations for the trail. Rifle, pistol, cameras and all other valuables and non-essentials were put in the cache. A $1\frac{1}{2}$-pound axe was whetted to a razor edge: a vast cooking of wolverine and beans was made, frozen on plates into rations and slipped into a sack: tea, oatmeal and salt were set aside, and a little wolverine fat: a light, eight-foot-by-six tarpaulin, with grummets at the corners and along one eight-foot side, was laid out; it had two long leather laces attached to two corner grummets, and leather loops to the grummets on the opposite long side; this was to be the lean-to shelter, and with it I laid one very light single blanket—my only bedding: not that I would not gladly have had more, but this was going to be all that I could carry over a long distance. Thank God I carried a furnace inside me, even on rolled oats and tea: it was nothing to be proud of, it was purely and simply a gift, and I had it—my circulation and internal heating arrangements were so efficient that I could travel and sleep out with the minimum of covering in temperatures at which most men would freeze. Last thing in the evening, with wolverine in mind, I put over the windows the heavy shutters that I had made and drove in the pegs: and here let me confess that there was not the slightest danger, on my present diet of wolverine and beans, of my forgetting this precaution. Far from it: all through the day, from matins to evensong, I "remembered the wolverine" with all the rustic simplicity and zest of a village choir.

It had snowed without stopping since January 26th, at least half the time heavily. It was cold as charity, however cold that may be—a long way below zero, anyway—and the snow was of an incredible fineness: every complicated crystal lay revealed in all its beauty on any dark surface such as the sleeve of a mackinaw jacket. A week ago the trail was good—and now it was going to be breaking trail every step of the way; and even round the cabin one sank on snowshoes over the knee into this powdery, almost intangible fluff.

February broke grey and cold and spitting snow. After breakfast I rolled up my eiderdown and put it in the cache. Then I lashed down the heavy tarpaulin over the cache, turned down the draughts in the stove, shut and barred the cabin door and put on my snowshoes. One last look around, and then I shouldered my pack and hit the river trail.

The trail was worse even than I had expected. I slugged away at it, in the bush and on the river, hot and sweating, up and down, a steady grind. Plodding downriver like that, leaning forward a little to balance the heavy pack, one had lots of time to think. The shoes were five feet long. Up came your right foot vertically, bringing with it sixty inches of mountain ash and babiche filling. As you swung it forward at knee height your left arm swung across your body to balance it. Down it went with a protesting squeal from the dry, cold-weather snow, and your weight became centred on it. The other shoe was coming up now and your right arm was swinging across: up knee high, forward and down—and you could go on doing that right to LaFlair's post at South Nahanni. And maybe beyond. It was like climbing an endless stair with a pack on your back and the added burden of working in a soft, yielding material that was almost like sand.

I came to Ram Creek, and up came the sun over the canyon walls—a yellow, sickly-looking orb, without heat and blurred by the flying snow powder. It glowed feebly through the cold curtain of grey cloud—but it lit up the surface of the snow, and I could see that here was trouble. Four winds—from the Lower Canyon, Ram Creek, the Dry Canyon and Deadmen Valley—had come together here and had cross-drifted the snow to an incredible depth. And it had not settled yet—nor had time or wind or any Chinook put a crust over it yet that would carry a man. And there was no way round.

That stretch of trail from Ram Creek past the Little Butte and down on to the Cache Riffles was the nearest thing to hell on snowshoes that I have ever struck. There was a three-inch crust on top of the drifts, but it was not strong enough to hold a man on a five-foot shoe, still less to take the pull and heave of a man with a heavy pack climbing out of a hole in the snow. For it was into a hole in the snow that you fell when you broke through that crust—you were in up to your waist, and your next step was on a level with your belt. Only by flailing away at the crust with the flat of the axe could one force a way through this barrier—and at an incredibly slow pace. "Sometime," I thought, "this day will end, and I'll be lying by a fire, warm and comfortable and drinking tea." It was hard to believe, but it was true and it kept me going.

I was working into the shadow of the Little Butte. Slowly it came abreast of me and then fell behind. The going was a bit better now down the slope of the Cache Riffles—and then a miracle happened: the Cache Rapid, at the foot of the slope, had overflowed, soaked into the new fallen snow and frozen again into an iron-hard highway. I clattered happily down its snow-free surface and into the Lower Canyon.

As you come round the point of rocks at the foot of the Cache Rapid a long reach of the canyon opens out—it might be a mile and a half in length, or it might be nearly two. At the foot of this reach the Nahanni fetches up against a towering wall of level strata, swings to the left and disappears. Just above the elbow of the bend is a timbered island, and on that island I planned to make camp. The wind was rising now out of the north-east and blowing dead up this reach of the river. There was a little daylight left—but, if I went on, my only camping places would be burrows between the rocks of timbered points or on the beaches, and the way the night was shaping up, the big sheltering spruce of this alluvial island looked more like home than any windswept shore. Furthermore, I had no wish to get myself involved with Gordon's stretch of open water this late in the day; so I broke trail down to the island and climbed up the south bank into the shelter of the trees.

It was a dirty night. The roar of the wind could be heard out on the open river: inside the trees one could feel it a little, and occasionally there would come the whirring thud of snow dislodged by the gentle movement of the branches. I chose two spruce about ten feet apart, more or less in line with the wind, and with an open space in front of them. I snowshoed quickly around the campsite, sharply striking each overhanging tree twice with the back of the little axe: that fetched down any loose snow which would otherwise fall into camp or on to the fire when the heat from the flames rose among the branches. Then I trimmed the two chosen spruce up to a height of about six feet, laying the small dead branches in a pile to serve as kindling. Next, off came the snowshoes, and one of them was used as a shovel to dig down to ground level, banking the snow up all round, but especially behind the fire-place where it would act as a reflector. Then I laid the kindling in the fire-place, together with a twist of birch bark from my pocket. A match was applied, and the little pile burst into flame: I nursed it carefully, adding bigger twigs and then branches and then a log or two—anything I could reach till it became a fire. I got the tea pail and filled it with snow, rammed in and pressed down, for this dry snow is nothing but frost crystals; it has nothing in common with the snow of southern lands, and there is very little water in it. I pushed back the blazing logs and set the tea pail on the ashes, right up against the hottest part of the fire—it was safe there and could not overturn. Next, I cut down a tall, dead spruce, about fifteen inches through, that was standing handy. I felled it behind the fire and moved alongside it on snowshoes, trimming the branches and flinging an armful on the fire to get more light to work by: then I cut through the tree and moved forward first one end and then the other of the big log till it lay resting on the snow wall at each end, just above and just back of the fire—between the fire and the big reflector wall of snow. The flames promptly curled round it, and soon it would be a glowing, radiant mass of charcoal on the surface, giving out heat all night and ready to burst into flame again at breakfast time.

I remembered the tea pail and lifted it out of the fire, using the little axe as a hook. It hissed and spluttered; there was nearly an inch of scalding water in it, and into this I rammed and pressed more snow, making a soggier mixture this time and setting it back where it stood before. Then I cruised around in the bush with the

axe, returning again and again with armfuls of soft, green spruce
boughs. These I worked into a mat in front of the fire and into my
bed, interlaced, underside up, and with the butts buried so that
all should be soft to sleep on. At one end was a treble thickness of
boughs—the pillow.

This time the tea pail was half-full of water when I looked, and
I jammed more snow into it, getting a pot full of ice water which
which was set back again on the hot ashes. Beside it, in the little
frying pan, lay frozen blocks of wolverine and bean stew, well
packed around with snow. Occasionally there would come a sharp
''spang!'' from some glowing log, and a fragment of charcoal
would fly out, perhaps into the stew. Let it stay there—it could be
fished out later. Soon the tea water was hot but not boiling: I

lifted it off the fire and drank two cupfuls of it to replace a little of the sweat that I had lost coming through the Ram Creek drifts. Then I filled the pot up once more with snow, this time for tea, and gave the stew a stir, setting it back on some raked-out coals.

While the tea water was boiling I set up the lean-to, tying the two long leather laces of the tarpaulin to the two spruce trees a little over four feet from the ground and stretching the tarp between them. It was then stretched back and pegged down into the snow and frozen moss with four tent pegs made from the dry spruce branches of the felled tree and driven through the leather loops. Snow was then banked around the back of the tarp and built into a wall at both ends, and camp was complete. The tarp had been set sideways on to the wind, thus allowing the smoke to be blown away: had it been set with its back to the wind, the fire smoke would have eddied back into the shelter.

Tea was made and set by the fire to draw while I piled up some eight-foot logs, end-on and with the butts lying over the snow wall towards me so that I could reach them easily from the mat. Then I kicked off my snowshoes and set them upright in the snow, stepped on to the spruce mat and stood before the fire, turning slowly around in the heat of it, thawing the ice on my moccasins and on the shoulders of my mackinaw. Soon a quick shake sent the particles of ice flying, and the moccasins could be scraped clean: and then—and how can I convey the faintest idea of the blissful comfort of it?—as I lay relaxed and warm on the spruce mat, propped up against the spruce pillow and the pack, down went the tea, hot and strong and tasting of spruce needles, closely followed by that most delicious wolverine stew. I lay back luxuriously and looked up at the sloping roof above me. Above it, I knew, beat down sixty-odd degrees of frost straight from the empty spaces of the Barrens, whipped up the canyon by this raving wind, but underneath from every point, from the snow walls and the back log and from the tarpaulin lean-to itself, the fire's heat beat down on me.

I roused myself after half an hour or so and put on snowshoes, mitts and a woollen hat. Wood had to be cut and dragged up to the mat; and for most of an hour I moved to and fro among the trees, cutting down dry spruce and cottonwood by the light of the fire, dragging logs out from under the snow and slashing off sound, dry branches. The big stuff, cut into six- or eight-foot lengths, was piled at one end of the mat and the small stuff and kindling at the other. At last it was done—and before taking off my snowshoes for the last time I went across the island to the main river. A fine snow was falling, so fine that it was only granules of frost. One could just see the white surface of the river fading out of sight between sheer, treeless walls, snow-powdered and forbidding, which themselves vanished from sight, but upwards and into the night. An eerie place.

Back by the fire all was warmth and comfort. Another pail of tea went down, followed by a frying-panful of oatmeal: and then I sat there turning and toasting myself, drying inner mitts on short stakes set in the moss, melting snow for the breakfast tea, warming my bare feet at the fire while I dried out the moccasins and socks worn during the day. I had with me a change of socks and moccasins, and I put them on, three pairs of socks and a loose pair of moosehide moccasins, dry, clean and warm. I would sleep in these, keeping the used ones to travel in.

As I sat there I made plans for crossing the open water. I had brought with me an eighty-foot length of trackline so that I could make a raft—and I sat gazing into the fire, planning the raft down to the last knot and brace. This wind would have to drop a bit, though—but, used by now to the vagaries of the Nahanni winds, I easily put that worry off for the morning.

Half-dozing in the warmth I fell to wondering who had passed this way before—what manner of men they were and how they had travelled. It was a good camping place, this island, in summer or in winter—I wished I could see all that it had seen. Only thirty years ago there would be the Klondikers—a few small parties of resolute, mustachioed men, poling their boats in summertime, dragging sleds made from the boards of these same boats over the winter ice.[1] Few ever reached the Pelly River by this

---

[1] The late Mr. Walter Hanson, a rancher of the High River District in Alberta, told me that he and his party passed through the canyons of the Upper Liard in this fashion in the winter of '98—rebuilding their boats in the spring of '99 on the upper river.

route: the wild country got them—or the Indians.

But there were earlier visitors than these: one reads in the Hudson's Bay Company records that John McLeod left Fort Simpson on June 5th, 1823, with a small party for the South Nahanni. How far, one wonders, did he get up the river? Did he pass by this island, craning his neck at the marvels of the Lower Canyon? At any rate he found the Indians friendly and was back at Fort Simpson by July 10th, returning again to the "Nahanni Lands" in June 1824 when he persuaded one of the chiefs to accompany him back to the fort. That was a hundred years ago: the "explorers" of the twentieth century, we must frankly admit, arrived a trifle late on the scene. And again, in 1828, Governor Simpson planned to establish a post on the Nahanni, and the outfit of twenty-five pieces was expected to yield twenty to twenty-five packs of furs, "value about £2,000." That was a businessman's considered estimate—they must have known a thing or two about the Nahanni by that time.[1]

But, ages before this, came the nomad hunters—the wandering tribes of the great Déné race whose spearhead, the Apache and the Navajo, was only halted by the white man on the borders of Mexico. The Nahanni would be no main highway of this folk-wandering, but some parties must have come this way from the wild caribou uplands at the head of the South Nahanni and Gravel Rivers and the branches of the Pelly—driving onwards, fighting their way towards the grasslands of the south and the valley of the Rio Grande. And at this stage in my meditations, with clear, melodious trumpet note, I remembered the wolverine, and felt at one with the Déné in their urge towards the sun-lands—out of this damned black and white hell into some gentler clime where a man would have time for something else besides just trying to keep his belly full and himself from freezing. They had reason on their side, those old Déné hunters. . . .

The thought became vivid as thoughts do when a man is much alone: and I peered out beyond the fire into the leaping shadows and the driving snow. You'd think, by God, you could see them

[1]See extracts from Governor Simpson's letters—appendix.

now out there in the snye—a weary, shuffling parade of ghosts moving southwards, looking always over their shoulders for the alien clans who pressed behind. Simpson's men, too—but they were headed upstream on this night of dreams and fancies, fur-hatted, their guns in fringed and beaded covers and their—dammit, what was that? I sat up, wide awake and alert—I could have sworn something *was* moving in the snye. But it was only a grey snow devil spinning up the canyon on the furious wind.

Midnight and bedtime. I broke up fine twigs for kindling and laid them ready to hand: then I arranged some big stuff so that I could reach out and pull it on to the fire without getting up, and so losing heat. The tea pail was set where it couldn't freeze and then split with the expansion of the ice, and the fire was built up into a lasting blaze with the soundest of wood. Quickly I loosened my moccasins and my belt, put on my fur hat and tied down the earflaps: over the fur hat I drew on a woollen balaclava helmet, and on to my hands, dry woollen mitts with outer mitts of soft moosehide over them. Then I took off my stag jacket and rolled up in the blanket—a cheap, light affair, mostly of cotton, but it helped to maintain body warmth. Over my feet I laid the wind-break overalls, while the heavy mackinaw jacket was put over my shoulders. That was all; nothing had been overlooked, and in two minutes at the outside I was asleep.

The system was a simple one: a well-built fire lasts about two hours before dying down into a mass of glowing charcoal; at the end of two hours, therefore, the cold would wake me with a sting-ing sensation on the nose—there was not the slightest danger of being "frozen to death while sleeping:" long before that took place, acute discomfort would rouse one to action. And sure enough, at the end of two hours almost to the minute I woke up and peered sleepily at the fire. The big logs were burnt through; the ends glowed and sparked a little in the wind, and smoke wreathed this way and that from the pile of red-hot embers. I drew the charred ends together with a hooked stick from where I lay and threw on one or two small sticks. Then I rolled on a couple of bigger ones, and a sudden burst of flame rewarded my efforts. Now a real big one on top to hold the fire, and already it was warm again under the lean-to: in a few moments I was off to sleep again.

Two hours later the wind had dropped and the sky had cleared: the cold of the black, empty spaces that lie between the stars was beating down upon the island. Thirty-five below and dropping, I thought, as I made up the fire; for already the ice and the trees were cracking in the intense frost. So much the better—that would tighten the river up, and there would be less delay from overflow—and I dropped off to sleep again for the last lap of my six hours. The next time I woke it would be breakfast time, and after that I could pack up camp and make all ready for the trail, piling the last of the wood on to the fire and waiting for the first faint light of the new day.

Coldest of all was the hour before the dawn when the trees took shape again out of the shadows, and the topmost pinnacles of the canyon became outlined against the pale eastern sky.

The river swung to the left, then to the right again: soon the highest cliffs of the canyon, nearly 3,000 feet above me, were rose-coloured from the unseen sunrise, but the river still lay deep in the cold blue shadow of the walls. I had come now, I was pretty sure, to Gordon's rafting camp, but all signs of his activities lay buried under the deep snow. Plenty of ice had formed since he was there: would it hold right round under the canyon wall and let me pass? I hoped so: the idea of fooling about with a raft in this cold, even without wind, held no attractions for me at all.

I moved on round the point of the precipice, testing the ice, where it was clear of snow, with the back of the axe and finding it solid. In the other hand I carried a long, light spruce pole, held crossways. If I broke through there was just a possibility that the pole might bridge the hole and give me a chance of getting out: occasionally I sounded through the snow with this pole. Rocks lay scattered on the ice and bedded into it, but this morning there was no Chinook blowing to loosen others from their hold, and no bombardment fell from the cliffs above.

The light was growing stronger, and now I could see, away down the river, the glitter of open water and the ''smoke'' rising from it into the cold air. This was it—and, as I came nearer to it, I could see that it ran diagonally across the river from wall to wall; there was no way round by climbing and no timber handy for making a raft. Well, I supposed, I could go back and find a way round to Clausen Creek through the hills south of the canyon—and then I came close enough to see the bridge.

It was a poor-looking affair whichever way you looked at it. Close to the canyon wall there must have been a spring that was keeping the river open, for the water lapped right up to the base of the cliff which was coated with waterworn ice. But about twenty feet out lay a strip of ice running up and downriver and connecting two points of what looked like solid ice and snow. This odd-looking bridge was about sixty feet long at the most and ten or twelve feet wide at its narrowest. It was free of snow except for a slight powdering of new stuff fallen in the night, and it sloped slightly from the ends down to the centre as if the river had dropped away from it, and it had cracked and then frozen again in its new position. It was not all solid ice: a good deal of its thickness was water-soaked snow that had frozen into a white, crystalline mass. There it was, and you could take your choice—go back to a toilsome trail through deep snow and unknown hills with insufficient grub—or have a go at it. I cut a rock loose from the ice and skipped it across the bridge. It seemed solid.

I would try it—but not with this pack on my back; it might prove to be the last straw. I took the pack off and got out the eighty-foot trackline. I made one end of this fast to the pack and coiled the rest so that it would pay out easily. I whirled the axe around and sent it flying over: it landed with its shaft sticking up out of the snow, and I wished to God I was over there with it. Then, with the pole in my left hand and the coiled line in my right, I ran lightly out on to the bridge and down the slope, letting the line pay out as I went. Something cracked in the middle and made my heart miss a beat, and on the way up the opposite slope, one snowshoe slipped on the ice and made me bring the other one down with a fierce slap as I recovered—but I was over and safe beside the axe, and that was all I cared about. I turned round and hauled steadily on the line, fetching the pack over without ever letting it come to rest anywhere, and the outfit was complete.

I put the line away into the packsack with the feeling of satisfaction that only comes from taking a calculated risk and getting away with it. From behind me, just as I was congratulating myself on my riverman's instinct, came a dull snapping sound: I spun round just in time to see the centre of the bridge, on the far side of the hollow, sag into the river. The water flowed over it putting more and more pressure on to my side of the centre. From it, too, there came a click, and then, very gently and with a sound almost like that of a sigh, the whole central mass of the bridge, some four hundred square feet in area, subsided into the Nahanni. It was all done in very orderly fashion, without any fuss or noise, and now all that remained was a bumping sound from under the ice, fading gradually away downriver, becoming "small by degrees and beautifully less." That was what happened also to men who went under the ice, I thought—they bumped and banged away downstream and fetched up in some sunless, subaqueous jam, there to remain till May set them free, bloated a bit but still fairly well preserved until they were ground to a pulp between the milling ice blocks of the spring break-up. . . .

I looked for a moment or two at the dark, swirling water that ran where the bridge had been and then hit the trail again, this time in more reverent frame of mind. Turning and twisting to avoid overflow and open water, I made my way through the remaining eight miles or so of the Lower Canyon without much trouble. Once I found, with the hammer head of the axe, shell ice over deep overflow near the Green Island, and had to back up a bit and try elsewhere; and once the pole saved me when, prodded into a snow hollow, it went straight on through without ever reaching bottom. Below the Big Spring, where the arctic grayling lie in summertime, was the greatest stretch of overflow, spreading over the ice and into the snow in a viscous, lava-like flood, liberally besprinkled with feathery "frost flowers." But there was room to pass by, and well on in the afternoon I came to the Hot Springs. I wanted to see what they were like in wintertime, and I was heading towards them when a curl of smoke appeared from the chimney of one of the old Indian cabins on the opposite shore. A man came out and stared upstream towards me: he waved and shouted something: then he turned and called into the cabin, and two or three more men came out and stared in their turn. These were white men and not Indians: and yet last May, when we appeared, the Nahanni was silent and deserted as it had been for years. Now what was going on?

The 1929 boom was going on; and fur prices were high. Canada was reaching northwards again in a premature wave of expansion which was to break and come to nothing with the depression of the thirties—only to surge forward again ten years later. The men who had had homesteads on the frontier, north of the Peace River, from which they could trap and hunt, now found their peace disturbed by an oncoming tide of farmers, alongside of whom existence for a man who liked a bit of elbow room soon became impossible. There was only one thing to do, and that was what the nomad hunter has always done when menaced by the plough—get out. So they got out, to the Liard, to Hay River, to the Mackenzie—northwards, anywhere where there was good hunting and room to turn around in—and in so doing they in turn threatened the contentment of other men who were there before them, driving them a hundred miles deeper into their mountains or their barrens.

And now, at the height of the flood, the human tide had lapped up to the walls of the Lower Canyon. It would have liked to go further, but those frowning walls had made it pause. This was in the days before the registered trapline had come into being, and the results of this human flood were confusion and the overlapping of traplines—and trouble. The North was changing: the advent of the plane was one more factor in this breakdown of the old order which, in a few years' time, was to make necessary the creation of huge "Native Hunting and Trapping Preserves," closed to all outsiders: and in one of these, the Mackenzie Mountains Preserve, a little affair of some 70,000 square miles, now lies the South Nahanni.

Greathouse, Southard and Quinlan, Carl Aarhuis and Ole Loe—the Nordic races were in the van as usual. The first three had a cabin a little way down the Nahanni, while Carl and Ole were up Jackfish River. Nothing would do but that I should pull in and stay overnight—never mind if it was still daylight. So I went in to the warm, dark, crowded cabin and downed some tea with bannock and honey, and limbered up my tongue which had had almost six weeks' holiday.

Gordon had gone by, they told me, around Christmas, hitting the high spots for South Nahanni: the story of the open water in the canyon had gone the rounds, and now, from odd bits that they told me, I began to see that Gordon had laid it on with a shovel. I didn't know yet exactly what kind of a jackpot he had got into (and, evidently, out of), but it had quite certainly lost nothing in the telling. Then I began to see why: these men believed that I had stumbled on to the lost gold of the Nahanni in 1927 and had gone out that fall, returning with Gordon in 1928 to stake out claims. His sudden appearance, therefore, in the wintertime with a fast team of dogs, was quite understandable—he had gone down to Fort Simpson to file our claims with the nearest mining recorder. This satisfactorily explained to them (though not to me) his continued absence, and now the questions came piling in—What was the country like up above? Had we caught much fur in Deadmen Valley? and, above all, What was the Lower Canyon like? How had I got through?

My mouth was full when this question came: I was evidently being pumped, and I needed time to think. I chewed away and then slowly swallowed a mug of tea. After all, there was no need to look very far for material: that affair of the ice bridge was pretty nearly made to order—though, here and there, I could see where one could improve on it a little. I embarked on it and told such a hair-raising tale of the hazards of the Lower Canyon that I not only impressed my audience but scared myself stiff all over again into the bargain. "God," they said, in awe-stricken tones at the end of it all. "That kind of a trail and nothing but wolverine to chew on. No, sir—not for me"—and Deadmen Valley had peace for a little while longer.

After I had eaten I put on my snowshoes and crossed the Nahanni to look at the Hot Springs. Out from the base of the cliff they flowed, warm as ever and steaming in the cold air. The snow lay right up to them, getting slightly less deep as it came really close; but the feature of the place was the enormous thickness of hoar frost on every twig and bough—everything was festooned with great, glittering ropes and cables of rime, outlined against the dark spruce and the clear, green sky of evening. It was going to go down to over forty below in the night, one could feel the sting of it already out over the river. And here, tangled up in all this fantastic tracery of frost, it felt colder yet. I was glad to get away from the evil-smelling, sulphureous place and back to the river bank and the beckoning light of the old cabin.

Camp the next night was on an island in The Splits, a little way above the Twisted Mountain, and from there I came, in one more sleep, to Jack LaFlair's post at South Nahanni.

Gordon had gone by a day or two after Christmas, Jack said. He had bought some grub there, and one or two things that had been lost in his Christmas Eve frolic in the Lower Canyon—and Jack went on to give me his version of the spill into the Nahanni and the firing of the big driftpile. It sounded like a good story, the way Jack told it, and I was becoming eager to hear it at first hand from the star performer in it.

There was no news at all from down the Liard. The snow was very deep, Jack said, and nobody was travelling unless he had to. There was no trail broken, and there was no sense in just going at it in bullheaded fashion: how about laying over for a spell and giving Gordon a chance to show up? He was probably hung up somewhere with a heavy load, deep snow and nobody to help him break trail.

It was a very kind invitation, and I decided to lay over for two whole days and, if there was no sign of Gordon, hit the Liard on the third morning. I then bought some odds and ends of grub from Jack to throw into his grub pile, so as not to be a burden on him in that way, and I also bought a gaudily striped wool and cotton blanket, five feet by seven, weighing four and a half pounds. It was the best light blanket Jack had, and it was to see me down to Fort Simpson and back to Deadmen Valley.

By the next morning it had warmed up to zero. The sun blazed
down out of a cloudless, deep blue sky: not a breath of air was
moving, but away up on the summit of the Butte we could hear
the distant rush of a Chinook that never came down to river level,
some three thousand feet below: it was not strong enough to roll
back eastwards the mass of cold air that lay heavily over the plains
and in the mountain valleys. But it made things very pleasant: we
could sit outside in the sun against the warm south wall of the
cabin—Jack telling stories of the Nahanni country and of those
few, but magnificent, years of the fur trade when the Lamson,
Hubbard Company fought the Bay for the fur—when the incom-
ing boats of trappers and independent traders (and Jack was one
of these) were met on the beaches at Fort Simpson by the buyers
of the rival companies, and prices went sky high. "I thought
they'd all gone crazy when I got down to Simpson," he told me.
"It was just like a madhouse. And then I tumbled to what was going on—luckily before I'd made a deal. Oh, man! . . ." And here
followed a revered silence.

It was beautifully warm, and we were thoroughly comfortable,
inside and out. I had made porridge for our breakfast, for without
it I am no man. Jack had one regular breakfast which never
varied: he had a vast frying pan, about fifteen inches across; in
this he constructed one tremendous hotcake, thick and heavy,
which he cut in V-shaped slices as one would a pie. It was the
grandaddy of all hotcakes—and a steady diet of it would have
killed a lesser man.

But not Jack; and as for me, I had the digestion of an ostrich: so
we ate slabs of this thing for breakfast, with golden syrup and
bacon, porridge and coffee; and then went at it again, later in the
day, with butter and jam and a moose steak and more coffee, till it
was all gone and we had to think up something else for supper. A
fine, body-building diet, and one guaranteed to hold cold weather
at bay; and I felt most comfortable, sitting there in the sun and
stitching away with a moccasin needle and sinew at a shapeless-
looking piece of moosehide. Jack took moosehide in trade from
the Indians, and I had bought sufficient from him for a pair of
big, gauntlet mitts. Jack had a pattern, and we had cut the two

pieces out with great care: now they were taking shape; they were being sewn, turned inside out, with a herringbone stitch, and I was not a little proud of the result when I had them finally completed—they lasted for years and were the best and warmest pair of outer mitts that I have ever had.

Amongst other things, Jack told me that mule deer had just arrived on the Nahanni from the south. He had never heard of them being there before, and he pointed out their range to me—around a couple of little, lion-shaped buttes that rise from the flats between the Nahanni and the Liard. "Between them and those far mountains," he said. "But don't tell the Indians what I've just told you. They'll get on to them soon enough, and I'd like to see the deer get established."

He had a garden there by Nahanni Butte, and he planned to have a row of choke-cherries in it; he was fond of their jelly. There were some at the Hot Springs, at the mouth of the Lower Canyon; would we bring a couple of bushes down for him when we came out in May? I said we would; and when the time came we brought one, and Stevens and I planted it for him.

The sun went behind a cloud, and it felt chill in the sudden shadow; we went in and tackled that hotcake again and some moose mulligan and tea, and then sat and smoked and talked for a while; Jack's tongue, too, had been getting a bit stiff from lack of exercise, and he was glad of the chance to give it a run. Suddenly he sprang up from his seat and walked smartly to the centre of the store. Above his head and running the full width of the building was a polished spruce pole that I hadn't noticed before. "Be getting soft if we sit around like this," he said, and as he spoke his hands smacked on to the "horizontal bar" with gymnasium precision: in a second or so he was hanging from it upside down with his arms folded across his chest, a triumphant, bat-like figure. "Beat that for time," he said with a grin. I tried. Then he performed some further stunt, and I followed him through all kinds of weird contortions till the sunset light was fading behind the first of the lion buttes. The Indian village was deserted; they were all away hunting, which was just as well, for the story of the two mad white men discovered hanging upside down in the trading post would have lost nothing in the telling.

When the display was over I put my snowshoes on and broke trail down out of the mouth of the Nahanni and for a mile or so down the Liard. If Gordon was trying to make it in late to the post that night he would find it handy—or I would find it useful myself if I went down to look for him. The snow was very deep, even after a day's settling in the sun.

The next day was the same: Chinook away up on the Butte, warm (around zero) and dead still down on the river level, and a blazing sun. The mitts were finished and looked like a first-rate job: they were duly admired and then laid aside on the bench while we sat out there in the sun, talking. Jack was of French Canadian stock, but the family had crossed the line into Maine, and the name had gradually become changed from la Fleur to LaFlair. He was a self-educated man and read all he could lay his hands on, and I learned that day much of his outlook on life and his personal history. He had drifted down the Slave River and on into the Northwest Territories in a boat that was little more than a box, and he had fallen in love with this beautiful spot at the foot of Nahanni Butte and made his home there. He never left it, and he died there in the fall of 1950.

Again there was no sign of Gordon when I ran down the river in the twilight, and after supper I began to make ready an outfit for the trail. Jack, however, broke in on my preparations. The weather was so perfect, he said, that somebody surely must show up soon: George Boudin had gone by, not so long after Gordon, on his way from Fort Liard to Fort Simpson, and he hadn't come back either. And there were others, too, due to make a trip up the river—they couldn't *all* have gone through the ice. And then we began, all over again, to try and figure out what might be holding them: an epidemic of some kind brought in by these new-fangled mail planes? Or a gold rush? That might be it; and they had all stampeded off to stake, leaving the fort deserted, much as the men of Forty Mile on the Yukon River did at the news of Carmack's strike on the Klondike. Anyway I had better stay another day before pulling out—and life was so pleasant here at the foot of Nahanni Butte that I saw eye to eye with Jack and stayed.

So another monstrous hotcake was made next morning, and another perfect day slipped by. I snowshoed up to a point on the Butte whence I could see the Liard winding away into the blue, shimmering distance where the forest faded into the immensity of the boreal sky; but there was only the white, staring emptiness of the mile-wide river, unbroken by any tenuous thread of trail—no far-off procession of men and dogs could be seen, toiling over that frozen surface towards the Nahanni. So down again I came to the hotcake and the moose, and then to our postprandial contortions on the horizontal bar, with the afternoon sun streaming in at the open door, until it was time for the evening run down the Liard. And once more there was nothing to be seen.

That night I packed. I left the old blanket and the trackline behind, and added nothing to my personal gear but took all the food I could carry. It was a hundred and ten miles to Fort Simpson by river, the snow was deep, and there was no trail broken: it was going to take time—and so I loaded up with tea, sugar, butter, bacon, hardtack biscuits, rolled oats, raisins, a little salt and a little bit of cheese that Jack was able to spare me. I baked a bannock to do me for the first day and packed it where it wouldn't freeze—and next morning, by the light of the stars, I hit the Liard.

For a day or two it stayed around zero with the sun blazing down out of a cloudless sky. The sun's heat was reflected by the great expanse of snow, and I travelled with my hat and mitts stuffed into the pack, my jacket and shirt thrown wide open, and the sweat running down into my eyes and falling off the end of my nose in great drops into the snow. It was in this warm weather that I stopped overnight with Ole Lindberg and his Indian wife, a woman of the plains Cree, in their cabin on the right bank of the Liard: from the cabin one looked over to the Grainger River country, which was Ole's trapline, and to the great buttresses of the Nahanni Range where it swept up out of the Liard Plain, with never a foothill to mar the splendid upthrust of the mountain wall. Ole was one of those men who have a passion for firearms of all descriptions, and we spent a good part of the evening looking over his arsenal: the taking down of the Mannlicher-Schönauer bolt had defeated him up to now, and I was able to demonstrate that to him, together with a few details on the Luger action that were new to him.

He took a look at my pack. "You'll kill yourself breaking trail in this snow all the way to Simpson with that weight on your back," he said. "I have a little toboggan that I don't need. Take it and put your load on it—you'll find it easier."

Without a word Mrs. Lindberg got up and disappeared outside, returning with a small toboggan about five or six feet long by fifteen inches wide, well curved up in front. She set to work on this with wax and a flat iron till it carried a beautiful polish on the running surface: then she fastened a light line to the nose of the toboggan and spliced a short piece of line on to the longer one, making a V. On to the ends of the V she put two loops of moosehide, wide and soft: these would fit over my shoulders so that I could take the pull from them and travel with my arms free. Two lines ran along the edges of the toboggan so that a load could be lashed down to it. Mrs. Lindberg handed me the little sled with a smile. "Much better, I think," she said, and then pointed to the heavy old pack and laughed.

It *was* much better. That pack weighed forty-six pounds on Jack LaFlair's scales, and it felt a whole lot better on the toboggan than it did on my shoulders. The toboggan came nosing along after me in the little white-walled canyon that my snowshoes made for it, bunting into the walls occasionally, pulling easily over the warm-weather snow—and then, when it dropped again to forty and fifty below, grinding after me heavily and lifelessly as though it were being hauled over a pathway in the sand.

The weather changed suddenly as I was making a noonday meal on the Long Reach of the Liard—frying bacon, raisins, butter and rolled oats all in one glorious hash, keeping an eye on the tea pail and watching two young bull moose playing out on the glittering surface of the river. They circled round and round each other, coming very close and taking no notice of me at all: then quite suddenly they seemed to become aware of my presence and to take alarm. Away they went, side by side, in that long-reaching, awkward-looking, deceptive trot that has fooled many a hunter—and, as I watched them cross the river, the sun faded into a grey, racing bank of cloud and from the northeast came the moaning of the oncoming wind. I scoffed up the heartening mess in the frying pan, gulped down the scalding tea and hit out for the centre of the river: the snow was a bit more windpacked there, and the going was easier. The storm hit me head on, and the banks faded from view in the driving snow: I moved over a little to keep the south bank just in view; somewhere there, six or seven miles ahead and by a little island, was the cabin of Rouillé and McNeill, and I didn't want to miss it on a day like this. I came to it in the dusk and found it deserted: a sheet of paper lay on the table. "Left on February 3rd," it said. "Back in ten days. Make yourself at home and leave plenty of kindling when you go. R. and M." They were travelling with dogs, of course—had they, too, gone to Fort Simpson? Was all the world jammed down there at Simpson?

The cabin stood on a high cutbank looking straight north across the Liard, and all night long one could hear the howling of the wind as it raged up the river, driving before it the dry, hissing snow, piling it in drifts round the cabin like blown sand. The dawn showed nothing but a furious whirl of snow, eddying for perhaps a moment and then driving onwards. The river had vanished, blotted out in the universal greyness of the storm—even from a bush camp one would hardly venture out against this wind. By the light of a candle one could just see the thermometer outside the window: twenty-two below, it said. I re-lit the stove, rolled up in my blanket again and closed my eyes. The light was getting stronger, day was breaking—but as far as I was concerned, it seemed to me that old Jorrocks had the right idea when he said, on a certain occasion, "Let it break—it owes me nothing."

Late that afternoon, as I sat writing at the table by the window, the wind dropped and the sky cleared. The last tattered wisps of storm cloud thinned out and vanished, and the low outline of the Nahanni Range appeared once more in the west, nearly forty miles away and black and sharp against a cold, green sky. I finished my letter, and then went out and felled a dead tree, and sawed it up into stove lengths to replace the wood I had taken from the woodpile. Then I came in, lit a candle and set about getting supper. It was getting colder, I noticed: it was thirty-seven below, and the mercury was jammed tight down on the needle, so it was still dropping.

The wind rose again with the dawn, straight out of the northeast. After a few miles it rose to a screaming blast that almost rivalled that of the Meilleur River Gate, and this it maintained all day and into the night. There was an active relentless ferocity in this wind: here and there the ice was hummocky beneath the drifted snow—broken by the fall Chinooks and piled up and frozen again into huge jams—and this necessitated special care in the placing of the snowshoes. One step would be more than knee-deep into the snow, while the next might meet with some sharp ice pinnacle an inch or so beneath the surface. It was no time to make the mistake for which the wind was obviously waiting—no time to catch the rim of a snowshoe on one of these points of ice and so tip over, spraining an ankle or twisting a knee. And so all day I plugged on towards Birch River, watching the snow for signs of piled-up ice, sometimes shielding my face with my hands and always rubbing gently now a cheekbone, and now nose or chin, with the soft back of my mitts, as these exposed parts became numb with the cold. After dark I came to Birch River, and turned up it to Joseph Marie Coté's cabin. Thank God there was a light—Joe was at home. At the sudden uproar from his dogs he came to the door and peered out: "Come in, come in," he said. "This is no fit day for a sacré wolf to travel."

For a while talking was difficult; one's lips become stiffened and numbed and refuse to come together to frame the words, just as fingers and thumbs seem to lose touch sometimes after a very cold winter ride, and fumble aimlessly with the latigo strap in a vain effort to unsaddle. The stove's heat and a mug of hot, black tea, stiff with sugar, restored to me the power of speech, and I made full use of it in a brief, sizzling exposé of weather conditions on the Lower Liard in February, as they appeared to me, winding up with, "And what's the matter with this damned river? Any place I've ever been, when it got *really* cold the wind dropped. Here it rises. Why? Does it always do this?''

''Pretty much she does,'' Joe said. ''The colder she gets the harder she blows, and always upriver.''

The next day there was a good deal of hummocky ice: with the strain of hauling the toboggan through the ever-deepening snow the *mal de raquette*, the snowshoe sickness, was now beginning to appear in the right ankle, and this day made it worse. After an hour or two's travel a dirty, yellowish-looking ball climbed up out of the trees on the right bank and hung suspended in the sky, glowing feebly like a badly cleaned lantern. It was the sun, rayless and without warmth, tracing its low arc across the southern horizon; one could look it straight in the eye without blinking and see, streaming across its face, the infinitely fine snow that never ceased falling and which was whirled up the river in grey, ghostly eddies and convolutions by the savage wind. The banks and the outline of the forest showed dimly through the driving snow powder, and the trail, winding around the hummocks and made with such effort, remained only for a little time: very soon it was filled in again and levelled off by the wind, and the surface of the river was once more smooth and clean as though no man had passed that way at all. No midday halt was made that day, and lunch was a handful of raisins and a hunk of bannock and bacon eaten on the trail.

I planned to make camp near Poplar River, and in the late afternoon I plodded wearily along towards a point of trees on the north bank that seemed to offer shelter. But it was an old Indian camping place, and there was not a stick of dry wood to be found, nor was the shelter good enough. As far ahead as I could see, the north shore looked hopelessly inhospitable, but through the gathering gloom I could just make out what seemed to be the dark mass of spruce, dead opposite on the south bank. That meant crossing the river which was about three-quarters of a mile wide here; however, there was nothing else in sight, so I walked back to where I had left the toboggan, hitched myself on to it and started across. Halfway over I put the edge of my left snowshoe on to a point of ice that must have been just below the surface and took a spill into the snow, wrenching my left knee as I went down. That wasn't so good; and it was dark, and camp was still to make.

The little flat didn't look at all promising. The trees were too far apart, and there wasn't much dry wood—and I cruised around, peering into the darkness, looking for a possible campsite somewhere out of this wind that thrummed and whistled through the sparse timber. There was a little mount there, out in an open space, and I stepped over to one side to avoid it; some animal had made its burrow in the side of the mound—no, by God's truth, it hadn't, though! It was the top of a door that I could see, and the mound was the peaked roof of an old cabin; and I moved over to the door and stamped and kicked away at the snow until I was able to squat on my snowshoes and toboggan down into the cabin without knocking my brains out on the lintel.

The floor was bare of snow except where a little had fallen in through the doorway and the two empty window frames. The remains of a pole floor seemed to be underfoot, and I gathered a few chips together, took some birch bark from my pocket and built a tiny fire on the floor. By its light I looked the situation over. The cabin had been long since abandoned, but the roof looked fairly sound. The snow was almost up to the eaves—a forty-below wind might be raging up the river, but not a breath of it could come in here. The pole floor would provide ample firewood, supplemented by a little heavier stuff from the bush, and in the doorway was any amount of clean snow for tea and cooking. It was very late, and one knee and one ankle were a bit out of plumb—this was undoubtedly the place to camp; and I kicked some snow over the little fire and went off for the toboggan.

Soon I was established in there, lying on a mat of spruce branches beside the brightly burning fire. Wood lay piled in the doorway, and the fire was burning on the ground where I had ripped up the floor poles: the only trouble was the smoke which eddied around inside and was finding some difficulty in getting out of the place. However, there was always a five- or six-inch layer of smoke-free air right down on the floor, so I found myself eating my supper lying down, shovelling the food into my mouth with my face practically in the frying pan.

In the night I woke with a start; something had fallen across my feet. I drew the fire into a blaze and saw that it was a rotten roof-pole, with turf and sod frozen on to it, that had come tumbling down. I threw it aside and looked up at the roof which seemed to be sagging slightly. With the heat of this fire under it would it hold? There must be five feet of snow on top of it anyway, plus its own weight of poles, ridgepole and sod. Just then a blast of wind came roaring and blustering through the trees, and I decided that the roof had damn well *got* to hold—till I was through with it, any-how. It was over forty below outside, and an open camp on this windswept point would be no place for a Christian. So I dropped off to sleep again, for I was dog-weary, and the old cabin was warm—beautifully warm, and I slept for a long time, to be roused after three hours or so of dreamless sleep by a light that seemed to be getting stronger.

"Sunrise! Overslept!" and I sat up, vexed, stupid with sleep, and rubbing my eyes. But it was not sunrise, it was something far more serious than that. Up the log walls in two places, by the door and under a window, the flames were licking gaily—a few more minutes and the old shanty would be properly ablaze. I jumped up, grabbed a snowshoe and shovelled snow on to the burning logs from door and window: the flames went out, and the cabin became an inferno of smoke and steam. Gasping and choking I roused up the campfire on the floor and then heaved some more snow on to the steaming logs. My fire had evidently crept through some punk wood, sawdust and chips and so reached the walls: it might break out somewhere again while I slept, but all I could do now was to lay a barrier of snow between the fire and the walls and prop the heavy roof up by sheer will power. Then I slept soundly for another hour, waking to find the flames licking up the walls again in the same place as before. This was getting to be a habit; it was not easy, I could see now, to put out a fire in dry old logs with snow alone because the snowbank melted away from the log wall, leaving a space between them: this space then acted as a funnel for any available draught to fan into flame the smallest lingering spark in the half-rotten wood.

After breakfast I plastered every trace of fire in the cabin with a thick covering of snow till all seemed to be extinguished. Then I scrambled out, hauling the toboggan after me, and took a farewell look at the roof and its monstrous pile of snow. If I had got a proper sight of that roof in daylight, the evening before, would I ever have dared to camp and light a fire beneath it?

At L'Ile du Cap there was a huge piled-up jam of ice blocks to negotiate, and then scattered smaller jams. And then the low walls of the Lower Canyon of the Liard began to rise on either hand: this was the Lower Rapids; the river was half to three-quarters of a mile wide here, and there was no escape from it—no sheltering trees or wooded points offered refuge from the searing wind. There was only one break in the canyon walls that I knew of for certain, and that was where the Big Stone Creek came in from the south. I headed for it and reached it in good time, with daylight in hand. The creek had overflowed and then frozen again like iron. I left the sled sitting on the ice and clattered up the creek to look for a camping place: without the drag of the toboggan and with a firm, hard surface to walk on, I seemed to move absolutely without effort, and I had the curious feeling of being pushed from behind.

The little canyon of Big Stone Creek goes straight south for a hundred yards or two and then swings east. I knew that bend; I had waded up to it two summers ago on a blazing July day when the thermometer on our boat ticked up a hundred and seven in the shade; fat, ripe wild strawberries were growing there then, close to a great drift of old snow; and I had noticed, in the angle of the bend, a little shelf or bench that might now give me a camping place.

Late that night, as I lay stretched out before the fire, listening to the howling of the wind out on the Liard, I knew that I was lucky to be tucked away in the gorge of the Big Stone Creek. It was well over forty below, the snow was a little heavier, and the wind on the open river was blowing a full gale. Caught by some accident out on the Liard and between those canyon walls, no man could have lived through that night's storm. Here, in this nest in the snow up on the bench, it was not too bad. Wood had not been too plentiful, but there was lots of alder, and I had a huge pile of that—an encouraging sort of wood when dead because a man can snowshoe up to a standing tree of it, eight to ten inches thick, and hit it a clout with his mitted hand; down comes the tree, and a child can carry it back to the fire to add its clear, sparkless flame to the blaze. Squaw wood, some people call it contemptuously, but I felt most grateful to it that night as I toasted myself at the glowing fire. The snow was hellish deep, and more was falling: I had dug down with a snowshoe nearly five feet to make my campsite, but that made it all the warmer now, with the white walls reflecting the heat from every side. Now and then an eddying gust blew a whirl of snow powder under the lean-to, but, on the whole, camp was pretty snug.

The morning was decidedly less cheery: the bellowing of the wind as it raved up the Liard was disheartening, and it was most foully cold.[1] This was the fourth day of the storm, and nobody else, or course, was fool enough to travel—indeed, it was almost impossible to travel with dogs pulling much of a load on a day like this. I had pushed on from Joe Coté's cabin in spite of his urging me to stay and wait for better weather, and now I had the bull by the tail and couldn't let go—I had to get out and travel, whether I liked it or not: I couldn't sit here just grinning at the campfire all day.

There was a Hudson's Bay Company cache about eight or nine miles away, at the foot of the rapids. Nobody would be there but, if my knee and ankle got worse, I could probably camp there and take enough grub to keep me going till I could travel again, paying for it when I reached Fort Simpson. So I hobbled on down the river, helped quite often through the stretch of rapids by the hard, firm road of overflow: then the snow got deep again and the going bad, though there was no more piled-up ice. The wind never let up, and most of the time that day I had to go along with my head down and my hands in their big, gauntlet mitts over my face. Even so, I froze my cheeks a little for the first time and, unable to swing my arms freely, found my hands getting cold.

---

[1]When I reached Fort Simpson I checked the temperature for these last few days on the government thermometer. The maximum for this day was forty-five below zero.

The end of the trail came just after I had spotted the roof of the Bay cache in a clearing on the right bank: the *mal de raquette* suddenly took complete charge, and I found myself unable to move an inch. Something had to be done about it right away, so I fished my blanket out of my packsack, put it over my head and shoulders and sat down on the toboggan with my back to the wind—one small insignificant splash of colour in the greyness of the storm. While I massaged my ankle I chewed away at a hardtack biscuit and made an estimate of the distance from where I was sitting to the cache—it looked a long way for a lame man. The snow came hissing past me as I sat there, and when I rose to go my trail had all but vanished; all that remained was the hollow round the toboggan, and even my blanket was drifted over with an inch or so of fine snow.

At the foot of the river bank, below the cache, I found a trail up which I slowly and painfully hauled the toboggan. As I topped the rise and moved forward into the trees a great clamouring of dogs broke out: there were tents back there—and, as I looked, an old Indian emerged from one of them, stared at me and then came forward, holding out his hand.

"Bad day!" he said as we shook hands, including the whole desolate scene in one sweeping gesture. "Ba-ad day!" and he pointed to a tent. I took off my snowshoes and unlashed my pack: the Indian put the shoes and the little sled up on to a rack on which dog sleds, camp gear and other snowshoes were piled, out of reach of the dogs—and in a couple of seconds I had stepped out of the bitter wind and into the warmth of a red-hot, roaring camp-stove. A place was made for me on the spruce mat, and I sat down gratefully and loosened my mackinaw—the temperature had risen rather suddenly for me by about a hundred and thirty degrees.

I had fallen in with a hunting party of Slave Indians—three families—on their way south to Trout Lake, and denned up here waiting for the storm to pass. They had water ready melted, so I made tea and thawed myself out and gave them news of the Nahanni country in a queer mixture of English and French. I had met some of them two years previously almost at this very spot:

they remembered me, and apparently they knew that I had been again up the Nahanni and were now under the impression that I had snowshoed down all the way from the Flat River, which they called the Too-Naga.

Later on they brought out fiddles and mouth organs, and a concert started up. Here and there I could detect a tune that was known to me such as "Loch Lomond" or "Camptown Races," or those old-time northern favourites "Turkey in the Straw" and "Bonaparte's Retreat." But to all these tunes of an alien race they contrived to impart a certain haunting monotony of rhythm that had in it all the melancholy, hopeless desolation of this frozen land—a rhythm that was well suited to the season and the place.

I dozed off, lulled by the warmth and by the low-pitched voices as they chanted in time to the music. The old man roused me later on and led me to an empty tent which was to be mine for the night. There was a stove in it, and a spruce mat and some wood. I lit the stove and then went out and cut more boughs and more wood: soon I was comfortable and cooking my supper by the dim light from the draught hole of the stove: things were not too bad at all, though I could see that the night was going to be a cold one for me—a small campstove cannot hold a lasting fire without being fed pretty steadily, and a tent holds no heat: it is warm just so long as the stove is going.

Later in the evening I found that one of the young men was going next day to Fort Simpson with an empty dog sled, so I made a deal with him to throw my sled and packsack into his cariole and travel with him; somehow, I figured, I could keep up with him. The name of that Indian I could not catch: it sounded like Carolus, so Carolus he became to me.

That night it dropped to fifty-three below. I slept somehow, rolled in my blanket and my tarp and dreaming of the roaring campfires of the last few days. At intervals I sat up and prodded and fed the stove into activity once more but, putting it mildly, it was a disturbed night, and I was glad when breakfast time came round and I could put on the porridge. And then Carolus stuck his face in and said, "I think better we go," and we loaded up and hit the trail by the feeble light of another dirty dawn.

That Indian was fresh and rested, and he lit out down the Liard
as if the devil himself was right on his tail. In front of him went his
dogs going all out, for they had no load to pull and the trail was
well broken: it was drifted over and almost invisible, but it had
been used all winter, packed down by snowshoes and then drifted
in by the wind, and the process repeated again and again till it
was a wall of solid snow right down to the river ice. It wouldn't
quite support a man without snowshoes of some sort: running in
moccasins alone one would break through. But small trail shoes
were all that one needed: Carolus had them, while I had still only
my five-footers, and I clattered after him in these, cursing them,
my knee, the *mal de raquette* and the Indian right straight from the
heart. We were out to make Fort Simpson by nightfall: ''All
right,'' I thought, ''even if I never walk again,'' and I hung on
like grim death in the wake of the flying Indian.

Again the maximum was forty-five below. There was the same
damned wind and the same mad-looking snow devils whirled up
the surface of the river. And there was no dodging this icy blast:
we were travelling fast and, when running, one needs to look
ahead and one's hands must be free to swing. And so the tears
drawn by the wind ran down our unprotected faces and froze on
our cheeks, and Carolus froze his face a little and I froze mine a
bit more—and the miles went by.

Around midday Carolus swung in towards the west bank on a
well-beaten trail and urged his team up into the bush. I climbed
painfully after him and found a great mat of spruce boughs there,
with a windbreak of boughs and brush piled all around. In front
of the mat smoke curled from a still-warm fire. Carolus mumbled
something about ''Matou here last night—good,'' and blew the
fire into flame, while I rooted into the pack and unearthed a frying pan and tea pail. The ice slid off our faces, and very soon the
tea water was boiling. Carolus had only some strips of moose fat,
so we threw them into the frying pan along with boiling water and
the last of the raisins, butter and rolled oats—it was Simpson
tonight or bust, now! I made tea like ink and recklessly flung in
the last of my sugar. Carolus, I was sure, had none; he was count-
ing, poor trusting fool, on the all-providing white man—in this

case, a broken reed.

Warmth and energy flowed back into us as we lay and rested there and ate and drank. The cold ebbed slowly from lips and chin, and it became possible to discuss the trail ahead of us. The discussion was quite short, and I can reproduce the whole of it in detail:

Carolus: "I guess we make Simpson tonight."

R.M.P.: "I guess so."

And silence fell again upon the camp.

The afternoon for me was a hell of stabbing pain and awkward movement. As the light faded the snow became a little heavier, and the east shoreline vanished into the storm: my world, as seen through a curtain of frosted eyelashes, was a vast, white emptiness through which a dog team and an Indian were running at a steady jog. They had always been there, and they always would be there—there was no end to it. And I must always keep just behind—always the same distance—and I must never lose ground, no matter what speed the fleeing ghost in front of me chose to travel. And a couple of hours went by.

Suddenly the dog team broke out of the straight, floundered through some deep snow and then seemed to get on to a well-broke trail that ran straight towards the west bank. Carolus followed cursing a blue streak in his own tongue. The dogs went up the bank and into the bush with Carolus after them. A devilish uproar of dogs broke loose: men were evidently here. I topped the bank just in time to see Carolus disentangle his team and swing them about: they had imprudently hit straight towards the spruce by the cabin where Sammy and Bloody Poilu were tied—the Indian didn't know how lucky he was to get them away so easily from those two hellhounds. In a tree nearby a rifle was hanging—a queer-looking rifle with a home-made stock to it, hand-hewed out of birch. I had made that stock; it was Gordon's Mauser—and as I stood staring at it he came out of the cabin and ran towards me.

The cabin was Harry McGurran's. He had moved up there from Simpson, with his wife and family, in the last few days. Fed

up with waiting for the storm to end, Gordon, Ludovic Mac-
donald and Ian Macaulay had made up a convoy and pulled out
of the fort that very afternoon. The other two men were headed
for Fort Liard, and Gordon had had to wait at Fort Simpson till
they were ready to leave: one man alone can't break trail for dogs
and a heavy load in deep snow and make any sort of time; and it is
customary, anyway, to travel two or three together if it can be arranged—the Mounted Police prefer it and sometimes insist on it
in the winter storms.

After supper I sat on a bunk in a corner of the cabin, listening
to Gordon's story of his Odyssey. In the swamping of his canoe in
the Lower Canyon on Christmas Eve he had lost almost all of his
own grub but had saved the dog feed. So he dealt himself a bit of
that and lost no time on the trail down through The Splits to
South Nahanni: in fact he travelled quite a bit in the dark and
gained little by it, for he went almost clean under the Nahanni ice
just below Jackfish River and had to stop and make camp there
and dry out. That and his Christmas swim in the Canyon, plus
the devil dance around the blazing driftpile in his birthday suit,
probably did him a bit of no good, for he was a pretty sick man for
the first fifty miles down the Liard. Then, luckily, he recovered
for he travelled the remaining sixty miles or so in the big blizzard,
when four and a half feet of snow fell on Fort Simpson and the
Lower Liard, arriving in Simpson almost out of grub and with his
face nicely frozen—just like mine was now. Finally the mail plane
had been long delayed, and by the time it reached the fort more
snow had fallen. Then a cat-and-mouse period had ensued during
which the various would-be travellers for the Liard—individual-
ists and non-co-operators to a man, or they wouldn't have been in
the N.W.T.—sat around eyeing each other to see who was going
to be the goat who would lose patience and get out and break the
trail for the rest. It becomes finally a question of who can least afford further delay: Gordon got fed up with the performance and
organised this little convoy of three—and here they were at Harry
McGurran's, ten miles from the fort. Carolus and I must have
run twenty miles that day.

And now I was unfit to travel—the knee was extremely painful and my right foot and ankle were so swollen with the *mal de raquette* that every bone had vanished utterly—five podgy-looking toes stuck out from a pudding-shaped object that had lost all resemblance to a foot. So in the morning we slung our load into McGurran's cache, I paid off Carolus and was loaded into the cariole, wrapped in my blanket and Gordon's eiderdown, the dogs were hitched up, and we hit the trail for Simpson.

It had dropped to fifty below in the night, but the wind had dropped also, and now the sun was shining out of a pale blue sky, and there were only a few glittering particles of frost falling. A thin, small breeze, keen as a sword blade, was blowing from the north-east. I lay there, snug and protected in the cariole, listening to the squeaking of Gordon's snowshoes on the cold, packed snow, and to the squeal and slither of the dog toboggan beneath me. The dogs made no sound: there were five of them now—Poilu and Mam'selle and their two sons, Sammy and Quiz, and a husky Gordon had bought in Simpson called Spud, a humble unobtrusive beast: he had to be that, I thought, to be allowed to live and eat alongside our bunch of wolves. The puppies had been sold—and I remembered with a smile their comical antics around the home cabin in Deadmen Valley.

By twisting my head back I could just see Gordon's nose sticking out beneath the furred hood of his parka. It was the only bit of him that I could see, and it was bobbing up and down as he ran behind the toboggan, holding on to the long oak handles.

"Frozen your face yet, Gordon?"

"No, not yet, George. But don't worry—I will."

We always dressed alike—the same khaki shirts, the same heavy, dark blue mackinaw, the same red scarves—and it was only fitting that we should arrive at the fort with the same sort of frost patches on our faces, around which we should have to guide our razors, looking, as a result, like two identically trimmed poodles.

I was very warm and comfortable and becoming rather sleepy, when I heard Gordon speak to the dogs and felt the toboggan swing off the trail into the deep snow and come to a stop. Two loaded sleds squealed past going in the opposite direction, and I heard Gordon move away on his snowshoes. There was a mumbling of men's voices from a little distance, and then several pairs of snowshoes squeaked back over the protesting snow towards the cariole. Frost-rimed faces in frosty-looking fur hats and wolverine-lined parka hoods broke into my small patch of blue sky: Gordon rubbing his nose and cheeks, Harrington and McAra of the R.C.M.P. from Fort Simpson, and an Indian. The two policemen and I exchanged greetings.

"Matthews tells me," Harrington said, "that you've just broken trail for us all the way from South Nahanni? And you travelled alone?"

"Yes."

"Well, shake hands again. And let me tell you this—if ever you're overdue or in any trouble up in those mountains of yours, don't count on the police sending out a patrol to look for you. After this solo trip of yours we'll just figure you're all right wherever you are and that you'll show up sometime!"

Which was one of the greatest compliments I've ever had paid to me.

And then we parted. The two policemen were travelling with two dog teams and two Indian fore-runners, making patrol up the Liard to the British Columbia boundary. Nobody in Fort Simpson, Gordon said, had ever heard a whisper about the impending patrol—firstly, perhaps, because there was not much sense in advertising a patrol ahead of its time—but also, no doubt, because even these Olympians were men, too, like the rest of us, and didn't mind having a bit of trail broken for them, free of charge. In this instance, owing to my unscheduled trip, they got the whole thing handed to them on a plate. "We followed your trail the whole way to Jack LaFlair's," Harrington told me in the police barracks the following May. "Sometimes we got off it a bit, but we always worked back on to it again. We used your camps and your tea places, all the way. . . ."

The squeal of the toboggan over the snow and the warmth of the eiderdown were making me sleepy again. This was the way to travel, there could be no doubt about it—and I began to speculate drowsily upon the reputations that some of the old Hudson's Bay Company officers had built up as travellers. Sir George Simpson, for instance, and many another. What did they do? They sat in canoes with their top hats rammed well down on their heads, or in carioles well wrapped up in their furs, looking like the traditional Mr. Noah of the Ark or the Czar of all the Russias according to the season of the year, while skilled men plied the paddle or drove their dogs for them, and took the hardship and the weariness, the rain and the snow . . . just like me, with Gordon driving the dogs. . . .

I was roused from my dreams by Gordon shouting to the dogs: we were going uphill, and the trail was no longer smooth.

"Where's this, Gordon?"

"Coming up out of the snye on to Simpson Island. Right behind the Mission. And, since you made rather a point of it, while you were snoring away down there I've kept my promise and frozen my face!"

"We'd better have a look at that bookshelf of McIntyre's," Gordon was saying. "He said we could borrow a few, and we might just as well; we've read everything we've got about six times over, and I can make room in the load. . . ."

It was the day of departure, and we were up at the R.C.M.P. barracks, straightening up the dog feed account and saying our farewells. I was in travelling shape again and, what was equally important, the cold snap was over. The north wind was gone, and it had warmed up to ten below; it was probably Chinooking at South Nahanni, but ten below was pretty balmy for Fort Simpson; now was the time to hit the trail while the going was good.

Fort Simpson had been a pleasant interlude. We had stayed at Andy Whittington's "hotel," the only hostelry on the Mackenzie, but many other ports of call had been open to us—Inspector Moorhead's house, Flynn Harris's well-stocked library, the Bay, the Wireless Station. . . . But, above all, the barracks where our dogs were corralled and fed and where we were welcome at all times of day to read, write, gossip and bathe the injured foot that held us in the fort.

We invaded McIntyre's room and picked out a couple of the Everyman classics, an Oppenheim or two and *The Lives, Heroic*

Deeds and Sayings of Gargantua and his Son Pantagruel by Dr. Francis
Rabelais. The last one would take some reading, and it looked as
if it would improve our vocabulary to boot. And now all that remained to do was to hitch up the dogs and pull out.

McIntyre and Johnny Robb were there to see us go. "We'll see
you in the spring," McIntyre said. "And 'Patterson's Porridge'[1]
is on the police menu from now on: the indent for raisins and
cheese is going up; that's one souvenir you're leaving behind!"

I had taught them that bush breakfast mixture of mine, and it
now seemed certain that, as long as the tradition lasted, the
Mounties of the Liard-Mackenzie country would be a fatter and a
better nurtured race of men, impervious to storm and frost. That
was some slight return for all their kindness to us.

The afternoon shadows were lengthening when we left the fort.
We jogged easily up the Liard trail in the twilight and slept that
night at Harry McGurran's.

Next morning it was down to forty below again with a strong
wing blowing upriver and drifting the snow. We hit the trail in the
half darkness and in a blinding whirl of snow dust: we were
travelling south this time, with the wind, so that we didn't have to
worry about freezing our faces: Gordon, however, was none too
happy about the dogs.

"With this wind behind them," he said, "it'll drive the snow
right into their coats, next to the skin. It'll melt there and then
freeze again till their coats are just a mass of ice: then their insula-
tion'll be gone, and they'll freeze at night. If it goes on like this
we'll have to stop."

However, we travelled on. I was running with my snowshoes
on, feeling for the hard-packed trail under the new snow, occasionally stepping off it to one side or the other, then back on again
with the next step. The dogs followed me, and Gordon ran
behind, without snowshoes, taking part of his weight on the
toboggan handles. We went for some miles like this, and the day
lightened, bringing with it no cheer: it was grey and foul and getting colder and altogether worse.

[1]See Chapter 2, page 69.

Something happened to the husky's harness, and Gordon halted the team and stepped off the trail into the soft snow to go forward and fix it: with surprising suddenness he disappeared right in up to his hips, just like the sawed-off lady in the conjuring trick and a worried look came over his face.

"I'm in about a foot of water," he said. "We'll have to get to shore and make a fire."

Some warm spell far away to the westward had raised the Liard, or else the river ice had sagged beneath the tremendous weight of snow: whichever it was there was a flow of water and slush coming over the ice, insulated from the frost by three or four feet of snow, and Gordon had found it. He clawed hold of the solid wall of the trail and hoisted himself back onto it: I pulled his snowshoes out from under the lashings and laid them ready for him, and then I set to work and broke a trail to the bank which was about a quarter of a mile away. Up I went: the axe whirled and the chips flew, and by the time Gordon stuck his nose over the crest there was a nest made in the snow and a fire was blazing against a big, fallen tree: slowly his frozen moccasins and socks became limp again, and he was able to change into dry things. And while he did that I went on upstream through the trees: there was something there that I had seen from the river—a cabin roof or something very like one. . . .

Sure enough there was a cabin, old and deserted but fairly windproof: cheesecloth and flour sacking covered its two windows, and the stove had no damper and was rusty and full of holes, but the door was sound and there was a good log floor: it would do. I went back to Gordon, and we had lunch by the blazing fire. Out on the river it was one hell of a day by now: it must have been about fifty below, and a screaming storm was driving from the north, worse even than the jewel of a day that Carolus and I had spent together on this stretch of trail. A man alone could have travelled on south, but with dogs—no.

That storm raged for three nights and two more days—a period upon which I shall always look back with kindly memories. We had only opened certain business letters in Simpson, but now, comfortably installed in the old cabin (and by "comfortably" I mean that, if we wore fur hats and our complete outdoor clothing all the time and kept near the stove, we were warm and sheltered from the howling blizzard outside), we fell upon the Christmas mail and discovered all kinds of exotic luxuries. There were letters to read and papers, a vast plum pudding, a box of excellent cigars, some most expensive chocolates and a medium-sized Stilton cheese that came if you whistled to it. In the evenings, when the dogs were all seen to and the chores done, we would lie by the stove on our eiderdowns full of plum pudding, perhaps smoking a Ramon Allones or dipping into the gorgeous, half-frozen chocolates, reading out loud, by the light of the two flickering candles, some Rabelaisian titbit. . . And then, from the river, would come again the screaming of the wind, the stovepipes would rattle, and the shadows dance in the wavering candle light—and the old ruin would seem most incredibly snug.

On the third morning the storm weakened: by noon it was clear and utterly still, and we hit the river trail for the Hudson's Bay cache and the Indian hunting camp where I had sheltered on my way down. And a devil of a trail it was: packed down all winter by the Indians, it now stood, a wall of solid snow, practically ice, from the river ice to the surface. The storm had swept the softer snow away from it on both sides until driving a dog team along it was like trying to drive it along the top of a wide garden wall.

It got worse as we neared the cache where the Indians had been travelling to and fro: the heavily loaded sled would teeter over to one side and perhaps flop right off the trail into the soft snow in spite of all Gordon could do on the handles: then we would have to brace our feet against the wall of the trail and haul the sled back on again by the lash ropes—no easy feat when wearing snowshoes. With the constant stoppages the dogs became sulky and balky, and at the slightest change of rhythm they would stop of their own accord and look round at Gordon in a maddening sort of way as if they were laughing at him. His patience was fading fast; the breaking point was obviously not far ahead. And there was nothing I could do: I couldn't lead the dogs, the trail was like a rock already without my assistance, and I couldn't run alongside the sled and steady it. The camp and cache were in plain view, about a mile ahead—it would be better if I removed myself.

"Give me the key to the Bay shack, Gordon, and I'll go ahead and cut wood and get a fire going for supper."

"A good idea," he said, with a face like a thunderstorm. "This is a one-man show the way this—trail is just here. I may shoot these bloody dogs shortly. . . ." He was speaking with great restraint.

I greeted the Indians, opened up the cabin and lit the fire. I cut and split some wood, and then I took a couple of buckets and went out on the trail to the river and the waterhole. The trail dropped steeply off the little bluff down to the river and there, right on the edge of the high bank, I found the Indians—every man, woman and child. They were motionless; their mouths were open but no sound came from them; they faced downstream, their eyes shone with pleasure and enjoyment, and their common attitude was one of acute, terrier-like interest: I thought they had gone mad. I, too, looked down the river. Perhaps four hundred yards away, or a bit less, in the yellow light of a perfect sunset, the outfit was coming up the trail at a tremendous speed with Gordon jogging happily after them: he would soon be here at that rate, I thought. And there was nothing odd that I could see about the performance— just a dog team travelling: these Indians must be cuckoo. . . .

Suddenly the picture changed: Gordon exerted some slight leverage on the handles to keep the toboggan on the trail, and the five dogs stopped dead as if on a word of command: the toboggan slid up against the huskie who promptly bit Quiz in the back end, while the other three sat down with their tongues hanging out and looked round towards Gordon, wagging their tails gently backwards and forwards on the snow.

Gordon said afterwards that he could have borne it with patience if they hadn't wagged their damned tails at him.

I saw my partner raise two arms towards the sky and stand thus, motionless, for perhaps a couple of seconds. The Indians nudged each other and smiled: this was what they had been waiting for—about the fourth encore, I gathered later.

Gordon walked slowly forward till he stood by Poilu. Suddenly

he broke out into a wild torrent of cursing: he swore with drive
and power like the Nahanni in flood time; he cursed viciously,
fluently and with imagination; he damned every abject dog in
turn and took its ancestry apart separately; then he took the team
as a whole and consigned it to various hells, including, in this section, a certain prideful eastern city. Then he rambled off into the
bypaths of theology, mythology and demonology till one wondered whether the whole assembled company would not be struck
dead. It was zero and perfectly still, and every blistering word
clicked into place with an audible snap. It was the best thing those
Indians had ever heard, and they were appreciating it, but I, who
had once shocked an Australian gunner with the savage virulence
of an impassioned curse, was appalled.

Gordon went back to the rear, took a gaily coloured, Cree dog-
driver's whip from under the lashings and swung it round his
head. The crack and a blood-curdling yell reached the little party
on the bluff simultaneously: the dog team cringed and crept forward, gathering speed. . . .

I mention these delays because they alone can account for the
welcome vision that was vouchsafed us on the following morning.
The going was easier above the Indian camp: the trail had to be
broken, but it was no longer cocked up in the air above the surrounding snow, and the dogs were working well. They plugged
forward steadily with Gordon handling the toboggan. I would run
ahead for a stretch, then back to the outfit and then forward
again, thus making, in effect, three men over the trail to pack it
down and give a firm footing for the dogs. We were going up the
Lower Rapids towards midday when, on one of my return trips to
the toboggan, I saw, away downstream, a man come into sight
round the point of a cliff. His head was down, and he was leaning
forward and travelling fast: his arms were swinging wildly to
counterbalance the lurching gait of a man on snowshoes. I whistled
gently and pointed: Gordon stopped the dogs and looked back;
dog teams and more men were coming into view. He turned to
me with a grin spreading slowly over his face.

"Well, I'm damned," he said. "I must say they kept it quiet
well. The dirty dogs—if it hadn't been for that storm we'd have

broken trail for them all the way to South Nahanni. They're travelling light, I see, so now the joke's on our side. It would be a shame to hold them back. . . ." And we began to laugh: it was the old cat-and-mouse game, and we had bought it properly. No ill-will ever attached to these performances; it was always a simple case of devil take the foremost which, in this instance, had been us.

Jonas Lafferty was coming up, flailing away at the trail like a man possessed. His head was still down, and the first thing he saw was Gordon's snowshoes. He halted and looked up, staring wildly.

"Morning, Jonas," we said cheerfully.

"Gosh," he said, "we thought you'd be further ahead than this. You both came down in such damn' terrible weather we thought you always travelled in storms."

Gordon pointed to the dogs. "Police dogs," he said, "not huskies. Wind behind. Too much snow drifting. Freeze their coats."

"We should have thought of that," Jonas said sadly.

We pulled out, and one by one they passed us, a convoy of fur traders, shouting cheery greetings. They were all on foot behind their sleds except D— of the H. B. Co., the dreamer of strange dreams and Jack Stanier's partner to be.[1] He was riding in his cariole like an archbishop: most regrettably he was in the lead, for his sled, top heavy with his shifting weight, fell frequently off the trail, to be dragged along half on its side by the struggling dogs until it chose to climb back again of its own accord on to the level. The trail was thus largely spoiled for those who came behind, and D—, like a certain racehorse, was "damned by all who followed him."

We caught up with them in the evening; they were camped, as luck would have it, on the very point where I had passed the night in the burning cabin. We pulled up to the fire, unhitched the dogs and made supper, and, as we did so, a breath of warm air from the west came sighing through the spruce, spilling the snow from the laden branches: it was the Chinook, the first whisper of the distant spring. Coming right on top of the intense cold it felt as if

[1]See Chapter 1.

the poplar buds were on the point of bursting into leaf: parkas and
fur hats were thrown aside, mitts were taken off, and men moved
casually and easily, while the dogs, sprawled on their spruce mats
with the gentle breeze ruffling their coats, stretched, yawned and
slept in comfort as though winter had never been.

The fire sank in the night some three feet into the snow: breakfast was eaten at dawn, and the party sat around on the edges of
the vertical-sided pit, toasting its moccasined feet above the glowing embers down below. After we had loaded up and hitched up
the dogs Gordon and I snowshoed back into the bush to inspect
the old cabin that had been my refuge from the storm. But there
was nothing to be found—only a smooth, white hollow in the
snow and a couple of scorched trees. I looked at Gordon and he
looked at me, and without a word we turned away towards the
open river where the sun, the emblem of life, was climbing over
the glittering tree tops into the warm blue sky.

By the afternoon the warmth was softening up the trail: a little
more and it would have been impossible to travel, so we decided
to move in future by moonlight while the Chinook weather lasted,
and to camp and sleep in the warm part of the day. We pulled in
that evening to the Rouillé and McNeill cabin: they were at
home, and altogether there was an appalling pile-up there of men
and dogs: we humans slept in the cabin, jammed together on the
bunks, on the floor, on the table and under the table, while outside there must have been sixty dogs, or more, all huskies or
variations on the husky theme except for our four Alsatians. It
was full moon and, in the distance, timber wolves were howling.
Invariably it would be one of our Alsatians that had to answer
with its sharp, piercing bark (they never howled) that cut through
the deepest slumber. The other three would chime in with an explosion of sound and, before the weary sleepers could get out
more than a strangled growl of wrath, sixty huskies would lift
their heads to the moon in a long-drawn, melodious howl of in-
describable sadness. It was more than human nerves could stand.
Quietly we rose, fell over a few people, warmed up the stove and
cooked breakfast. Then we hitched up our little bunch of
songsters and fled up the river ice at full speed, black silhouettes

against the moonlit snow.

And so it went, and we travelled in the night frost by the light of the moon, and on into the morning until we began to break through the hard surface of the trail. And the bell-shaped mountain, the Butte, came closer, and the dim, blue shadows on the wall of the Nahanni Range began to be seen as clefts and coulees. Through the sunlit afternoon we slept, men and dogs, waking to suppertime and sunset behind the mountains—for it was March and the days were lengthening.

The convoy of the fur traders was strung out now, and the snow froze at night into a harsh pattern of diamonds made by the passage of many snowshoes, and on this, before the sun could soften it, the straining dogs would cut their feet. So we fitted them with moccasins—little round bags of moosehide tied at the first joint—twenty paws to fit into twenty little sacks at midnight before starting, each one with a muttered, "Hold still, blast you—don't you know I'm trying to do you good?" And if we lost dog moccasins that was the least of our worries—the trail was littered with them, scattered by those ahead of us.

The Chinook and the warm sunshine put a glistening "skin," a faint crust, on the surface of the snow and, as one rose and fell with the snowshoes, up and down, the sun flashed from the glittering crust with a weird, mirage-like effect. Soon snow glasses were making their appearance and shady hats, while others ringed their eyes with charcoal, thus achieving a curious wall-eyed, even clownish, appearance. Of all the travellers I alone remained unaffected by this blaze of light.

The fur traders went on towards Fort Liard, but we turned aside into the mouth of the South Nahanni with myself in the lead feeling for my old trail, now buried deep under the February snows. As I went to and fro, breaking trail ahead of the dogs, I noticed far behind, away down the Liard, a moving speck. Slowly it resolved itself into a man and a dog team and it, too, turned into the Nahanni, following our trail. Shortly after we had arrived at Jack LaFlair's post, a well-matched team of dogs struggled up over the bank followed by their smiling, dark-goggled owner. It was Johnny Sanderson of Fort Simpson, the grand champion, the ultimate, indisputable winner in the cat-and-mouse game. Breathing never a word of his impending trip he had let the complete zoo get well clear of the fort: then, in perfect weather and with a trail like a paved highway, he had broken all records to South Nahanni. It was game, set and match to Johnny, there could be no doubt about that. Reverently we stepped forward and congratulated him.

6

Awakening of the River

"The sap was rising in the trees, and daily the trickle of unseen steamlets became louder as the frozen land came back to life."

Burning Daylight, Jack London

Jack took a look at his three guests and disappeared into the cabin to start supper on its way. In the course of the evening he produced a couple of the verbal distortions for which he was famous: talking of a new building that he was going to put up in the coming year he remarked that he planned to start the "excavication" for the cellar as soon as the frost was out of the ground, and later, replying to a question of mine about the Indians' names, he said that they all had two—an Indian name in their own language and a Christian name, a white-man name, such as Amos, Joseph or Paul—"all Bibolical names," he said. "The priests wouldn't give them anything else. . . ."

Long before daylight Gordon and I hit the trail. Jack was up to see us off, and as we left he shouted after us, "Be sure, now, and bring me down a choke-cherry for my garden. You'll find them at the Hot Springs. Don't forget." We reassured him and pushed on up the Nahanni by the light of a low moon. Down on the river it was cold and still, but around the summit of the Butte the Chinook was whispering gently to itself. The day was going to be warm.

Poole Field had gone up the river, Jack said, and was trapping somewhere up North Pass Creek, the creek that led out of the

245

elbow of The Splits towards the North Nahanni. We had some
business with him so, on the second day out from LaFlair's post,
we turned aside from the river and followed his trail. . . .

Three days later we came out from the shadow of the Little
Butte and into Deadmen Valley. The Chinook was still blowing,
and the trail had been good. The open places in the Lower Canyon had frozen over, and there had been a good deal of overflow
which had converted the deep snow of January into solid ice over
which the sled slipped easily without any effort from the dogs: only
in the last few miles, from the Little Butte to the cabin, did the
snow lie deep enough on the river to give us trouble.

All was well at the cabin. A wolverine had investigated the
stovepipe and had a good go at my window shutters, but had
given it up as a bad job and turned his attention to the cache.
There the overhang of the platform and the sheeting of tin on the
uprights had defeated him, and he had contented himself with
clawing at a fish-net that he could just reach between the poles.
We opened things up and dug the woodpile out, and, while I
shovelled a tremendous pile of snow off the roof, Gordon got a fire
going and packed the toboggan load into the cabin. Soon we were
at home, and life fell back into the normal routine of the trapline,
sweetly and easily as though it had never been disturbed. The
weather completed the illusion: our very first dawn in the valley
broke grey and cold with the wind in the east and the snow driving up the river. Winter had resumed its sway.

With it came a run of marten, and we were kept busy from
dawn to dusk out on the line and through the evenings dealing
with the fur. The weeks slipped by and, with the approach of
spring, we began to think of our light canoe, marooned down in
the Lower Canyon where Gordon had left it at Christmas. We
still had our business to complete with Poole Field, and that involved a trip to South Nahanni. We waited for a good spell of
weather, and then Gordon threw a light outfit into the cariole,
hitched up the dogs and hit the trail for Nahanni Butte and Jack
LaFlair's. I broke trail for him as far as the Little Butte and
watched him running down the Cache Riffles and out of sight
behind the Island. . . .

I camped that night up Ram Creek and got back home the following afternoon with a couple of weasel and a nice marten in my pack. I threw the door open, lit the fire and put the tea pail on the stove. Then I sharpened a knife, hunted up a fur stretcher of the right size and sat down to fix up the marten. . . .

A shadow fell across the pool of sunlight on the floor: I looked up and saw an Indian standing in the doorway. Not being addicted to jumps and sudden starts I contrived to show no surprise, which was the reverse of what I felt. "Good day," I said. "Come in and sit down. I make tea soon."

The Indian stepped in over the sill log and sat down on Gordon's bunk without a word or a sign or any faintest flicker of expression on his face. I pushed the marten aside and put another stick in the stove—and turned round to see a second Indian standing in the doorway, as completely expressionless as the first. Soon he, too, was seated on Gordon's bunk, and this went on until eight graven images had silently taken their places in the cabin. There they sat watching me intently; no murmur came from them nor any sign, and the place looked like some primitive woodcut that might well have been entitled "The Council House."

So these were the Nahanies, the people, Michael Mason had written, who were hostile to strangers. Right at this moment one friendly word would have met with a ready response from me—if they could speak at all, which I was beginning to doubt. I busied myself with the tea. For the first Indian I had left my own tea pail boiling on the stove. After three or four had turned up I put a large pot on to warm up. But now, for this mob, I filled and set on the stove the big, lidded, aluminum bucket that we had used for rendering the bear's lard; and at the sight of this bucket with its promise of much tea the Indians nudged each other and grinned. They were thawing out, physically as well as mentally, for the day was cold.

While the water was heating I asked a question or two and was answered by signs: they had come, it seemed, from the west, and they pointed towards the Meilleur River. How, I wondered, had they gone up from South Nahanni? Up some river in the Yukon Territory?

They seemed quiet enough and peaceful—and I thought of the sinister reputation that rumour had assigned to them. Here was I alone with them, and, by all the rules, I ought very shortly to be headless. Yet there was no sign of immediate action, and they were intensely interested in the preparations for tea. The water was boiling now in the bucket: I threw in a huge handful of Orange Pekoe, followed it up with about half a pound of sugar and stirred the bubbling concoction vigorously with a stick. A murmur of satisfaction went round, and from a shadowy corner came, in a deep voice, "*Lots* of tea!" followed by a quiet chuckle. So they were not mute, after all.

Chief Factor Edward Smith, writing from Fort Simpson in November 1829, says of these Indians: "In return for good usage they are obedient and willing to please—in their general character there is something secret and treacherous and once irritated very sanguinary—numerous and in a rich country might be very independent if it were not for their habits of indolence."[1]

Yet another Indian appeared in the doorway, a burly, cheerful figure with an Old Bill moustache, wearing a black and red check mackinaw and a flat-brimmed Stetson hat which, I found later, he would stick to even in the coldest of weather: heaven alone knows what miracle of circulation kept his ears from freezing. This was Barney,[2] a Yukon Indian who lived with the Nahanies: he spoke pretty good English, and the rest were finding their tongues. Soon the ice was broken and I was hearing of their journeyings: they had come from the Beaver River in the Yukon by a pass to the head of the Meilleur. They had gone in from South Nahanni over the windswept plateaux of the Tlogotsho by dog team, with their families, to the Beaver after freeze-up, and they were making their winter hunt in there. This was the trip that they always made in to LaFlair's post before break-up in the spring to trade some of their fur for the various things they had run out of: tea and sugar were amongst these so this inky brew that I had made

---

[1] "The Hargrave Correspondence," Vol. XXIV, The Champlain Society.
[2] Another Biblical name, be it noted—Barnabas.

for them was doubly a treat. They would be back this way in a few
days, they said, on their way back in to the Beaver River for the
spring beaver hunt; and when that was over and done with and
the rivers had gone out they would make skin-boats out of moose
hides whipped on to wooden frames, and in these they would run
down the Beaver, families, dogs, toboggans and furs all piled in
together, and down the Liard to South Nahanni.

They must have been well tanked up on tea by now, but they
stayed with it manfully and drained that bucket to the last dregs.
Then they rose up and departed, without a word or a smile, and I
sat there and scratched my head and thought, well, it was probably their way of doing things, and anyhow I had done for them
as those other Indians had done for me on the Liard when I was
tired and cold. And I got up and tidied things away and started
again on the marten.

Presently I heard the squeal of a snowshoe on the hard-packed
snow outside, and there was a slight thud on the roof—then more
squeaks and squeals and more thuds. I went out. Silently and
without any word or even any flicker of a smile they were coming
up from the river and leaving on the corner of the cabin roof each
man a good-sized chunk of moose meat. Then they drove away, a
long line of dog teams, down the river towards the Lower Canyon. Chief Factor Edward Smith knew what he was talking about
when he wrote, a hundred years ago, "In return for good usage . . .
they are willing to please."

When the Indians returned Gordon was with them. They
camped all around the cabin for one night and then went on their
way over the divide to the Yukon. The next thing to heave in sight
was three of the men that I had met at the Hot Springs cabin in
January—Greathouse, Southard and Quinlan. They had spent the
winter doing a little trapping here and there, and waiting, we had
thought, for the gold rush that Faille or myself or Charlie McLeod
was expected to start. The Lower Canyon had so far saved us from
a visitation, but it now became apparent that, failing the gold
stampede to the Flat River for which we were all poised, they had
a plan in reserve: this was to wait till a plain and safe trail had

been broken for them through the canyon and then to follow the Indians to their hunting grounds on the head of the Beaver River, there to horn in on the beaver dams and get themselves a good catch of beaver pelts with the minimum of effort and no time wasted in looking for a good country of their own. They were all experienced northern travellers, Greathouse especially being well known throughout the Barrens and Southard in the Yukon. Just how their scheme would have panned out it is hard to say, for we have seen that these Indians, once irritated, could be "very sanguinary." However, poetic justice was on the side of the Nahanies, and the plan was doomed to fail most spectacularly.

For the moment they camped on us. They had plenty of time, they thought; they liked our valley (we thanked God they had not cared to venture into the canyon earlier in the winter), and Great-house and Quinlan hunted, without result, for moose while Southard made an equally fruitless attempt on the beaver in the dam up Trowel Tail's Creek. We were pleased to see them for one day, mildly entertained for the second evening, polite for the third. Then things began to get a bit "old," and the situation deteriorated fast: the cabin that was roomy for two was bedlam for five, nothing was right for old Greathouse and, to crown everything, he set a couple of traps on our line to the Bald Mountain basins. This could not happen today and should not have happened then: a dangerous row was rapidly approaching.

Greathouse saved the situation. He didn't like the way Gordon was making the hotcakes for supper. He would show us the way it should be done, and I marvelled at the alacrity with which Gordon handed over the outfit to him.

"There's the works," Gordon said quietly. "The batter's in that pot and the frying pans are hot: now go to it your way and let's see some real hotcakes." And he shoved one of the frying pans on to the hottest part of the stove and went and lay down on his bed and filled his pipe.

Then I saw which frying pan it was that Gordon had set ready for Greathouse, and it began to dawn on me that we were on the threshold of great events. The frying pan was a damnable thing of Gordon's that I had many a time cursed: it had a hinged handle that folded over into the pan, and Gordon had carried it in the eastern North all the way from Norway House to Chesterfield Inlet. He liked it because it fitted so neatly into the load in the cariole, but nobody else loved it at all. And to Greathouse, in the dim evening light in the cabin, it looked just like any other frying pan, solid, innocent and without guile.

Talking nineteen to the dozen the old man dropped the first ladleful of batter into the hinged monstrosity: he had rolled up his sleeves, I was glad to see. The bubbles appeared on the surface of the pancake and a little smoke rose from the pan. "And then you flip her," Greathouse went gabbling on. "One brave flip like I'll show you—none of your knives or egg slices. Like this. . . ." And he flipped, bravely enough—even, one might say, rashly. . . .

The results, to his partners, must have been startling. The hinge, of course, immediately came into operation, but the hotcake stayed with the pan up to a certain point. Then centrifugal force began to take effect, and the hot mess of batter took wing and plastered itself over the old man's face, rather in the early Chaplin manner. The smoking pan completed its half-circle and landed its searing rim square on Greathouse's wrist, fetching out of him an agonised yell and causing him to hurl it blindly across the cabin where, as luck would have it, it struck Southard in the back of the neck. Wiping the batter from his face and shouting at the top of his voice his comments on all "damned greenhorn frying pans," Greathouse rushed furiously out into the snow, hotly pursued by Southard who was under the impression that his partner had gone suddenly mad and had tried to assassinate him. He had been deep in Sir Clifford Sifton's treatise on the fur trade, and consequently all this had come as rather a shock to him: he was using very strong language as he left the cabin.

Gordon and I rolled to and fro on our beds quite silently. My partner's face was crimson and distorted, and so, no doubt, was mine: the tears rolled down our cheeks: this was more than one could reasonably have asked from one small hotcake. But it was not yet all: further mischief was in store. Quinlan, after staring at the wreckage for perhaps a minute in a bewildered sort of way, suddenly realised that something funny had happened and went

off into a high-pitched, whinnying scream of laughter: it evidently
took him some time to get a full grasp of a new situation, but there
could be no doubt about his enjoyment of this one once its
subtleties had been resolved for him. And throughout the evening, at intervals, the memory of it would be too much for him,
and shrill, stallion-like noises would intrude on the sulky peace
that Greathouse and Southard had patched up between themselves. Greathouse could bear it no longer. He had lost face ir-
retrievably before us, and now one of his own partners was
screaming at him intermittently like a jackass. There was a splitting row right after breakfast among the members of the trium-
virate and, as a result, Quinlan hitched up his dogs and hit for
South Nahanni, and Southard and Greathouse shoved off on the
trail of the Indians. They had one big sled between them with a
canoe on it and their stuff in the canoe: no skin-boats for them,
running down the Beaver River. Peace reigned once more in
Deadmen Valley, and a day later, a strong Chinook, with the
very breath of spring in it, began to blow.

   To complete the Greathouse saga, the would-be beaver hunters
got well up the Meilleur and into the alpine country where I had
followed the moose in January. The further they went the warmer
the Chinook became till at last the snow started to rot, and they
began to break through the trail into the soft snow beneath. Then
their snowshoes, which were Indian-made and filled with
babiche,[1] began to soften and sag in the waterlogged snow and
eventually broke down. There was no sign of the Indians: the sled
slipped sideways on some mountainside, and the loaded canoe
crashed into a rock and got a hole smashed into it: Southard cut
his knee badly with his axe. One way and another they were in a
pretty bad fix; there was nothing for it but to turn back. Somehow
or other, with bits of dog harness and odds and ends, they made
their snowshoes usable again. Then they had a stroke of luck—the
weather turned cold and tightened up the snow for them but, even
so, they were exhausted when they arrived once more at the wind-

[1]As opposed to a factory-made, white-man shoe in which the filling would be
waterproofed.

swept gate of the Meilleur. They pushed on down the flats and camped somewhere close to the Nahanni. Southard's knee was a poor-looking sight by this time, and they had no bandages or surgical outfit of any kind.

Then they had another stroke of luck. Morning and evening I began to notice a faint mist up at the head of the valley. I knew there was open water up there, a place where the Nahanni never froze, and I knew that, in cold weather, it "smoked"—gave off a steaming fog where the water met the cold air. But this weather was not cold enough; it rarely went below zero. I pointed out this peculiar mist to Gordon and, as he had some marten traps up that way that he wanted to pick up before the river broke, he drove off one morning with the dogs to investigate.

That evening he was back with the tale of disaster. It was their fire smoke that I had mistaken for mist, never dreaming that anybody could be camped up there: for while we knew that they would be in difficulties owing to the Chinook we had no idea that fate had thrown the whole bagful at them and that they had been forced to retreat to the valley. The knee, Gordon said, was a mess, and they had nothing to tie it up with but an old, dirty shirt. And after the hinged frying pan episode nothing would induce Greathouse to come to the cabin where he had made such an ass of himself, while Southard couldn't travel owing to his wound: it was therefore up to us. So we sorted out bandages and disinfectants, lint and ointment, and Gordon set out the next morning and did a proper job on Southard's knee. And there they camped, waiting for open water: the Indians trapped their beaver undisturbed, Greathouse hunted in the upper end of the valley, and our trails never crossed again.

The gurgling of the newly-awakened Wheatsheaf Creek was very soothing, and the late April sun was hot. The water was running in a miniature canyon of ice in the centre of the frozen stream, cutting it wider and deeper day by day. The valley was coming back to life after its winter sleep and here and there, on the south-facing hillsides and ridges, were patches of brown and green. The creek ice was also rotting at the edges where it touched the warm, sunny bank on which I was lying: very soon now the tremendous pressure of the water from a thousand streamlets like this one, and from rivers like Prairie Creek and the Meilleur, would burst the ice of the Nahanni; and then. . . . And I half-closed my eyes the better to enjoy a vision of long reaches of blue water alive with gabbling wildfowl and their banks a pale mist of tender green. For a moment I could almost smell the sweet scent of the poplar buds. . . .

The second volume of McIntyre's Rabelais slipped from my hand on to the spruce needles. I jerked awake and picked it up: it was dedicated, I noticed, "To the soul of the deceased Queen of Navarre." It had travelled a long way in space and time since the Doctor paid that tribute to the ghostly lady four hundred years ago in far-off Touraine.

There wasn't a thing to do that afternoon but loaf and read. We had been out before dawn on the hard-frozen snow picking up the last of the traps, and the dogs had carried down from the mountain, in their canvas panniers, the last of the bones and scraps of the moose we had killed in October, for the supply of dog feed was running low. Now Gordon was busy down at the cabin doing some baking and mending one of the dog-packs that had got torn: a couple of feet of sloppy, waterlogged snow in the bush made travel impracticable—a snowshoe would pick up twenty pounds of the stuff—and, what with one thing and another, this dry bank up against the old spruce tree was a good place to be till it froze and put a crust on the snow again. My shirt dangled from a branch, socks and moccasins were thrown beside me on the ground, and I lay there very comfortably in mackinaw trousers, twiddling my toes in the sun. I found my place again: Panurge and Pantagruel were off to consult the Oracle of the Holy Bottle. . . . And I dozed off once more in the warm afternoon sunshine.

A stone clattered suddenly, and from a little way upstream came the sound of breaking ice. Instantly awake I found myself staring at a bull moose who was standing on the creek ice, perhaps twenty yards away, looking at me. He was outlined in gold where the rays of the sun struck through his hair. He turned away, climbed the far bank and faded into the bush: he had not been unduly alarmed.

There was no time for shirt and socks. I slipped my feet into the moccasins, whipped the strings round my ankles and tore through the bush to the cabin. Gordon was busy at the table, and he looked up inquiringly as I ran in through the open door, grabbed my rifle off its pegs and turned to go.

"A moose," I said. "Crossed the creek at that sunny bend going west. If I get him I'll fire two signal shots. Bring the works—axe, knives and the rest. And a mackinaw or something—shirt's up creek. . . ." And I left on the run.

"Get him," he called after me. "We need him."

I crossed the creek and plunged into the bush on the trail of the moose. The sun was dropping into the west, and the shadows of the spruce lay cold and blue on the sodden snow. The moosehide moccasins were soaked through at the first step, and a load of snow, dislodged from an overhanging branch, caught me squarely on my bare shoulders and ran down my back; there were many more of these—but, after all, one couldn't get wetter than wet, though the feeling had gone out of my feet, and I did wonder, once or twice, how many sharp snags I was sticking into them. And there were compensations: the effort to gain ground and to make use of the big animal's tracks in the deep snow kept me warm, and, dressed as I was in my own hide and in wet woollen trousers, I was making my way through the bush without a sound. And the wind was right.

Here and there the moose had stopped in small clearings to browse on the willow tops. He was heading west, and, if he kept this up, we would run out into the open behind the old cabins of the Klondikers; there was a big muskeg and a lake between them and the mountain slope, and there might be something there that would delay him for a little while.

Sure enough that was where I found him—on the far side of the muskeg, amongst some red willow, browsing on something there that I couldn't see. I circled round to the south to get the sun out of my eyes, keeping in the edge of the timber. Then, as soon as possible, I fired, taking a long shot and using a small, dead poplar as a rest. Down went the moose, only to rise again as I drew near and break into a clumsy run. I fired again and killed him just as he was coming to the edge of the dry ground and the trees.

I fired a couple of shots for Gordon's benefit and immediately, as if at that very signal, the sun went down behind the mountains of the Meilleur. Instantly the sharp crispness of the frost could be felt, and in my sodden, half-naked condition I was well able to appreciate the change. To keep warm I went to work and stamped down the snow around the moose until there was a firm place on which to skin and cut up. Then I went down into the muskeg and swung like an ape on a number of the old, dead spruce that were standing there. Down they came, crashing into the snow and myself with them, and then I dragged them up to the moose and piled them there. Soon there was a blaze going with the flames leaping high—where the devil could Gordon have got to? He should have been here by now. Suddenly he appeared on the far edge of the muskeg and behind him, floundering through the deep snow and carrying their canvas packsacks, came four dejected dogs followed by a particularly woebegone Mam'selle. But they brightened up when they saw the moose: supper, they knew, was about to begin. . . .

A week or so later we woke one morning to a grinding, bumping, thudding uproar from the river—the Nahanni ice was on the move. The main run continued for about two days with the enormous blocks thrusting, shoving and slamming at each other, upending sometimes and turning over under the tremendous pressures till the ground shook with the force of the collisions. Somewhere down below our camp the ice was jamming and, when that happened, the water and the floating ice would rise and rise until we began to wonder. . . . And then the jam would give way and the whole mass would get on the move again with a devastating rush, taking with it tall trees and whole sections of river bank. By the third day a low and shrunken Nahanni was running freely between beaches that were strewn with enormous blocks of ice: more ice was still coming down the river but no longer in sufficient quantity to jam.

Our beach was free of ice and so was the mouth of Trowel

Tail's Creek. That was all to the good for we had established a camp beyond the river north towards the mountains, and now, by watching our chance and dodging the running ice, we could get across again by canoe. There was a bit of country over there in which we were interested, and we could reach it easily over the frozen snow in the early mornings: there were beaver in the dams across the river; the game was coming back to the valley and heading for the sunlit slopes around Prairie Creek; there were mallard on the open waters and partridges drumming in the bush—and we took it in turns to travel and hunt that country: three days across and three days based on the cabin, and a lunch and a meeting always arranged at the change-over. This system gave us just the right amount of contact and kept us out of each other's hair. We had been a long time together, and now we needed either some new blood or a change of scene. Small things began to loom large: Bloody Poilu, for instance, mistook my shaving brush for a bone and ate it, lock, stock and barrel, and when I berated him for an overfed pot hound, Gordon took this as a personal reflection on his dog feeding and was annoyed accordingly. And for a long time now each man had fried his own moose steaks in his own frying pan: Gordon liked his cooked to leather (as I saw it), and I liked mine to be what he called raw; it was better to cook your own, and then you only had yourself to blame if it wasn't the way you liked it. . . .

The evening of May 12th was clear and still. I was feeding dogs outside the cabin and thinking about getting my own supper when I heard the rattle of a paddle on the floor of a canoe and the sound of footsteps down on the beach. Presently Gordon appeared coming up the bank.

"I thought you'd like to hear the glad tidings," he said. "I was up to the mouth of the Second Canyon this morning, and there's a wall of ice right across the river there, thirty feet high at least. Of course, this much water's getting through somehow, but there was no gap in the wall that I could see. If the river's dammed up behind the ice. . . . How far would a thirty-foot dam back the water up in that canyon?"

"Three miles anyway," I said. "It's not very fast there."

"Well then, if that ice barrier collapses all at once, something pretty notable in the way of a flood's going to come down this valley. I was worried about the canoe so I came back to make it safe. We'd better carry it up into the bush beside the other one."

So we did that and then set about getting supper. We got out the last of the coffee, and we were just debating whether to fling it all into the pot and make one glorious brew of it, or whether we should use only half and spin it out for a couple of evenings, when the faint beat of an engine sounded from upstream. We stared at each other for a moment and then dashed madly for the beach, just in time to see Starke's scow run down the riffle and swing into the home eddy. Gordon was ahead of me with an excited mob of dogs at his heels: he was shouting a welcome to Stevens who was in the bow with a coiled line in his hand.

"George! George!" he bawled at me above the uproar of the dogs, "Throw on *all* the coffee!" It was not a *very* magnificent gesture but it came from the heart, and it was the best we could do in the way of a welcome. . . .

They had had an exciting run down from Caribou Creek through canyons walled with ice, racing down riffles side by side with floating bergs. There was a way through Gordon's ice barrier, apparently, that could not be seen from the north shore—an ice canyon, it seemed, cut through the jam on an angle and not more than two or three times the width of the scow. It only opened up to view at the last moment, Starke said: until then they thought they were going to smash straight into a solid wall of ice under which the Nahanni was somehow finding its way. Through this gap was pouring the whole river in a green, purling chute with a drop of about ten feet and a monstrous standing wave at the bottom of it, and at it the Black Pirate rammed the scow with Stevens flat on the fore-deck, hanging on to the ring-bolts.

"It was like being on a toboggan," Stevens told us, "coming down a green hill of water—and that ice flying past within a few feet. And then the wave: we took that green—right through it—whoosh! I'm a bit wet and so's Jack: did Gordon say something about coffee? Because we have something here that'll go well with it. . . ." And with justifiable pride they produced the last bottle of the case of rum with which they had set out from Waterways two years before.

They had run down, risking the ice, for two reasons: firstly to get out while they could before the extreme low water that follows the spring break-up should make it impossible and tie them up at Caribou Creek; and secondly, Starke said, because Stevens' birthday was on May 11th and mine was on May 13th, "and Steve was bound we'd be here on the 12th and celebrate them both together in spite of rocks, ice and all the perils of the deep."

"Perils of the shallow, you mean," said Stevens. And then to us: "Lead us to the coffee before we freeze and we'll start with a round of coffee royals."

Late that evening Stevens and I stood arm in arm on the river-bank. Second Canyon Mountain and the western range showed darkly against the afterglow of a cloudless sunset, but the north-eastern wall of the valley from the Lower Canyon, past Prairie Creek and far up the deep cleft of the Nameless Creek, shone against the darkening sky with the golden, evening light gleaming from its winter snows. Behind us there streamed, from the cabin door and windows, yellow shafts of candle light: the place was lit up like a church, recklessly as befitted this festive occasion, and from within came the murmur of men's voices: Starke and Gordon were deep in serious debate.

"All this," Stevens was saying, "is ours. All of it! All!" and he included the Nahanni, the bush, the wide flats of Prairie Creek and the shimmering magnificence of the northern mountains in one tremendous sweep of his free arm that almost flung us both down on to the beach. "We do what we please—and who is there to stop us? We go where we please—and others follow in the trails we make, if they can. Mostly they can't. When we're hungry we kill King George's moose or his caribou: we ask no man for anything. Who's like us?"

R.M.P.: "Faille."

Stevens: "Yes, and good luck to him wherever he is. And what might we have been? You might have been Secretary of the Bank of England and useless as hell on a river, and I might have been fat and running a greengrocer's shop in Kensington. But we had

the sense to get out while we were young, and now we're monarchs
of all we survey, lords of this magnificent—er—magnificent. . . ."

R.M.P.: "Domain?"

Stevens: "That's the word—domain. Better than that, too:
why, we're kings, emperors. . . . That reminds me, we ought to
go and sing a few Christmas carols to those solemn old goats in
the shack. . . ."

"For God's sake, you two kings, make less noise about it. Gordon and I have important matters to discuss." It was Starke's
voice that came rumbling out of the cabin.

Nevertheless we sang to them.

The days passed pleasantly enough. We hunted a little. Somebody got one more beaver, and we feasted on beaver tail and the
last of the bacon. And Starke demonstrated new and better ways
of making sourdough bread. But it was no use: the demon of
restlessness had entered into me; the sight of the open water had
made my feet itch; I had a little appointment to keep, and I
wanted to be on the move. It was useless for Starke and Gordon to
point out that we were better off where we were: I wanted to get
down to Fort Simpson in order to catch the first plane out, and I
made a perfect pest of myself about it, with Stevens partly on my
side, until at last Starke in desperation said: "Oh, for heaven's
sake, let's get him out of here and down to Simpson Island, and
then we can all camp there in misery instead of up here in comfort. Maybe that'll make him happy. . . ." So that was settled and
we made ready to go.

We would load our outfit and fur and canoes on to the scow,
Starke said, and all run down together: there was lots of room.
That wouldn't do for me either: what—miss the last chance of
running down through the Lower Canyon in a canoe? Nothing
doing! I would take the little canoe and the shot-gun and go ahead
and have camp all made and a fire burning at the Hot Springs
landing by the time the others got there—and have all the fun of
the trip, and some ducks as well.

"All right," Starke said good-naturedly. "Take a few more
risks. Run your little pea-pod of a canoe once more through the

canyon: you don't know what it's like at this low stage of water. But you'll find out: hitting a rock in the Cache Rapid's a shorter road to a funeral than it is to a wedding, but have it your own way. . . ."

So the last day came, and I raced away down the valley in the sixteen-footer with the canoe's nose cutting into the dancing glitter of the morning sun. The familiar woods and hills marched by, and the black gate of the canyon came closer. The Nahanni was low and utterly clear: down through the green water I could see the shadow of the canoe flying over the stones: it was a perfect day, windless and hot, and the canoe answered to a touch: risk be damned—I was in paradise.

I circled for a while in the big eddies of Patterson's Lake at the mouth of Ram Creek: it was hard to believe that it was here that I had flogged my way on snowshoes in February, inch by inch almost, through those tremendous drifts. But now the ducks rose from what had then been ice and snow, and by the time I turned to run down the Cache Riffles two butterballs and two mallards lay at my feet in the canoe: the duck-shooting excuse had been justified. . . .

I beached the canoe just above the Hot Springs Creek. There I cleared out a camp ground, cut spruce boughs and wood and got a fire going: I hung a tarpaulin over a leaning tree so that the scow party would see it easily and have plenty of time to manoeuvre for a landing; and when they came and found all ready for them, including boiling water for tea, even Starke had to admit that there was something to this business of sending a courier in advance.

Armed with towels and soap we took the trail to the Springs. The grass was green in the meadow there: the snow had gone from that favoured spot and the violets were peeping through, and there we loafed and bathed and sunned ourselves, in and out of the hot water and sprawled on the grass, till the shadow of the cliff fell on the little clearing and it was time to stroll back to the river. We sat late that night round the fire, talking and watching up and down the long, calm reach, hoping for a moose but seeing none. Next morning I rolled out with the first light of the sun, silenced Sammy's welcome with a scowl and quietly cooked my breakfast. Then I slid the canoe into the water and fled: the others were snoring gently, each under a tree—dead to the world as the Seven Sleepers. I would see them in the evening: I was to have a camp ready for them in the calm water by the foot of The Splits, while they were to grub up and bring with them a choke-cherry for Jack LaFlair. We had marked down a very fine specimen for this purpose back by the Springs.

And so another perfect day went by and the ducks rose nicely, and again we sat late by the fire. But when the dawn came the rain was falling and we had put up no shelters, so we threw canoes and everything on board the scow and ran down the last eight miles of the Nahanni, intending to breakfast with Jack LaFlair.

But Jack was away. His boat was gone, the cabin door was padlocked, and the windows were closed and shuttered. There was not a screw showing anywhere that we could turn with the fine point of an axe, and we stood there in the rain, staring disgustedly at the door and thinking of all the good things that were standing (we hoped) on the shelves inside: jam and marmalade, raisins and chocolate, all the sweet things for which our insides were clamouring. And, in Starke's case, potatoes: that was what he wanted. Jack grew them at South Nahanni and, with any luck, there should be some in the cellar. Starke had been talking of little else in the last week and now, muttering something about "being thrown on the resources of our own ingenuity," he disappeared over the bank, returning shortly with the well-equipped tool-box of the scow.

He did a beautiful job of house-breaking. Carefully and delicately he removed the front window, leaving not one visible mark on the shutter or the battens for, as he truly said, we didn't want to put any ideas into the heads of the simple, untutored Indians. Our own consciences were clear: Jack had invited us all to make use of the place in his absence and had even promised to leave potatoes for Starke. He had simply forgotten to tell us where the key would be hidden.

Soon, one by one, we were wriggling through the window, and very shortly Stevens discovered a bunch of keys and was promptly shoved out into the rain again to see what he could do with the padlock. He soon had the door open, and then he and I brought up the two grub boxes from the scow. Gordon lit a fire in the stove, and Starke got a bucketful of his beloved potatoes from the cellar and started to peel them. Everything was very peaceful and domesticated, and Stevens and I left the others to get breakfast and went over behind the counter to get a selection of canned stuff from the shelves, listing it so that we could pay Jack for it in fur when we ran into him at Simpson or wherever he was.

We did ourselves well, and I could see nothing more that we needed when my eye was caught by a bunch of patent cigarette lighters hanging from a nail by their chains: I turned to examine them, wondering what the Indians could want with them when a match or a piece of glowing charcoal was always so much more re-liable. Stevens was a foot or two behind me and facing the other way: he was rummaging, with idle curiosity, in the shelf under the counter, and I heard him say, "Here's a funny place for a man to keep his six-shooter—in his tool-box, behind the counter . . . ," and I felt him turn towards me. There was a roar and a flash within an inch of my right ear, and half a dozen of the lighters fell to the ground, their chains severed. I stared at the remaining lighters for perhaps a second and then slapped my head down on the cupboard top below the shelves, clasping my hands behind my neck—a curious reaction, but I was not certain what had happened and was dumbly under the impression that a second whatever-it-was might be on the way. . . .

But nothing came, and I cautiously raised my head and looked around. Stevens was standing behind me, white as a ghost, with a Colt .45 in his shaking hand, staring at it as if he had seen the Gorgon's head. Starke was sitting by the stove, puffing at his pipe and peeling potatoes as if nothing had happened, while Gordon, quite white and with a strained expression on his face, was march-ing out of the cabin. Nobody spoke. Silence lay on the place like a wet blanket. I made one effort to lift it: I was feeling better for, after all, a bullet gone by is a bullet gone by, and I said what a treat it was going to be to have some marmalade for breakfast again. But nobody answered me. Gordon returned, green this time, and fried some of Jack's bacon and potatoes, and breakfast was eaten under a perfect pall of silence. At the end of this solemn feast Gordon got up without a word and went over to the counter where the Colt was lying. He took out the cartridges and the one spent shell and fiddled with the thing.

"Did Jack leave the gun at full cock?" he asked Stevens.

"Yes. Of course, I should never have touched it but. . . ."

"Well, no wonder it went off. Jack's got it filed down to a hair trigger so fine that it'll go off if you just shake it. Picking it up was enough: look. . . ." And he cocked the revolver and shook it, and the hammer fell. Jack evidently, rightly or wrongly, trusted the Nahanni Indians about as far as he could throw them and kept this weapon in a state of instant readiness, under the counter where he could grab it in a split second. The click of the hammer loosened everybody's tongue, and in the ensuing babel I got a chance to ask Gordon what made him go striding out of the shack like a grenadier on parade right after Stevens' shot.

"Went out and was sick, old man," he said simply.

The rain had stopped and the clouds were breaking: it was turning into a perfect day. Nobody felt like travelling; we would cook and wash and shave and enjoy this last day on the Nahanni to the full. And Stevens and I would plant the choke-cherry. We fetched it up from the scow and we found a shovel, and then we wandered round trying to decide where Jack would want the thing: finally we elected to plant it bang in front of the cabin door, six feet away from the threshold, "because he'll be sure to notice it there."

So there it was planted and well watered; and then Stevens said it ought to have a fence and rail around it like a park tree; so I made and pointed four posts and Stevens drove them in, using the back of an old axe with a split head as a post-maul—"the last job it'll ever do," he said. While he did this I hewed out four neat, squared rails, and then I went down over the bank to get a brace and bit. The tool-box lay on the shingle, and I was just going to bend down to it when a rifle shot cracked out from up above. I stood there looking out across the river: they were probably shooting at a goose or a beaver but I couldn't see for certain, and I bent down over the tool-box. As I stooped something flitted just over my head with a vicious "Wheet!" and plunged into the river; I could feel the breath of it ruffle my hair. A moment later Stevens appeared on the edge of the bank.

"Did you find it?" he asked.

"Yes, I've got it. Was that the old axe that you threw over just now?"

"Yes," he said. "We've packed it far enough. To hell with it; we've got others that are sound. Why?"

"Oh, I just wondered. . . ."

Things usually come in threes, I thought, and this made three. First at the Cache Rapid by water, last summer, and then in the cabin this morning by fire. And now by cold steel. . . . What was that Stevens was saying? We ought to give it a Latin name like the botanists do?

I couldn't remember the Latin for cherry, but the innocent little bush was duly labelled in most improper fashion: we burned the dog-Latin inscription into a board with a red-hot iron. Then we backed away and admired our handiwork.

"Jack'll like that," we said.

"He will if he doesn't break his neck over it, trying to get into his cabin." This from Starke who was sitting on the bench outside, smoking a pipe in the sun and looking on, as one who watches children at their play. . . .

Late that evening Gordon and I sat at Jack's table making our last will and testament. This curious document was a joint effort, and it was in Jack LaFlair's favour. To him, with every legal phrase that we could remember, we bequeathed, devised, etc., various treasures and articles of camp gear that he had admired, together with our library of two volumes. Jack read everything that came his way, and I have often wondered how much or how little he made of those two rather specialised books, *Jorrocks' Jaunts* and *Pickwick Papers*.

Starke and Stevens had gone to bed on the scow, and we had thrown our beds down on the grass outside. The sun had set behind the mountains; not a breath of wind was stirring and, in the calm radiance of that perfect evening, the peace of the North, which is a thing beyond all imagining, lay softly upon South

Nahanni. Somewhere outside a frog was croaking, and into the cabin there blundered, with gentle hum, a large and amiable mosquito. From the direction of the oven came a pleasant sizzling sound: a goose had incautiously put its head in the way of Gordon's bullet and was now paying the penalty of its rashness. A beaver, too, had been the victim of a lucky shot; there would be beaver tail for breakfast, and we would go down the Liard on cold roast goose and beaver stew. All was well.

I got up and tried the goose with a fork. Done to a turn he was, and we lifted him out and set him on the table to cool. Then we went out into the evening, closing the door behind us.

Afterword

From our camp on Fort Simpson Island, while we were waiting for the Upper Mackenzie ice to go out and for the first plane of the season to come in, we slowly disposed of the outfit, leaving one or two of the larger pieces for Gordon to sell later on, down the Mackenzie.

Fort Simpson is 800 miles by river (with one portage) plus 300 miles by rail from its nearest supply base—Edmonton in Alberta. Being a natural-born trader, and having in his favour this cogent argument of 1,100 miles of heavy freight charges, Gordon eventually sold everything we owned in common for more than the whole outfit, including the grub, had cost us in Edmonton to start with; so we had the trip, with the use of the canoes, traps and so forth, for nothing, while the fur, the photographs, the experience and any further by-products were all clear profit. And we did very well out of the fur.

As to the Nahanni Legend one realises now that it was much ado over very little. But while its feet were of clay, the Legend itself was strong—strong enough, with the help of the Falls and the canyons, to keep the Nahanni country from being overrun by the white trapper under the old, easy-going regulations prior to the establishment of the Mackenzie Mountains Game Preserve. The vague folk memory of some old massacre or defeat, moreover, kept the Mackenzie River Indians from going back west beyond the first ramparts of the mountains; and Gordon, when he was managing Wrigley for the Northern Traders in 1929-30 and trapping on his own account in the intervals of trading, had only to travel thirty miles west from the Mackenzie to get into virgin marten country into which the Wrigley Indians would not go—for fear, they told them, of the Mountain Men, the dread haunters of those lonely uplands. Thus, even to this very day, the Nahanni country has remained uniquely protected.

Appendix

EXTRACTS FROM TWO LETTERS CONCERNING THE SOUTH NAHANNI

1.—From George Simpson Esqre., Governor of the Northern Department of Rupert's Land [for the H. B. Co.], to Andrew Colville.

"York Factory. 8th Sept. 1823."

"The tract of Country [i.e., the Nahanni country] alluded to . . . is little known and I had directed my attention thereto last winter while in Athabasca; Mr. McLeod was to have sent a small party to explore it this season, but if it is not done I have arranged with Mr. Smith [Chief Factor Edward Smith, then in charge of Fort Simpson] that it will be attended to next year. Mr. Black will be able to give us some information on this subject as he is like to fall in with the Nohanus [Nohanees?], and you will observe by my correspondence with McLeod that I have turned my attention very particularly to the affairs of Mackenzie's River. . . ."

2.—A Dispatch from George Simpson Esqre., Governor of Rupert's Land, to the Governor and Committee of the Hudson's Bay Company.

"Mar. 1st, 1829."

"I have made arrangements with Mr. Smith that a new post shall be settled on the Nahany River, for the convenience of the Nahany Tribe . . . which will require an Establishment of Six Men besides the Clerk in charge, with an outfit of Twenty Five pieces Goods, and may be expected to yield about 20 to 25 Packs Furs, value about £2000."

269

Glossary

babiche . . . . rawhide, not smoked but merely dried and cut into strips.

bar . . . . shingle or sand-bar in a river, but sometimes also used meaning delta, alluvial fan or gulch dump.

Bay (the) . . . . customary abbreviation for the Hudson's Bay Company.

butte . . . . a conspicuous, isolated hill or mountain (pronounced bute).

butterball . . . . buffle-head or spirit duck.

cache . . . . a safe storage place for food and equipment—usually, in this book, a platform or shelter built high up on upright poles or sawed-off trees.

as verb—to hide or to store away.

Cache Rapid . . . . rapid at the head of the Lower Canyon of the Nahanni, now sometimes called George's Riffle.

chaudière . . . . cauldron—the boiling, surging water at the foot of a fall or rapid.

coulee . . . . used where the Scottish "corrie" would apply and also of any deep valley cutting back into a hill or mountain.

divide . . . . watershed.

Dolly Varden . . . bull trout or char—a relative of the arctic char of Europe.

271

gate . . . . a narrow cleft in the mountains, usually the pathway for a stream.

jackpot . . . . a scrape, fix or tight corner.

kicker . . . . outboard motor.

kini-kinik . . . . bear-berry.

Liard . . . . Cottonwood (French). The original names of the Liard River were Rivière aux Liards, or the West Branch (of the Mackenzie).

lick . . . . a natural salt or mineral lick used by the wild animals.

mal de raquette . . snowshoe sickness—much the same as the Navy's "immersion foot," or trench foot: caused by cold, lack of circulation and over-strain.

mulligan . . . . a stew into which every available ingredient and condiment has been thrown.

muskeg . . . . swampy stretch of peat moss, often sparsely treed with stunted spruce.

North Westers . . . men of the North West Company, the Hudson's Bay Company's rival. The two companies amalgamated in 1821.

outfit . . . . can refer either to the equipment of an expedition or to the expedition party itself or to any body of men—e.g. "the whole outfit was tired and hungry. . . ."

outside (the) . . . . out of the North—civilization.

pack . . . . as noun—the pack or packsack one is carrying, or, as verb—to carry.

parka . . . . a hooded, smocklike garment, Eskimo in origin and variously made—a protection against winter storms.

partridge . . . . ruffed grouse.

pong . . . . the noise made by logs contracting and nails drawing in the walls and roof of a cabin in intense cold.

prospect . . . . a discovery of mineral not yet fully proven or marketed.

pry . . . . as noun—a lever, usually a long pole.

as verb—to prize or to lever.

riffle . . . . a chute or slide of water in a river, usually in shingle or broken rock and not in solid rock.

right bank . . . . . . the right-hand bank of a river as one faces *downstream* (and similarly with the left bank—always facing downstream).

R.C.M.P. . . . . . . Royal Canadian Mounted Police

sashay . . . . a stroll or promenade. Hence used colloquially for a trip or journey.

scow . . . . a flat-bottomed, punt-shaped craft of varying size, with flush fore and after decks.

scree . . . . a slope of loose rock on a mountainside.

slicker . . . . long oilskin raincoat.

snye . . . . small channel between island and mainland in a river, or offshoot channel. Backwater.

Starke's Rock . . . originally the name of a rock in the Cache Rapid but now given to a very big rock at the head of the Cache Riffles.

swamp . . . . verb—to trim the branches off a fallen tree or to clear out a trail.

tamarack . . . . the American larch.

tarp . . . . commonly used for tarpaulin.

timberline . . . . . . the limit of trees on a mountain.

Tlogotsho . . . . . . "Big Prairie Mountains"—the mountains originally referred to as the Ram Mountains and which form the S.W. boundary of Deadmen Valley. Named by the author after questioning the Indians: name officially adopted sometime in the thirties.

whiskey jack . . . . Canada jay.

voyageur . . . . French Canadian term for wilderness traveller by river. Later, a North West Co. or H. B. Co. engagé employed in the river transport between posts.

DIMENSIONS OF CANOES USED:

Prospector: 16 feet long, by 36 inches maximum width, by 14 inches deep. Weight 75 lbs. Freight: 18 feet long, by 46 inches maximum width, by 18 inches deep. Weight 130 lbs.

THE WORD NAHANNI

On p. 4 we have Michael Mason's translation of this word. In *The Indians of Canada* (by D. Jenness, National Museum of Canada, Ottawa.) on p. 427 the term Nahanie is translated "people over there far away," and was applied in the early nineteenth century by the Slave Indians of the Lower Liard to the Indians further up the river. At that time the Indians of the South Nahanni River called themselves Esbataotinne or Goat Indians.